DEAR GREEN SOUNDS

DEAR GREEN SOUNDS

GLASGOW'S MUSIC
THROUGH TIME AND BUILDINGS

GLASGOW
CITY OF MUSIC

a UNESCO Creative City

WAVERLEY BOOKS

Published 2015 by Waverley Books, an imprint of The Gresham Publishing Company Limited, Academy Park, Building 4000, Gower Street, Glasgow G51 1PR.

Published in association with Glasgow UNESCO City Of Music.

Text copyright © 2015 Glasgow UNESCO City Of Music.

www.glasgowcityofmusic.com

www.waverley-books.co.uk

Photographs and Illustrations are copyright © and acknowledged as detailed in the Picture Credits listing.

Design: Mark Mechan

All rights reserved. No part of this publication may be reproduced, stored in a retrieval system or transmitted in any form or by any means, electronic, mechanical, photocopying, recording or otherwise, without the permission of the copyright holders.

Conditions of Sale: This book is sold with the condition that it will not, by way of trade or otherwise, be re-sold, hired out, lent, or otherwise distributed or circulated in any form or style of binding or cover other than that in which it is published and without the same condition being imposed on the subsequent purchaser.

ISBN: 978-1-84934-193-6

Printed and bound in the EU

Contents

Introduction	Kate Molleson	6
Glasgow Cathedral		
Before the Reformation	Elaine Moohan	17
After the Reformation	Gordon Munro	21
City Halls	Tom Service	24
The Royal Conservatoire of Scotland	Keith Bruce	35
The Scotia Bar	Ewan McVicar	42
Theatre Royal	Conrad Wilson	51
Empire Theatre	Alison Kerr	61
St Andrew's Halls	Hugh Macdonald	67
Rottenrow	Ewan McVicar	81
The Pavilion	Ewan McVicar	86
Barrowland Ballroom	Graeme Virtue	95
BBC Scotland	John Purser	104
The Piping Centre And The College Of Piping	John Purser	113
The Apollo	Graeme Virtue	119
Glasgow's Grand Ole Opry	Martin Cloonan	126
Postcard Records	Vic Galloway	132
The SECC	Martin Cloonan	140
Sub Club	Malcolm Jack	147
King Tut's Wah Wah Hut	Vic Galloway	157
Mono	Neil Cooper	162
The Glasgow Royal Concert Hall	Tom Service	169
Acknowledgements		178
Bibliography		180
Picture Credits		182
Index		186

INTRODUCTION

What makes a city musical? Glasgow's cultural history is all fits and starts: centuries of reformation and migration, industrialisation and depression, great wealth, deep problems, sporadic regeneration. Today the place is sprawling, stylish in parts and rough around the edges. And yet, or so, it is a blazingly musical city.

This book aims to capture the spirit of that musicality. It could never have been written as one unified story. Glasgow became a UNESCO City of Music in 2008 thanks to the countless kinds of music that coexist on these streets. Delve into the demographics and it's easy to see where that diversity comes from: Glasgow has always been a meeting place. It's a city built by Celts and Romans, the Irish and Highlanders and recent communities too numerous to list here. Each has contributed its voice to the urban soundtrack. Glasgow's music has been born of piety and poverty, pride and sectarianism, poor decisions and grand vision, bedroom pipedreams, and politics with a 'p', large and small. Incomers have sung of exile, community, isolation and integration; suburbs have bred songs of boredom, aspiration and sheer devilment. Classical music took off relatively late here but blossomed with the wealth of the Second City of the Empire, where merchants woke at 6 am to sing madrigals, and more than 100 choirs were going strong by the turn of the 20th century. Glasgow was flourishing and had something to sing about.

How to encompass such a raucous place in just one book? I could have attempted a great sweeping chronology or designated a chapter to each major genre or big name. But music and cities don't work like that; there are too many loose ends, blind corners, one-offs, crossbreeds.

Ultimately this is a book about music and place, so it seemed right to celebrate the buildings themselves: those hallowed and not-so-hallowed places where Glaswegians have flocked to hear, play, sing and shout their music over the centuries. Some venues are still standing, others tragically gone.

This book has taken shape as a series of snapshots. Each chapter focuses its lens on one of the pubs, ballrooms, clubs, concert halls, streets, recording studios, societies or holy places that have hosted the music made in Glasgow since the Middle Ages. Countless other buildings could have been included and countless other stories could have been told. There can be no comprehensive guide to this messy, mischievous city – and that is part of its great charm.

A Brief Look Back

Glasgow began as a fishing and trading village on the River Clyde. Its streets were laid to the sound of bone flutes, wooden whistles and folk songs. The Roman post of Cathures (c. AD 80) introduced chime bells and pipes of a different tune. Later, Celtic traders with their own songs settled in the area, and in the sixth century St Mungo built his church where Glasgow Cathedral now stands, where early Christian chant was sung and where this book's first chapter begins.

The earliest reference to an organ in Glasgow dates from 1520. By the onset of the Reformation there were more than 50 song schools across Scotland, and Glasgow's 16th-century choristers were well versed in Gregorian chant and part singing. Life outside the kirk walls bustled to jigs and reels, ballads and airs, pipes, clarsachs, fiddles (mentioned in Scottish documents from about 1450 onward) and drums. The vast majority of music from this period was never written down, and still more was lost during the destruction brought about by the Reformation. In August 1560, the Scottish Parliament abolished the Mass and adopted Calvinism. Only the song schools of Edinburgh and St Andrews survived the first zealous wave of the Reformation. Whole churches were razed, destroying centuries' worth of manuscripts and the means of employment for at least a generation of musicians. Church music was reduced to a handful of simple psalm tunes. Organs were frowned upon by the new church – too decorative – and music on the streets was hushed up. Like most of reformed Scotland, late 16th-century Glasgow was a quiet place to be.

In 1579, King James VI threw a lifeline to Scotland's music. 'The art of musik and singing,' he warned

Right: Glasgow Orpheus Choir concert in the Winter Gardens at the People's Palace c. 1910.

Right: Colour lithograph poster by Charles Rennie Mackintosh (1868–1928) for *The Scottish Musical Review*, 1896.

in a personal decree, 'is almaist decayit and sall shortly decay without tymous remeid be providit.' He instructed all councils 'of the maist speciall burrows of this realme' to 'erect and sett up ane sang scuill with ane maister sufficient and able for instructioun of the youth in the said science of music.' Glasgow's post-Reformation 'sang schwyll' opened its doors in the 1630s under the instruction of 'maister' Duncan Burnett. The students sang in church but the psalms they intoned were much plainer than Scotland's earlier polyphony.

Gradually, power structures shifted. The clout of the church gave way to the wealth of the merchants who had made Glasgow the second largest city in Scotland (after St Andrews) by 1670. This class of nouveau riche indulged in playing instrumental art music at home. International traders introduced foreign manuscripts and instruments into the mix – notably the Italian violin, which had turned up in Scotland by the early 17th century. This more resonant instrument all but wiped out the medieval fiddle, and with it came new musical inflections: English country dances, German hornpipes, ditties in the Italianate sonata style. The latest French fashions (lutes, virginals, clavichords, violins and viols) had already started filtering in with Scotland's French queens. Louis de France, the most famous music teacher in Scotland during the late 17th century, taught privately in Glasgow homes from 1691. All very cosmopolitan!

Glasgow has always been a hub for Highlanders and Gaels, whose wandering came and went between Scotland and Ireland. The collapse of Highland communities in the decades after Culloden channelled an influx of Gaelic speakers southwards and the first stages of the Clearances brought more laments of exile to the city. The gap between Glasgow's urban rich and poor grew alongside its industrial wealth, but culture paid less attention to class boundaries than social conditions did. Private soirees in the fine homes of the Trongate segued between rustic airs and refined imported tunes in a genre-defying blend that you'd be lucky to find nowadays.

Even Glasgow's church music eventually began to loosen up. More churches in the city meant more precentors; more precentors meant more musical activity, and more room to manoeuvre. One bizarre permutation of the strict church rules was the 'psalmody-rhyme' – the practice of singing nonsensical lyrics to psalm tunes so that church choirs could practise their music without bandying about their sacred words. Imagine a foursquare psalm tune with these jaunty lyrics:

Above: Crowd at Queen's Park bandstand, summer 1955.

I gued and keekit up the lum,
The skies for to behold,
A daud o' soot fell in my e'e,
Which did me quite blindfold.

- Enter the Scottish Enlightenment, with publishing houses, such as James Aird, printing treatises on 'musical improvement' and debates raging as to whether churches should be allowed organs. In 1785, Glasgow's Episcopal Chapel imported a Snetzler from Edinburgh and local Presbyterians began referring to the church as 'the Whistlin' Kirk'. The minister at St Andrew's in the Trongate was a keen fiddler himself and installed an organ in 1808; the Lord Provost wrote to sternly inform said minister that he would be held personally responsible for 'any breach of peace which might possibly be occasioned by the innovation he had attempted to introduce.'

Glasgow's first purpose-built performance venue appeared as late as 1752, when a wooden booth was put up next to the old Bishop's Castle. It was burned down a year later by a pious rabble denouncing the place as a house of evil, but still – the tide was turning. Wealthy homes were kitted out with pianos and began hosting glee clubs and music societies. In 1756 city magistrates launched free music lessons for 'parishioners of good character'. Migrant workers brought new folk songs

Right: Govanhill Recreation Ground, early 20th century.

Opposite, above: Copland's phonographs advertisement, 1909.

Opposite, below: Famous Hungarian composer and pianist, Béla Bartók, arriving in Glasgow for his concert in St Andrew's Hall, November 1933.

and dance into the city. In 1796, the Assembly Rooms opened its doors for high-society soirees and dancing; in 1799, the Gentlemen's Subscription Concerts set up a series of regular private events. Within the first few decades of the 19th century, Glasgow's musical culture shifted from Reformation clampdown to industrial-scale entertainment business.

Glasgow's new industrialists had the time, taste and money for musical patronage. From the 1820s, William Euing, insurance underwriter and broker of West George Street, ran a glee club called the Glasgow Larks that met at his home every morning at 6 am. The first specialist music journal in the UK, the *British Minstrel*, was published out of Bath Street. Richard Adams, music-seller of Buchanan Street, founded his own amateur orchestra.

Meanwhile there was a growing supply of, and demand for, public concerts. Italian opera companies regularly came through town; as Conrad Wilson details in his chapter on the Theatre Royal and opera culture in Glasgow, the great Italian diva Angelica Catalani gave performances in Glasgow in 1808, for which seats could booked at Mrs Wright's grocer's shop on Argyle Street. Jenny Lind sang *La Sonnambula,* and *La Fille du Regiment* at the Caledonian Theatre. The short-lived City Theatre burned down in 1845 when special effects in the haunted glen scene of *Der Freischütz* went awry.

Glasgow's first official music festival was held in 1821. Four days long, opening with a 'grand symphony' by Beethoven (sadly there's no record of which number), the festival featured an orchestra of miscellaneous amateurs whose performance was, according to audience reports, fairly awful. But they were ambitious. Also on the line-up were Mozart's *Jupiter Symphony* and *Magic Flute* overture, 'some works by Haydn' and a selection of Burns songs. The Italian violin virtuoso, Paolo Spagnoletti, was guest soloist and Madame Catalani returned on popular demand. Newspaper reports tell of one cobbler who couldn't afford the ticket price but was so determined to hear Catalani sing that he broke into the theatre, hid in the space between the ceiling and the roof slates and was only discovered

(and arrested) when plaster began crumbling onto the audience below.

The city's workforce wanted entertainment and plenty of it. Pubs on the Saltmarket converted back rooms into 'singing saloons' for cabarets and sing-alongs, but the crowds soon outgrew the small spaces and proprietors notched things up a gear. Purpose-built music halls sprang up, from the Royal Princess's Theatre in the Gorbals (whose owner Harry McKelvie is credited with creating pantomime) to the venue that became the Theatre Royal in Cowcaddens, now home to Scottish Opera. These velvet-upholstered, dime-a-dozen comic stages produced some of Glasgow's most iconic artists: even Will Fyffe, born a Dundonian, wore his allegiance on his sleeve when he penned his anthemic 'I belong to Glasgow'.

The Victorian class system established a new musical dichotomy – high and low, refined and rough – and the moral trappings to go with it. Glasgow's Social Reform Society tut-tutted over the potential of singing saloons to corrupt the workforce and provided alternative entertainment in the form of 'respectable' concerts. But crowds soon bored without their music-hall fix and the Society concerts became a bizarre melange of comic and serious, elegant and lairy – a kind of pops variety show with a moral message attached.

- Indigenous classical music in Glasgow was almost exclusively amateur for most of the 19th century. After all, there wasn't anywhere to study music at college level until the founding in 1890 of Glasgow Athenaeum's School of Music, later the Royal Scottish Academy of Music and Drama, now the Royal Conservatoire of Scotland (see Keith Bruce's chapter for more detail on the institution's various name changes). One of the few 19th-century Glaswegian classical talents to achieve international fame was the pianist, Frederic Lamond: born in Lynedoch Place in 1868, his father was a weaver; his mother was killed in a steamboat collision on the Clyde. Lamond found his way to Germany, befriended Brahms, Tchaikovsky, Wagner and Richard Strauss and became one of the finest Beethoven interpreters of his day.

Glasgow was slow to produce its own classical crop but had no shortage of esteemed visitors. Chopin, Joachim, Sarasate, Sullivan and many more passed through town in the late 19th century, and there were venues to welcome them. Kibble Palace was shipped up the Clyde on a barge in 1873 and reconstructed in the West End's Botanical Gardens, where it hosted concerts and exhibitions well into the 20th century. City Hall opened in 1841 between two cheese shops in the Candleriggs and installed an organ in 1853. As Tom Service charts, City Hall was easily the best acoustic in the city until 1877, when the magnificent St Andrew's Halls was built where the M8 now severs Bath Street. St Andrew's Halls burned down in 1962 due to a stray cigarette end at a boxing match. Hugh Macdonald's chapter sums up the poignancy of that fire, one of the great tragedies of Glasgow's cultural history.

Meanwhile, the roots of unionism and philanthropy formed on factory floors and around politicised dining-room tables. Music education suited the community service bill nicely and, as early as the 1840s, groups such as the Glasgow Mechanics Union ran music classes for 150–200 people at a time. The forerunner of the Musicians' Union was the Amalgamated Musicians' Union and in 1893 the Glasgow branch was one of the first to be founded. In 1891, the city held its inaugural *Glasgow Festival* – an industrial-scale event involving 8,000 performing participants. The buzz of amateur music-making lasted well into the 20th century. The iconic Glasgow Orpheus Choir (1901–51) was just one of more than 100 choirs active in Glasgow during the first half of the 20th century. An open-air amphitheatre in Kelvingrove Park staged orchestral concerts between the wars.

Below: Glasgow's first Gig on the Green took place in August 2000. The organisers were Mean Fiddler (the organisation behind music festivals such as the Reading Festival) and Regular Music.

Glasgow University, founded in 1451, finally appointed its first independent Chair of Music in 1929, the same year that the composer/musicologist Erik Chisholm founded his Active Society for the Propagation of New Music. As well as a fascinating (and still underrated) composer and conductor, Chisholm made extraordinary new music events happen. He brought Béla Bartók, to Glasgow on three separate occasions.

The orchestra that eventually became the Royal Scottish National Orchestra (RSNO) was founded in 1891 but remained part-time until 1951. The BBC Scottish Symphony Orchestra was Scotland's first full time professional orchestra, founded in 1935 but only a 35-piece studio band until 1967. Today it's one of the finest orchestras in Europe. In 1959 the Motherwell-born Alexander Gibson returned from studies in London to become the RSNO's first Scottish conductor. Gibson would prove to be one of the most influential figures on the Scottish classical music scene, founding Scottish Opera in 1962 and a contemporary music series called *Musica Nova* – which gave the UK premiere of Stockhausen's *Gruppen* and Schoenberg's *Violin Concerto* among many other achievements – in 1971. The Scottish Chamber Orchestra gave its inaugural concert at the City Hall in 1974. Today Glaswegians have the pick of three first-rate orchestral concerts almost every week.

• The term 'folk revival' is problematic, mainly because it implies that folk music had died out, but there's no question that the decades after the Second World War saw a reawakening of sorts. And as a meeting point for Islanders, Highlanders and Lowlanders, for rural Gaels and city folk, Glasgow's traditional music scene was where stylistic trends from around the country came to cross-pollinate.

For a long while the folk scene mainly happened outwith formal venues. Immigrant communities didn't tend to tout their ethnic colours in public; sing-songs around the piano at home, community centres or local pubs were the heart of most traditional music-making. Music hall and variety performers toured tenement back greens as court singers, standing in the centre of the shared garden singing popular numbers on demand. Families leaned out of their windows to listen and tossed in a few coins if they liked what they heard.

The institutionalisation of pipe music makes for weird and wonderful reading in John Purser's beautifully wry chapter. The Scottish Pipe Band Association was founded in 1930 and has held the World Pipe Band Championships in Glasgow Green annually ever since. The College of Piping was founded to 'preserve and promote' the highland bagpipe tradition, publishing the *Piping Times* magazine since 1948 and its first tutor book in 1952. The latter is still the bestselling bagpipe book ever issued. In the late 1990s, the National Piping Centre set up shop across town in an Italianate church at the top of Cowcaddens.

In the 1950s, a schoolteacher called Norman Buchan set up his Schools Ballad Club at Rutherglen Academy, where he encouraged the likes of Adam McNaughtan and Gordeanna McCulloch to think of song going hand in hand with urban politics. The socialist movement, the unions, the galvanising knock-on of American political song: this was the heart of the so-called folk revival, as Ewan McVicar's chapter on the old Scotia remembers from colourful personal experience. Paul Robeson sang in Queen's Park on May Day, 1960. The Whistlebinkies formed that same year – one of the first traditional bands to combine pipes, fiddles and clarsach. Matt McGinn, born in Ross Street in the East End, met Pete Seeger in 1961 and played with him and Bob Dylan at New York's Carnegie Hall. McGinn sang of life

on the streets of Glasgow. Adam McNaughtan kept a bookshop on Parnie Street and sang about post-war changes: the 'Jeely Piece Song' about the high rises, 'Oh where is the Glasgow I used to know?' about days gone by. In 1964, three librarians from the Mitchell formed The Clutha. They sang in broad accents and plundered historical characters from the library archive to populate their songs.

Clive's Incredible Folk Club ran for a few weeks between March and April of 1966 on the 4th floor of 134 Sauchiehall Street. The club's lifespan was brief but it left its mark, mainly in lending its name and an early platform to The Incredible String Band. Key performers during those short weeks included Matt McGinn, Hamish Imlach, Alex Campbell, Davy Graham and Bert Jansch; Billy Connolly played autoharp and Iain McGeachy – who later became John Martyn – could be found in the front row of the audience most nights. When Clive's shut down others took its place: the Glasgow Folk Club at 13 Montrose Street, the Marland, the Scotia.

In 1971, the Upper Clyde Shipbuilders went into liquidation and union leadership voted for a work-in. Huge crowds marched on Glasgow Green and benefit concerts were led by Billy Connolly, The Dubliners, Matt McGinn, Dick Gaughan, Hamish Henderson and others. Yoko Ono and John Lennon donated to the cause. After a year the government yielded.

• Glasgow's taste for Americana goes far back. Merchant seamen traded early blues and later Motown records down at the port, and by the 1930s and 1940s Glasgow was a dance capital of Europe. There were plenty of ballrooms to host the craze, notably the Barrowlands, which, as Graeme Virtue's chapter describes, opened above the scruffy market in 1934. Considering the impact the city was to make in pop music just a few decades later, it was slow to produce its own decent stuff. In 1963-64, a *Melody Maker* survey counted 350 bands working in Liverpool but just 12 in Glasgow.

Eventually Glasgow bands began touring Scotland – not so much playing ballrooms and concert halls as miners' welfares and village halls. The Alex Harvey Big Soul Band incorporated the exotic inflections of a saxophone and a conga player. Harvey was born in the Gorbals in 1935, won a newspaper competition in 1956 to 'find Scotland's Tommy Steele', played the Top Ten Club in Hamburg in 1960 and staged legendary shows at the Apollo in the 70s. The line between folk and rock blurred in Glasgow's bars and dance clubs.

Above: Sir Alexander Gibson photographed with the SNO, Kelvin Hall, 1975.

Billy Connolly founded the Humblebums with Tam Harvey in the early 1960s; Lonnie Donegan had a major hit in 1956 with 'Rock Island Line'; Lulu had a top-ten number with the Isley Brothers' song 'Shout'. The lead singer of The Poets, George Gallacher, trialled for Celtic FC; Simple Minds formed in the South Side in 1977 as Johnny and the Self-Abusers and did their first gig at a pub in Shawlands' shopping arcade. The short-lived Postcard Records operated out of a flat in West Princes Street, signing a cluster of bands that Vic Galloway's chapter describes as still shaping indie music today. John Peel christened the sound as 'shambling' for its rustic charm and wilful underachievement. Glasgow was the perfect breeding ground.

And so it went on. While the city was in its bleakest economic slump, a spate of iconic bands emerged from its streets. Many came from the outskirts: The Jesus and Mary Chain and Aztec Camera from East Kilbride; Teenage Fanclub, BMX Bandits and The Soup Dragons from Bellshill; The Close Lobsters from Paisley; Hue and Cry from Coatbridge; Wet Wet Wet from Clydebank. In the words of Tommy Cunningham of Wet Wet Wet, 'it was either crime, the dole, football, or music – and we chose music.'

Right: The Piping Centre with The Theatre Royal pictured in 2012, pre-extension.

Below: The Pavilion Theatre, with Cineworld (site of The Apollo) with The Glasgow Royal Concert Hall in the distance.

In Alasdair Gray's epochal novel *Lanark*, the protagonist, Duncan Thaw, asks an oracle to describe Glasgow. The answer comes bleakly, 'the sort of modern industrial city where most people live nowadays but nobody imagines living.' Later, when Duncan is a student at Glasgow School of Art, he and a friend stroll up to a vantage point north of Cowcaddens. They look south across the city and the friend says, 'Glasgow is a magnificent city. Why do we hardly ever notice that?' Duncan replies, 'Think of Florence, Paris, London, New York. Nobody visiting them for the first time is a stranger because he's already visited them in paintings, novels, history books and films. But if a city hasn't been used by an artist, not even the inhabitants live there imaginatively … imaginatively; Glasgow exists as a music-hall song and a few bad novels. That's all we've given to the world outside. It's all we've given to ourselves.'

Gray began writing *Lanark* in 1954 and published it in 1981. Nine years later, Glasgow was crowned European City of Culture with such success that the 'Glasgow model' was used in planning Liverpool's bid nearly two decades later. In 1983, Michael Kelly launched the 'Glasgow's Miles Better' campaign featuring the bright yellow face of Mr Happy. The Scottish National Orchestra opened the SECC in the autumn of 1985; the *Glasgow Jazz Festival* ran its first edition in 1987 with a bill that included Sarah Vaughan and Chick Corea. The Glasgow Royal Concert Hall and King Tut's Wah Wah Hut opened in 1990, The Arches in 1991. Chemikal Underground released its first single in 1994 and *Celtic Connections* staged its first festival the same year. Mogwai recorded seven live sessions for John Peel between 1996 and 2004 and Franz Ferdinand won the Mercury Prize in 2004. The revamped City Halls and Old Fruitmarket opened in 2006 and Donald Runnicles was announced as the BBC Scottish Symphony Orchestra's homecoming chief conductor in 2007. In 2008, Glasgow was granted the status of UNESCO City of Music.

Nearly a decade later, this book is a tribute to the bricks and stone, stages and people that have made Glasgow's music what it is today.

Kate Molleson, *Glasgow, 2015*

The contributors

Kate Molleson writes about music for *The Guardian* and *The Herald*. Previously she was a music critic and cycling columnist for the *Montreal Gazette* and assistant editor of *Opera* magazine. In her spare time she plays music and rides bicycles.

Dr Elaine Moohan is senior lecturer in Music at The Open University. Her main research interests are medieval sacred music and music in Glasgow in the pre-Reformation period and long eighteenth century.

Dr Gordon Munro is Director of Music at the Royal Conservatoire of Scotland and General Editor of Musica Scotica. His research interests include early Scottish church music and music education.

Tom Service writes and broadcasts about music for *The Guardian* and BBC Radio 3. His books – *Music as Alchemy*, on conducting, and interviews with Thomas Adès – are published by Faber.

Keith Bruce has been arts editor of *The Herald* in Glasgow for over 20 years. He serves on the boards of Glasgow Jazz Festival and Enterprise Music Scotland. He owns a tenor saxophone.

Ewan McVicar is an author, songmaker and storyteller. He was educated in Glasgow libraries and acquired his performing skills in Glasgow folk clubs, pubs and other venues. He has written several books and websites about Scotland's traditional songs, and composed over 100 songs with Scottish school children. He is currently heavily active in social projects in Uganda.

Conrad Wilson was staff music critic of *The Scotsman* from 1963 until 1991 and today writes for *The Herald*. He was the Edinburgh Festival's programme editor for 16 years, lectured on opera at Glasgow University and has written 19 books, including a major biography of Puccini for Phaidon, the authorised biography of Sir Alexander Gibson for Mainstream, and histories of Scottish Opera and the Royal Scottish National Orchestra for Collins.

Alison Kerr is a freelance journalist who writes primarily for *The Herald* and *The Scotsman*. Her research project *Stars in Scotland* charts the visits of stars from the movie, music and showbusiness worlds to Scotland in the 20th Century.

Hugh Macdonald was Head of Music at BBC Scotland and Director of the BBC Scottish Symphony Orchestra. He is now Co-Artistic Director of the Lammermuir Festival.

Graeme Virtue is a journalist and broadcaster who lives in Glasgow. He writes about music for *The Guardian*.

John Purser is a composer, playwright and musicologist who wrote the award-winning radio series and book *Scotland's Music*. When not lost in pre-history, he crofts with his American wife Barbara on the Isle of Skye, where he also lectures and researches for the Gaelic College, Sabhal Mòr Ostaig.

Martin Cloonan is Professor of Popular Music at the University of Glasgow.

Vic Galloway is an Edinburgh-based BBC broadcaster, journalist and author. His book about the Fence Collective, *Songs in the Key of Fife*, was published by Polygon in 2013.

Malcolm Jack is a Scottish freelance music and arts journalist based in Glasgow. He is Music Editor of *The Big Issue*, and writes for titles including *The Guardian*, *The Scotsman*, *The List*, *Metro* and *Time Out*.

Neil Cooper is an arts writer and critic based in Edinburgh. He writes about theatre, music and art for *The Herald*, *Map*, *The List* and *Line* magazine, and has written for *Scottish Art News*, *The Arts Journal*, *The Wire*, *Plan B*, *The Times*, *The Independent*, *Independent on Sunday*, *The Scotsman*, *Scotland on Sunday*, *Sunday Times (Scotland)*, *Scottish Daily Mail*, *Edinburgh Evening News*, *Is This Music?* and *Time Out Edinburgh Guide*.

GLASGOW CATHEDRAL

Before the Reformation: the auspicious choir of Glasgow

Elaine Moohan

Left: Glasgow Cathedral, viewed from W. Cathedral Square.

Below: Glasgow, antique map detail, late 16th Century.

The place where Glasgow Cathedral now stands is the very oldest part of the city. Glasgow's earliest surviving document shows that the piece of ground was designated as belonging to the church of St Mungo early in the 12th century, and it was here that, in the 1130s, work began on the cathedral. The stones were laid over the grave of Mungo himself – a sixth-century apostle and the patron saint of Glasgow, otherwise known as St Kentigern. With the cathedral came its hierarchical clerical offices and its key musical posts: most important of these were the 'precentor' and 'succentor' (or 'chanter' and 'subchanter', as they're sometimes called).

The precentor had overall responsibility for all music used during the cathedral's services. He rehearsed and directed the choir and recruited new members. He was also in charge of the sang school (the local term for a song school) where the choirboys were educated and where the choir probably rehearsed. In return he was given a house on

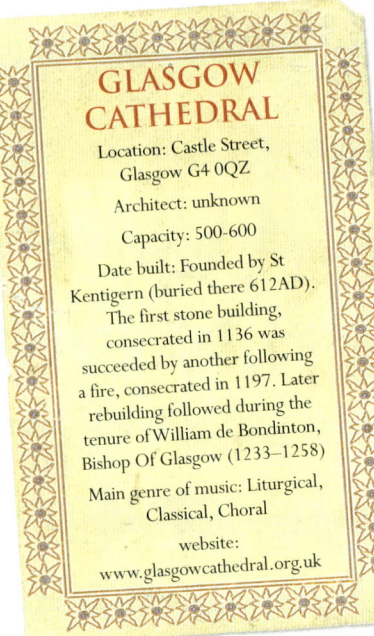

GLASGOW CATHEDRAL

Location: Castle Street, Glasgow G4 0QZ

Architect: unknown

Capacity: 500-600

Date built: Founded by St Kentigern (buried there 612AD). The first stone building, consecrated in 1136 was succeeded by another following a fire, consecrated in 1197. Later rebuilding followed during the tenure of William de Bondinton, Bishop Of Glasgow (1233–1258).

Main genre of music: Liturgical, Classical, Choral

website: www.glasgowcathedral.org.uk

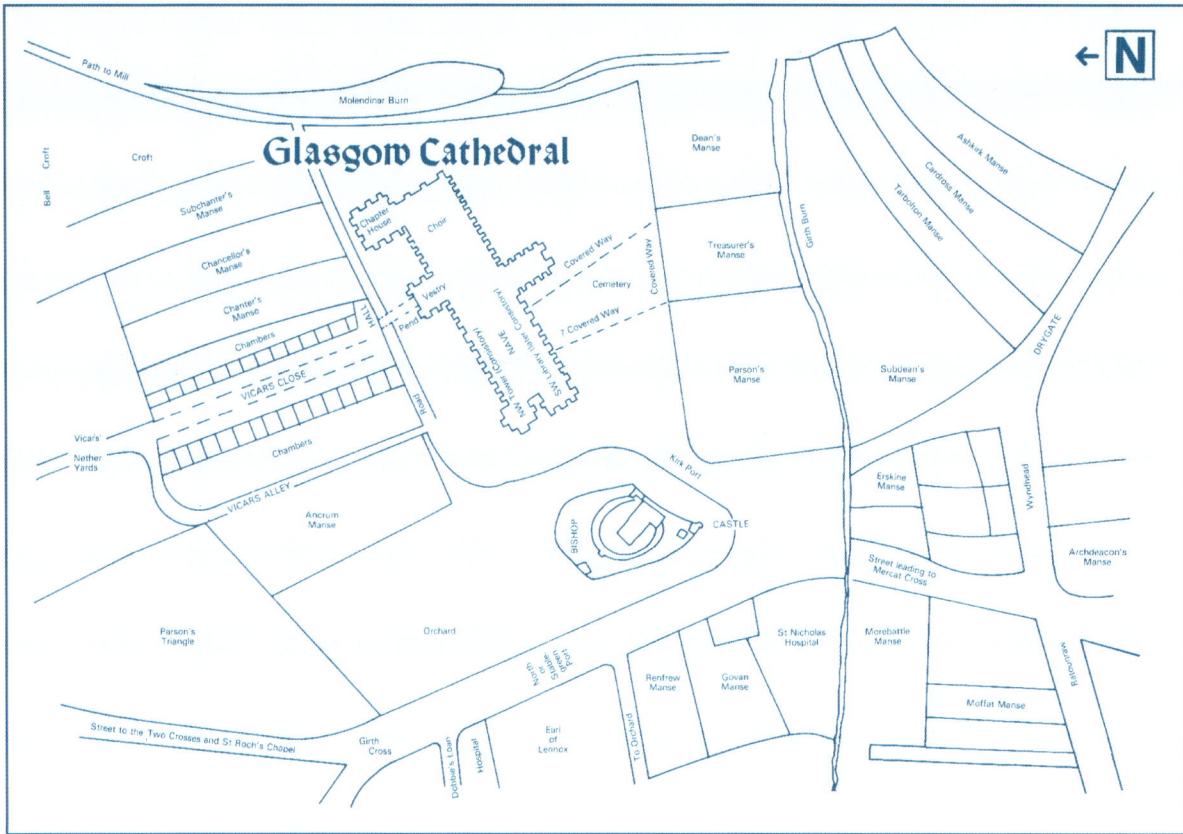

Right: Map of Cathedral Precinct showing the cathedral and its associated manses.

the north side of the cathedral and a modest stipend. The succentor, or subchanter, assisted the precentor in his duties with the additional responsibility of providing food and lodgings for the choirboys. He, too, was given a manse near the cathedral and a stipend.

It's hard to guess the size of the choir in its earliest years, but we do know that by the time of Bishop Andrew Muirhead (1455–1473) Glasgow Cathedral had 12 vicars choral (adult male singers), and by 1508 that number had increased to 18. It was Bishop Muirhead who built a hall specifically for the men of the choir on the north side of the cathedral, a two-storey building that functioned as their shared living quarters and housed the sang school. An inscribed lintel stone from this building still survives today and is currently housed in the nearby Provand's Lordship. The inscription reads:

> *Has pater Andreas antistes candidit edes*
> *Presiteris choro Glasgu famulantibus almo*
>
> [Bishop Andrew put up these buildings for the priests who serve the auspicious choir of Glasgow]

As for the choirboys? There is no documented mention of them until April 1427, when we know that the choir contained at least four unbroken voices in its ranks. The education and housing costs of these boys would have been supported by various bequests, including gifts of spur silver from the Crown.

Music is fundamental to the Catholic liturgy, so other churches in Glasgow also needed musicians among their clergy. The Collegiate Church of St Mary and St Ann was founded on the south side of the Trongate in 1525 and included three choristers and an organist who played daily and worked at the sang school. Choristers were typically required to be skilled in singing, letters

Right: Vicars Choral Stone, commemorating Bishop Andrew Muirhead.

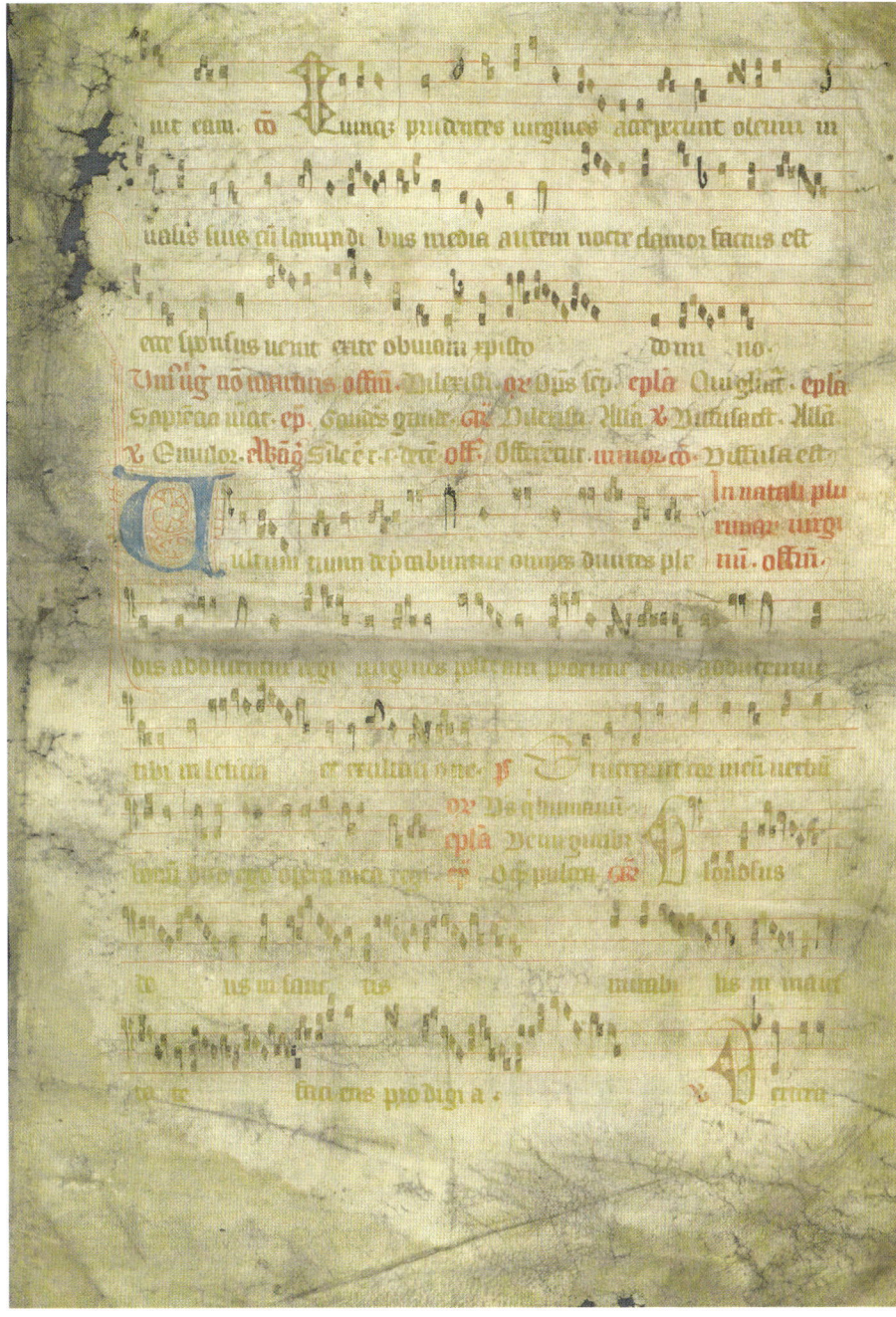

So what did these musicians sing? There are just a few pieces of music mentioned in the archives. For example, in 1454 the Dominican celebrant received a benefice (6 pennies and a gallon of the best ale in town) for celebrating anniversary Masses for the soul of one John Stewart, provided they sang the *Placebo* and *Dirige* in the choir as well as in a sung Mass. In another bequest, the Dominicans were given 10 merks by Matthew Stewart, laird of Castlemilk, for celebrating an annual Mass, a fee that doubled to 20 merks if the Mass was fully sung. This sort of evidence indicates the special recognition of a sung liturgy among wealthy worshippers and the belief that a sung Mass would bring greater heavenly rewards to the benefactor. Clearly the choir was worth paying good money to hear.

What did their music books look like? We know from an inventory of Glasgow Cathedral's library dated 1432 that the books used at daily services were kept in the cathedral itself rather than locked in the library. They were probably stored in a cupboard within a large book stand and would have contained the music required for all of the prayers that punctuated the medieval day. These included six noted missals and six graduals for celebrating Mass, plus three noted breviaries and seven antiphonals for singing the divine office. Sadly the books of the cathedral library no longer exist, having been lost or

Left: Liturgical fragment. The page belongs to a gradual, the book containing music for all the Masses throughout the year.

and science, and to this end they were instructed at the sang school in the art of singing plainchant, descants and part-music, and all of them would have had organ lessons. As with cathedral choirs of today, the boys were removed from singing duties when their voices broke, but they weren't booted out onto the street: there was provision for them to continue their education at the Grammar School for a further two years.

Right: Noted Breviary – Liturgical fragment.

destroyed over the centuries, but a few fragmentary pages of books likely to have belonged to that library still survive in Glasgow today.

This page belongs to a gradual, the book containing music for all the Masses throughout the year. It shows the ending of one Mass, the opening text for a second and the start of a third. This third Mass is identified in the rubric written in red ink at the right-hand side:

In natali plurimarum virginum

[Feast days celebrating several virgin saints all at once]

The book itself was designed to be placed on a large book stand and would either have been used by the precentor (or the succentor) to direct the choir, or by a group of singers all standing around it. The stave is 20 mm high and each notehead is 5 mm high; the notation needed to be big enough to be legible from some distance.

This fragment from a noted breviary contains music sung at matins, or morning prayer, on feast days of the apostles. Usually a breviary would only contain the text for the divine office, and the singer would need to have an antiphonal to provide the musical setting. In this instance, though, both the texts and the plainchant for the musical items are included within the same book. On this page the staves are only 10 mm high and the noteheads are 2 mm high; it would have been difficult for this book to be used by a large group of singers. It's more likely that it was placed on the book stand and used by the musician who was directing the choir.

After the Reformation: threttein comon tunes and some psalmes

Gordon Munro

John Knox's fiery preaching in 1559 led to rioting in various Scottish towns and the 'purging' of churches. The first Reformation Parliament (Edinburgh, 1560) abolished Roman Catholicism in Scotland and adopted a Calvinist Confession of Faith as drawn up by Knox. The impact on music at Glasgow Cathedral, as in all Scottish churches, was immense. Knox's regime banned the use of anything but simple, unaccompanied congregational psalmody, sung in Scots instead of Latin. In common with all other churches in Scotland, Glasgow Cathedral was stripped of its ornate artwork, books, vestments and organ. A long period of sobriety descended on the musical life of religious Scotland.

Sunday services in the Reformed Kirk were long. The 'reader', who also led the psalm-singing and was known as either precentor or 'uptaker of the psalms', led a preliminary service that lasted an hour or so and included scriptural readings, prayers and psalm-singing. This was directly followed by the ringing of a bell to mark the entrance of the minister and the beginning of his service: more prayers, more readings and a sermon with psalms before and after it. In 1595, daily morning prayers took place in the cathedral at 7 am and evening prayers at 5 pm, both with plenty of psalm singing.

As elsewhere in Scotland, Glasgow Cathedral's prestigious sang school probably didn't survive the Reformation: with no place for ornate choral music there was no need to train choristers. But a revival in music education began in the late 16th century and the sang school in Glasgow was up and running again by 1577, now in the control of the burgh council rather than the church. William Struthers, reader and precentor at the cathedral (now the High Kirk) was master of the sang school.

The music for the new Reformed liturgy was largely imported from England and the Continent. Struthers would have led his congregation and sang school pupils in the simple metrical psalm tunes of Knox's English congregation at Geneva, allowing one note per one syllable of text – nothing fancy or florid that might distract from the meaning of the words. Some of these tunes, like 'Old Hundredth', are still in use today. In 1587, Struthers's duties are listed as singing 'in the High Kirk from the ringing of the first bell to the minister's coming in'; he was also to 'appoint four men to sit beside him, beneath the pulpit'. These four men were joined by Struthers's sang school pupils, meaning that, to all intents and purposes, they formed a choir to help lead the congregational singing.

It's quite possible that this choir sang some of the four-part psalm harmonisations made by John Buchan, who in 1592 was appointed master of Glasgow's sang school and precentor

Below: Engraving of part of the Crypt of Glasgow Cathedral.

Above: Engraving of Glasgow Cathedral seen from the Necropolis.

Right: On the Outskirts of Glasgow with The Cathedral Beyond. Watercolour, artist unknown, c. 1840.

at the nearby Tron Kirk (formerly the Collegiate Church of St Mary and St Ann). Edward Millar, in his preface to the 1635 *Scottish Psalter*, describes Buchan as one of the 'primest Musicians that ever this kingdome had'. As well as being a gifted composer, Buchan was something of a maverick. In 1596, the High Kirk presbytery issued him with a stern warning to sing only texts 'contenit in the word of God' – non-scriptural hymns, they reminded him, were banned in the kirk. In 1600, Buchan and his sang school pupils took part in a colourful pageant to welcome James VI on his arrival to Glasgow.

Buchan was succeeded as master of the sang school by Duncan Burnett, another exceptional musician, in the early 17th century. Burnett's famous music book contains his own compositions (three pavans, variations on a ground bass and two song arrangements, all for keyboard), as well as keyboard music by William Kinloch and William Byrd, consort music by John Black and 44 psalm-tune harmonisations by Andrew Kemp, sometime master of the renowned music school in Aberdeen. It's very likely that some of Kemp's harmonisations would have been sung in the cathedral.

The names and salaries of many 16th- and 17th-century precentors are preserved in the records, but pitifully little is known about the cathedral's music during this period. It's likely that these men made use of the various Scottish psalm books published in 1625 and 1633 (linked with the Aberdeen music school) and in 1634 and 1635 (linked with Edinburgh and the Chapel Royal at Stirling). In the late 17th century, the cathedral's precentors possibly 'lined out' the psalms, as described in the 1645 *Directory for Public Worship*: 'Where many in the Congregation cannot read, it is convenient that the Minister, or some other fit person appointed by him … read the Psalm line by line before the singing thereof.' This most unmusical practice, imported from England, persisted until well into the 19th century in some parts of Scotland.

At the close of the 17th century, Glasgow burgh council sought to appoint one of the foremost musicians in Scotland, 'Louis de France', as master of its music school. Louis was to be engaged to teach 'the threttein comon tunes and some psalmes'. It's not known for sure whether Louis ever took up the position, but he would surely have been dispirited by the state of church music: a burgh that knew only 13 psalm tunes can't have been much inspiration to a musician of his stature. In 1781, the Church of Scotland leavened its diet of psalmody with the publication of scriptural paraphrases to be sung to the same selection of tunes; it wasn't until the late 19th century that hymns were introduced into worship.

Glasgow's Sacred Music Institution, founded in 1796, installed an organ in the cathedral's organ loft in August 1803 – probably the first organ in any Presbyterian church in Scotland. It wasn't used during church services, though, but for the rehearsals and public meetings that the Sacred Music Institution held in the cathedral. The Institution folded in around 1805 and in 1812 the organ was moved to St Andrew's Episcopal Church, nicknamed the 'Whistlin' Kirk' for its blatant musicality. It was another 50 years before the Church of Scotland finally lifted its ban on the use of instrumental music during worship in 1864. A few years later, in 1879, a magnificent 'Father Willis' organ was permanently installed in Glasgow Cathedral. This instrument has been rebuilt and enlarged several times. It was completely reconstructed by Harrison & Harrison in 1996, in the style of the original instrument, and continues to lead congregational worship in Glasgow's 'High Kirk'.

Music at Glasgow Cathedral was recognised as 'auspicious' as long ago as the late 15th century. The cathedral has always been a major centre of musical activity in Glasgow, and one of the most prestigious religious musical institutions in Scotland. These days it has an excellent semi-professional choir and hosts regular organ recitals and concerts. Things could have been very different, of course. Thomas Wood, a former Benedictine monk, set about trying to preserve the music of the Old Church in a lavish set of part-books compiled after the Reformation. He lamented 'notwithstanding of this travell I haue takin I can not vnderstand bot musike sail pereishe in this land alutterlye.' As we have seen, church music suffered a serious decline after the introduction of Calvinism in 1560 and from the mid-17th century until the late 19th century. But instrumental music is now a fully accepted part of worship in the 'High Kirk', and officially sanctioned musical tastes have become progressively more catholic. For proof, just take a glance at the four editions of the *Church Hymnary* (1898, 1927, 1973, 2005). The latest includes music ranging from plainchant to worship songs, as well as original harmonisations of 16th- and 17th-century psalm tunes. Wood's doom-laden prophecy has, thankfully, been averted.

Above: The Cathedral floodlit for Christmas, late 1960s.

CITY HALLS

Tom Service

When it opened in 1841, the City Hall in Candleriggs was the embodiment of a city's belief in the essential connection between mercantile success and cultural enrichment. George Murray's building was to be Glasgow's village hall – a place for politics, town meetings and culture to come together. The Hall's situation expressed that symbiosis as concretely as possible: a grand auditorium built over Glasgow's Old Bazaar in the Merchant City. It was a place where the developing cultural sophistication of its populace would go hand in hand with the burgeoning economic riches that Glasgow was responsible for manufacturing and distributing to all of those Imperial dominions over which the sun never set.

That idealised progress would only ever come true for a small percentage of its citizens, of course, and the squalor of much of Glasgow's living conditions for the workers who gave the city its greatness would be a blight that successive generations of politicians and city leaders would struggle with – or cravenly accept – throughout the 19th and 20th centuries and beyond. But from the start, the City Hall was a place that reflected Glasgow's hopes and dreams in its speeches and public meetings. It envisioned a richer existence than one solely focused on economics, either the hand-to-mouth struggle for survival in the slums or the Imperial excursions of the city's wealthiest merchants. In the new kinds of musical entertainment (or 'education', as the Abstainer's Union who ran the early City Hall's series of Saturday evening concerts called them), the City Hall was the theatre of a city's cultural dreams.

And it remains so today. Since 2006 it is in arguably its most effective incarnation since the 1840s as the home of the BBC Scottish Symphony Orchestra. That latest revamp has revealed the secret that Glaswegian music-lovers have long known: that the grand auditorium possesses one of the finest acoustics for orchestral music, above all for small and medium-scale ensembles, in the UK. Recent years make up one of the main periods of achievement for music at the City Hall; the others are its early decades from its foundation until the inauguration of St Andrew's Halls in 1877, and the years after the demise of St Andrew's Halls in 1962 when the City Hall again became Glasgow's de facto concert hall until the Glasgow Royal Concert Hall opened in 1990.

Betterment and bumpers: the early years

Both nationally and internationally, the City Hall's first musical seasons reflected Glasgow's aspirations to become a major player on the musical scene. By the mid-1840s the hall was attracting some of the biggest names in British, European and even American music. The tenor, John Braham, gave a concert in 1844, which, reported *The Herald*, 'was undoubtedly the finest musical treat which has taken place in Glasgow for many years'. In the autumn of 1846, the City Hall was hosting arguably the greatest showman of orchestral music, the conductor and impresario, Louis Antoine Jullien. *The Herald* describes how Jullien brought his band 'of about twenty crack performers, many of them, indeed, unrivalled on their respective instruments, the combined effect of which, under the admirable training of their accomplished leader, it is almost impossible to describe.' The paper's reporter has a shot at it in any case: 'The highest skill and cultivation were manifest, and Beethoven's *Symphony in A*, especially, was played with a degree of taste and delicacy for which we were scarcely prepared.' (Hard to believe that Jullien would play Beethoven's *Seventh* with just 20 players; perhaps the critic was too dazzled by the spectacle to count accurately the musicians on stage.)

The hall's international visitors inspired the organisers of regular home-grown concert series that took place at the hall. From 1854 the Abstainers' Union, those anti-alcohol upholders of temperance and sobriety, ran 'Saturday Evening Concerts'. Self-consciously

Right: City Halls, exterior view.

Right: BBC Scottish Symphony Orchestra at City Halls, photograph taken for their New Year 2015 tour in China.
© BBC, photo John Wood.

GLASGOW CITY HALLS

Location: 90-98 Candleriggs, Glasgow G1 1NQ
Architect: G. Murray, 1840. Refurbished 2003/2006 by Arup Acoustics, Civic Design, Arup Venue Consultancy and Arup Scotland.
Capacity: 150–1036
Date opened: 1841 (refurbished 2003/06)
Music: Choral, Classical; Home of the BBC Scottish Symphony Orchestra
website: www.glasgowconcerthalls.com/city-halls

designed to improve the cultural horizons of the population by luring them into the City Hall and out of the city's public houses on a Saturday night, these shows were a judicious mix of classical selections with popular and patriotic songs. Despite the natural impossibility of intoxication at any event promoted by the Abstainer's Union, they were big draws for a local audience of self-improvers. In 1858, *The Herald* opined that 'whatever difference of opinion there may be as to the measures attempted by the temperance party for carrying out their views, there can be none as to the highly useful nature of the recreation schemes of the Glasgow Abstainers' Union. The directors of this society, by their pleasure trips, soirees, and concerts keep up a constant round of unexceptional amusement' – in which the 'unexceptional' (the un-sensual, the non-lascivious) is to be regarded as part of the appeal.

In August 1858, *The Herald* had words of censure, not for the sober Abstainers' Union itself, but for the City Hall audiences. 'We would give the directors one word of warning, indeed, it refers to the only fault we had to find last season, viz, to put an end to, as far as possible, the indiscriminate habit of encoring indulged in by not the most intellectual part of the audience. To tax the good nature, and overtax the strength of the artistes is dishonest, and about as reasonable as to expect a pastry-cook to give a second tart gratis because the purchaser approved of the one he had paid for.' Encoring as the audience's decision, not the performers? That's a total inversion of contemporary audience-performer relations, at least at classical concerts.

There is evidence that the City Hall's broader project to educate and elevate the musical and social habits of the populace was accomplished. At the Abstainers' Union concert on 15 January 1859, 'The City Hall … was, as usual, crowded, and the concert passed off with great éclat', so *The Herald* reports. 'We are glad to see the working classes patronising these concerts so extensively, for we believe they could not spend a Saturday evening better than by attending the City Hall.'

But there's no better illustration of how far tastes had changed (and how far they still had to go to reach

Right: Candleriggs, looking towards City Halls.

modern ideas of canon, programme and reception) than a concert that took place on 7 January 1861. *The Herald* was again in situ to report on one of the greatest chamber ensembles anyone could imagine. How about this for a line-up: 'Monsieur Vieuxtemps, first violin; Signor Piatti, violoncello; and Mr Charles Hallé, piano; Herr Ries and M Schreurs, second violin and viola.' And yet neither *Herald* nor audience (the City Hall was 'well-filled' but not a 'bumper') was won over: 'The length of the compositions, despite their intrinsic beauty, richness, and rarity, and their interpretation by artists of the highest eminence, is fatiguing, and three or four such pieces in an evening become, in real truth, "something too much" for the patience of a promiscuous audience.' The audience heard Mozart's quartet *K387*, a B flat major quartet by Beethoven (whether *Op 18 no 6* or *Op 130* is not clear); Hallé played Beethoven sonatas, and Piatti presented Bach, a performance that drew the following from *The Herald*'s reporter: 'Signor Piatti's solo was a prelude and sarabande from Johann Sebastian Bach. The old-fashioned dance music of a century and a half ago was here revived, and – craving pardon for mention of such a subject in the present circumstances – we were rather amusingly reminded by it of the source of the breakdown negro terpsichorean accompaniments of the present time.' It's a remarkable review that reveals how distant and exotic mid-19th century listeners felt the music of Bach to be, and how the gulf between popular and serious entertainments was deepening. It also makes an extraordinary, even prescient, connection between the earthy rhythms of Bach's music and popular music – on this occasion, those 'breakdown negro terpsichorean accompaniments'. The adjective 'breakdown' reads like it has fallen down a wormhole in journalistic time, as if it had dropped from the 21st century to the 19th. It is, I promise, the original remarkable locution.

You can read just how far the City Hall and its audiences had come in developing a culture of performers and listeners in the line-up of concerts in February 1877. Charles Hallé gave what had become a 'customary annual orchestral concert' with his orchestra, offering audiences the chance to compare the recently established resident orchestra in Glasgow with the famous and already mature Mancunian band. 'Mr Hallé's orchestra has the immense advantage of comprising a much greater number of executants than the band conducted by Mr Sullivan,' considered *The Herald* (Arthur Sullivan had been conductor of the Glasgow orchestra for a couple of seasons; Hallé's orchestra had the advantage of about 20 more strings than Glasgow's ensemble). 'It is to be hoped that by another year the management of our orchestral concerts may see their way to increase the number of the Strings, for until that is done Glasgow cannot possibly hold a high position in the interpretation of orchestral music.' The compare-and-contrast wasn't all in Hallé's favour, however: 'It may be said with assurance that the tone quality of the first violins of the resident orchestra was distinctly superior to that produced last evening, just as the greater excellence of Mr Hallé's violoncellos and double basses must be frankly admitted.' And where Glasgow's woodwinds 'carry the palm … Halle's horns and brass hold "first position".' With a few more strings in the resident orchestra, *The Herald* thought it 'now quite apparent that our city can hold its own with any other in the country.'

Just a few weeks later, the proper accommodation for Glasgow's musical ambitions would open in the shape of St Andrew's Halls. 'Accustomed as we are in Glasgow with the City Hall, the contrast is very striking' wrote *The Herald* on going into St Andrew's Halls for the first time. 'This effect is probably due rather to the enormous height than the increased area, because, although the area is little more than half as large again as the City Hall, the cubic content of air space is more than two-and-a-half times as large.' Glasgow was ready to realise its musical dreams as never before. After 1877, the City Hall would continue as a venue for the

Below: Andrew Manze conducts the BBC Scottish Symphony Orchestra.
© BBC, photo John Wood.

Abstainer's Union concerts, New Year celebrations and 'Great Scotch Concerts', but until the conflagration of 1962, the centre for large-scale music in the city shifted irrevocably to the new hall. By the mid-20th century, the City Hall was a sleeping beauty of an auditorium, having been turned into a store and food control centre during the Second World War. It would take an amateur boxing match and a single cigarette to change all that in October 1962.

1962–1990: Accidental rebirth

On 27 October 1962, *The Herald* carried a huge advert on its front page: 'Invasion from Outer Space – Dramatic Bible Prediction on Verge of Fulfilment! Hear Kenney Lacey and Face the Future With Confidence!' There was also an amendment: 'Owing To Recent Fire At St Andrews Hall, Service Transferred To McLellan Galleries.' That fire was to prove as potentially apocalyptic for the city's musical ambitions as Kenneth Lacey's bible prediction. After the blaze that consumed St Andrew's Halls, Glasgow's planners faced a key moment in the cultural life of the city. The choice seemed a simple one: rebuild St Andrew's Halls, which could hardly have been more highly praised by its loyal audience, its orchestra and its international roster of classical superstars; or use the insurance money to create a major new cultural centre.

In the end neither happened, and instead the planners dawdled and fudged for the next 25 years. Elsewhere in its 27 October 1962 edition, *The Herald*

Below: The BBC Scottish Symphony Orchestra playing the Bernard Herrmann score for *Psycho*, live, in 2011.
© BBC, photo John Wood.

reported 'a real possibility that the City Hall in Candleriggs may be reconditioned and offered to the Scottish National Orchestra (SNO) for concerts. The hall was used for celebrity concerts before the war, and [Councillor John S Clark] described the acoustics as "just as good as, if not better than, St Andrew's Halls".' The optimistic Councillor Clark was a canny operator: it would cost just £36,000 to refit the City Hall, which would accommodate about half the capacity of St Andrew's Halls, while *The Herald* put the price of rebuilding St Andrew's Halls at £500,000. That reconstruction would have had to be in a different location, as the former St Andrew's site 'already lacks car-parking provision and is likely to encounter further restrictions on kerbside parking.'

Ultimately a combination of parking problems and lack of cash put the kibosh on any plans that the council might have had to rebuild St Andrew's. It was a devastating lack of foresight that would cost Glasgow a major part of its national and international reputation as a destination for the world's best orchestras and soloists. For the next five seasons, the SNO and Alexander Gibson (their principal conductor since 1959 and the first Scot to hold the post) gave concerts at the Gaiety Theatre on Argyle Street near Anderston Cross. Hastily refitted in 1963, this less-than-ideal venue was declared 'The Glasgow Concert Hall'.

The Herald called it an 'uninviting barn' and years of make-do frustration ensued at The Glasgow Concert Hall. It was only in the autumn of 1968 that the SNO moved into the City Hall as their new, but still hopefully temporary, home. On 10 October that year the orchestra played the first concert of their season, opening with Britten's setting of the national anthem and climaxing with Gibson conducting Mahler's *First Symphony*. *The Herald* was positive: 'As the evening advanced expectancy turned to delight as the cleverly constructed programme showed that for music of widely ranging tonal demands, the acoustics of the orchestra's new Glasgow home were superb. The choral pianissimo, which Britten's setting of "God Save The Queen" first falls on the ear, was completely audible at the back of the balcony.'

The sound of the City Hall won praise in subsequent seasons. Early in 1969, the SNO played Webern's *Op 21 Symphony*. 'It is not the easiest piece to open a concert with, but the acoustics of the Glasgow City Hall are nearly perfect for this composer, and with [conductor] Franz-Paul Decker … in control, every note of this precisely defined score was in place.'

Cellist Mstislav Rostropovich toured to Scotland with the orchestra in October the following year, playing Haydn and Britten in the Usher Hall in Edinburgh and the City Hall in Glasgow. Malcolm Rayment wrote that 'At times the volume level was reduced to a whisper, without either tone or precision suffering. Such passages – and they included much of Haydn's slow movement and Britten's scherzo – were so delicately treated that something was lost at the Usher Hall; but in the City Hall they were heard to rare advantage.'

These concerts were hot tickets. The potential audience would have comfortably filled a St Andrew's-sized hall if only Glasgow had one. 'As for the orchestra, it not only surpassed itself at these two concerts but its playing in general this season has reached and maintained an exceptionally high standard. This in itself is a strong argument for building a concert hall of adequate size in Glasgow as quickly as possible. Once again there were many who could not get a ticket for the City Hall.' Rayment's appeal, like all the rest, went unheeded. In the search for bigger venues, the SNO in the post-Gibson era (after 1984) would use the Kelvin Hall and the newly opened SECC, all of them equally 'uninviting barns' that felt exactly like what they were: unsatisfactory stopgaps for a solution that the city was unwilling to provide until the building of the Glasgow Royal Concert Hall in the late 1980s.

Rayment's modest proposal had another corollary, which was that the City Hall had its acoustic

Above: Matthias Pintscher conducting over 100 amateur muscians and strings of the BBC Scottish Symphony Orchestra.
© BBC, photo John Wood.

Below: Glasgow City Hall poster, 1892.

OLD FRUITMARKET

Location: 90-98 Candleriggs, Glasgow G1 1NQ
Architect: John Carrick (1882). Refurbished 2003/2006 by Arup Acoustics, Civic Design, Arup Venue Consultancy and Arup Scotland (2003/06).
Capacity: 1200
Date opened: As the Fruitmarket, 1882; became music venue in 1970s, refurbished 2006
Music: Folk, Jazz, Rock, Pop, World
Website: www.glasgowconcerthalls.com old-fruitmarket/

Opposite, above: City Halls, Fruitmarket interior, prior to refurbishment, 1994.

Opposite, below: City Halls, Fruitmarket refurbished, resounding to Celtic Connections in 2009.

Below: Fruitmarket, 1969.

limitations for the largest orchestral music. It wasn't just that the platform was too high (it felt like it was dozens of feet above you if you were a small child craning your neck to try and glimpse anything beyond the feet of the first violins). The hall's stage was simply too small to accommodate a Brucknerian or Mahlerian orchestra, and the acoustic strained at its limits in full-scale late-romantic music. In the late 1980s I felt that the windows might burst with the sound and fury of Mahler's *First Symphony* with Gibson's successor, Neeme Järvi, which pounded at the limits of the sonically possible. In fact, exploding those windows might not have been a bad thing, after they had been inexplicably covered up as part of the 1968 refurbishment.

The City Hall found arguably its ideal orchestral partner with the establishment of the Scottish Chamber Orchestra (SCO), which made the City Hall its Glasgow home from its first season in 1974. In its early years with conductor Roderick Brydon (1974–1983) and then with Jukka-Pekka Saraste (1987–1991), the SCO found a symbiosis with the scale of the City Hall and its audience in repertoire from Baroque to new music. It was a partnership that inspired probably the country's single most visionary project in contemporary music commissioning from a government body in the late 20th century: Peter Maxwell Davies's series of 10 *Strathclyde Concertos*, paid for by Strathclyde Council and each composed for one or more of the SCO's principal players (the last a *Concerto for Orchestra*). All of them were premiered at the City Hall between 1988 and 1996. Occasionally the SCO experimented with the much larger space of the Glasgow Royal Concert Hall (GRCH) after 1990, but returned, rightly, to the City Hall for its Glasgow seasons. The BBC Scottish Symphony Orchestra (BBC SSO) also found a natural home at the City Hall in the concerts it gave away from its broadcast base at Queen Margaret Drive – a taste of things to come after 2006.

But despite these positive relationships and the brilliance of some of the performances it hosted (such as the cycles of Beethoven and Sibelius symphonies that the Finnish conductor, Osmo Vänskä, gave during his time as chief conductor of the BBC SSO from 1996–2002), after the SNO made its permanent concert-giving home at the GRCH in 1990 the City Hall began to feel like a tired municipal sop to classical music's other institutions in Scotland. It was in need of a new purpose, and a major renovation of its public and backstage spaces, from

M. McCOMISH.
RUSSELL TURNBULL & Co
LOUDON & Co Ld
T NEALE
R.JENKINS & Co.
JOHN HENDERSON
JAM

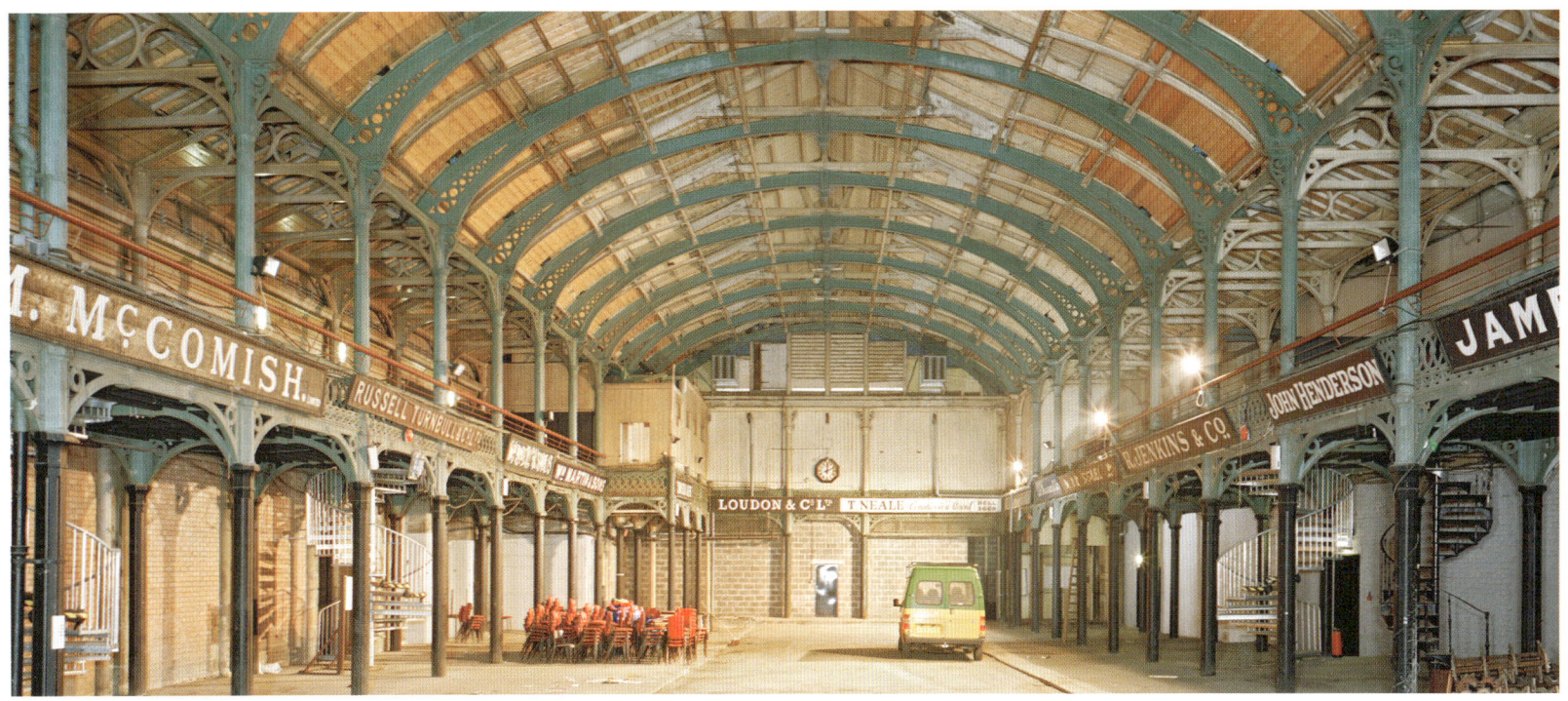

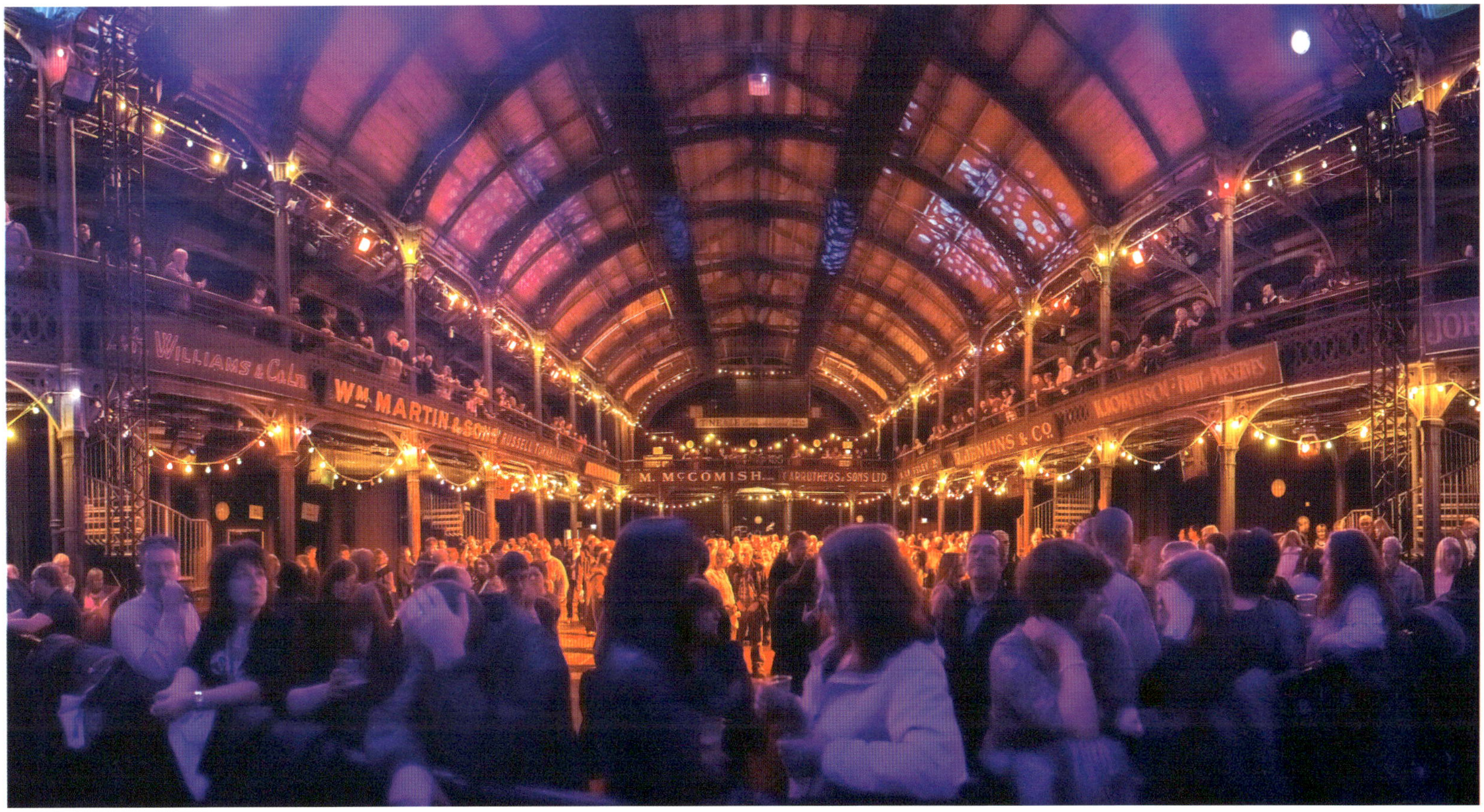
WILLIAMS & Co Ld
Wm MARTIN & SONS
M. McCOMISH
CARRUTHERS & SONS LTD
R.JENKINS & Co.

Above: Interior, City Halls, 1987. The organ screen was subsequently dismantled and sold, the organ having been removed to Chesterfield Parish Church, Derbyshire.

bars to stage, dressing rooms to foyers. And that is exactly what it got in a three-year overhaul from 2003.

Vindication: the Old Fruitmarket, the City Halls and the BBC SSO since 2006

The name is now plural. That's because as well as the reopening of the Grand Hall, the City Halls includes the neighbouring Old Fruitmarket as part of its performance portfolio. In fact, it had done since the 1970s. After it closed as a commercial site, the Old Fruitmarket was an occasional venue for rock and folk music. It was a richly atmospheric space (albeit more than a wee bit draughty before the 2006 renovation): a grand covered market on two levels with ornate ironwork and shop-front signs dating back to 1882. But the real flowering of the Fruitmarket, to mix some vegetal metaphors, came in its relationship with the *Celtic Connections* festival. Since it started in 1994, *Celtic Connections* has been based at the Glasgow Royal Concert Hall, but its irrepressible energy started to effervesce into other parts of the city from the late 1990s. Since 2000, the Old Fruitmarket has become an ever-more important part of the festival, hosting acts from the Animals to Irish flautist Michael McGoldrick and his band.

The renovation made the Fruitmarket a more comfortable and more flexible space for folk, jazz and rock, but it also became a crucible of multimedia and avant-garde performances. The central part of the BBC SSO's world premiere performance of James Dillon's *Nine Rivers* cycle in 2010 was an hour-long solo for percussion and video played in the Fruitmarket by Stephen Schick (before he rushed back to the main hall to conduct the orchestra in the concluding parts); the venue was the perfect space for the more intimate and extraordinary parts of the recent *Tectonics* festivals. And that's the genius loci of the Fruitmarket: that it can transform in an instant from party atmosphere to black-box performance-art arena. Using the main hall and the Fruitmarket together for an immersive experience was simply impossible before the renovation, and their current cross-fertilisation has opened up new creative possibilities.

Still, the most dramatic feature of the whole revamp was the astonishing transformation of the City Hall's main auditorium, now called the Grand Hall. The stage was lowered, becoming instantly more welcoming and more spacious. The effect of the replacement seats, floors, lighting, painting and uncovered windows was miraculous, physically and acoustically. Freed from its lino-clad municipal utilitarianism, the hall suddenly became a shimmering, light-filled place to hear music. The surfaces are now either white or wooden, so the hall seems bigger than it did before. It's a simple delight to be in the space, even before the music starts. The overall achievement was to preserve and amplify the best single feature of the hall – its acoustic – and finally to make it fit for purpose as a venue for orchestral music on every scale. Ilan Volkov's performance of the original version of Stravinsky's *Firebird* for more than 100 players proved the ability of the renovated space to cope with the most powerful orchestral panoply at the first evening concert in October 2006.

What the public doesn't see is equally essential: one of the most sophisticated recording and broadcast facilities in Britain, in which the BBC SSO's offices, studios, mixing desks and education programmes are integrated. Having everything on-site is the foundation of the orchestra's current success, since the band has the luxury – more like an essential if an orchestra is going to grow and develop – to rehearse and perform in the same place. You can hear that not just in its relationship with Donald Runnicles, who returned to his homeland to take over from Ilan Volkov as chief conductor in 2007, but in the whole range of concerts it performs and records, including a contemporary repertoire that no other orchestra in Scotland has the opportunity, or the ability, to handle. The City Halls are not just about the BBC, however: the Grand Hall continues to be the SCO's Glasgow home, a venue relished by the ensemble and Robin Ticciati, its principal conductor since 2009.

The City Hall's history should not have been as rich as it is. When St Andrew's Halls opened, that ought to have marked the end of City Hall's era as large-scale orchestral music's main auditorium in Glasgow. The scar that the 1962 fire left on Glasgow's musical culture is still evident today. But the way that City Halls has been renewed, and the way generations of listeners have imprinted their imaginations on its spaces, from Mozart to Mahler, Jonathan Harvey to James Dillon, makes this venue as essential to Glasgow's musical life now as it was in 1841.

Inset: Blue plaque on exterior wall of the City Halls.

Below: City Halls from Candleriggs.

THE ROYAL CONSERVATOIRE OF SCOTLAND

Keith Bruce

When the Royal Scottish Academy of Music and Drama became the Royal Conservatoire of Scotland at the beginning of the 2011–2012 academic year, the letters page and opinion columns of *The Herald* in Glasgow were filled with debate about the change. However, the new title of Scotland's premier institution for the teaching of the performing arts was only the latest of a whole series of name-changes and refinements of purpose that tell the story of an organisation which has always been developing and whose history is so complex that it contrived to mark its 150th anniversary in 1997, only six years after the School of Music celebrated its centenary in 1991.

The Glasgow Athenaeum came into being in 1847. Its classical name recalled the cultural foundation established by Emperor Hadrian in Rome and suggested a shift in direction from its roots in Glasgow's Commercial College two years earlier. If it was thought in any way grandiose, in the way that accusations of pretension greeted the 'Conservatoire' announcement in the 21st century, those reservations are unrecorded. The guest star at the Inauguration Banquet in Glasgow City Halls was writer Charles Dickens, then packing them in across the UK for readings from his work. The enthusiasm his novels showed for improving the lot of young people chimed well with the intentions of the

Left: Poster-covered wall of the Scottish College of Dramatic Art in Glasgow, 1955.

THE ROYAL CONSERVATOIRE OF SCOTLAND
(formerly the Royal Scottish Academy of Music and Drama)

LOCATION:	100 Renfrew Street, Glasgow, G2 3DB	DATE OPENED:	1988
ARCHITECT:	Sir Leslie Martin with Ivor Richards 1982-88 of William Nimmo & Partners	MUSIC:	Multi, Classical, Choral, Opera, Educational
		WEBSITE:	www.rcs.ac.uk/
CAPACITY:	various venues and capacities		

Athenaeum's founders, who provided classes in philosophy and literature as well as music, with art and drama also finding a home in the syllabus in the institution's first decades.

Initially housed in the Assembly Rooms in Ingram Street, The Athenaeum was ousted when the government bought the property to build Glasgow's central Post Office. Its first purpose-built home in St George's Place quickly proved far too small for the growing number of students – initially all male – and just five years later, in 1893, the Glasgow Athenaeum moved to Buchanan Street and the site it would occupy until the opening of the present building in Renfrew Street in 1989.

The broad-based education of the Athenaeum's initial conception quickly fractured into different colleges. Art and design were the first to make the move up to Renfrew Street and into Charles Rennie Mackintosh's celebrated Glasgow School of Art building in Garnethill. The Commercial College also departed, eventually to become part of the University of Strathclyde.

The Athenaeum's first session (1890–1891) was as the Athenaeum School of Music with Allan Macbeth as Principal. Originally from Greenock, Macbeth had studied in Leipzig with conductor Hans Richter and would serve the music school for the first decade in its new home, which boasted a concert hall, theatre, restaurant and gymnasium as well as classrooms. Productions of operas by Gounod and Offenbach were features of the sessions at the end of the 19th century under Macbeth's tenure, as was the introduction of a three-year programme of study for would-be performers and the acquisition of some highly regarded staff to teach them. They included pianist Philip Halstead, another student at Leipzig, who had performed the Mendelssohn *D Minor Concerto* at the opening of the Leipwig Gewandhaus in 1884. Violinist Henri Verbrugghen came to Scotland to join the new Scottish Orchestra, a precursor of the present Royal Scottish National Orchestra (RSNO), whose players also teach at the Conservatoire to this day. He led his own highly acclaimed string quartet and was a pivotal figure in the musical life of Glasgow until 1915. He was the soloist in the UK premiere of the Sibelius *Violin Concerto* in 1907 and was later conductor of the Minneapolis Symphony Orchestra. Verbrugghen conducted student performances of Weber's *Der Freischütz* during his time at the School of Music, while Halstead combined a career on the concert platform with nearly 50 years of teaching in Glasgow.

This auspicious beginning gave way to a time of less administrative cohesion at the start of the 20th century. Student numbers continued to grow, from just over 800 in Macbeth's first session to 3,000 in the year after the First World War. The School of Music was without a principal for most of that time, Macbeth's successor Edward Harper having resigned after just two years. It was a dynamic ex-Lord Provost of the City of Glasgow, coal magnate Sir Daniel Stevenson, who provided the impetus for the next great changes. Stevenson is remembered to this day in the name of the Conservatoire's concert hall.

On his initiative, a new Chair of Music at the University of Glasgow was combined with the post of Principal at what then became the Scottish National Academy of Music. Around the same time, the Glasgow Liberal Club, next door to the Athenaeum's Buchanan Street home, was acquired so that the new Academy could

Right: The Athenaeum Glasgow, Ingram Street was built in 1796 as Assembly Rooms. It was demolished for the building of the General Post Office in George Square.

Left: The Liberal Club, built 1907–9 and altered in 1928 for the Royal Scottish Academy of Music and Drama.

Above: Opening Soiree of the Glasgow Athenaeum, Charles Dickens in the Chair, City Hall, 28 Dec 1847, watercolour, by William Simpson.

expand on the same site. The man recruited to fill this big new job of Professor and Principal was William Gillies Whittaker. He was a great choral scholar, particularly of the works of Johann Sebastian Bach, and a conductor and composer who counted Gustav Holst amongst his friends. His innovations ranged from the establishment of degree courses to the introduction of the first dance classes. These were in the fashionable barefoot discipline of Dalcroze Eurhythmics and remained in the syllabus until the 1960s (and have recently been reintroduced to undergraduates). Whittaker also established a library of recordings as well as scores and books – the foundation of the Conservatoire's archive to this day.

It was Whittaker's successor Ernest Bullock whose influence and connections brought the Royal prefix into the Academy's name. While Whittaker was a dynamic self-made man of Quaker stock from Newcastle, Bullock had been organist and choirmaster at Westminster Abbey and oversaw all the music for the coronation of King George VI in 1936. He also provided some for that of the King's daughter, Queen Elizabeth II, in 1953, the year he left Glasgow to become Director of the Royal College of Music in London.

Although Bullock seems to have complained less about the workload of being both the University's Professor of Music and the Academy's Principal, his departure brought an end to that arrangement. Henry Havergal was able to give the Academy his full attention – and bring it much more into the public life of Glasgow. He had been Director of Music at Fettes College in Edinburgh at the age of 22 before moving to similar posts at English public schools, including Harrow and Winchester, so it is unsurprising that he was responsible for the expansion of the work of the Junior Academy that brought school pupils into the building for lessons at the weekends. He also expanded the number of recitals open to the public, particularly of chamber music. He recruited a number of expert performers to his staff and instituted the Friday lunchtime concerts that are a feature of the Conservatoire's programme to this day.

The Havergal name was to be well known in Glasgow long beyond his tenure. He departed in 1969 – becoming Principal of the College of Music in Jamaica at the age of 71 – and in that year his son Giles arrived to take over at Glasgow Citizens Theatre, beginning the period of its greatest acclaim. Henry Havergal had been widowed in 1962 and Giles's stepmother Nina has also been a pivotal person in the recent history of the Academy: she was the driving force behind the fundraising that created the Alexander Gibson Opera School development behind the new Renfrew Street, which opened in 1998.

Left: The Athenaeum in Nelson Mandela Place (formerly St George's Place), Glasgow, built 1886.

The move to the new building had begun under Principal David Lumsden, during whose tenure the Academy achieved the distinction of becoming, in 1981, the first conservatoire in the UK able to offer degrees. The move was completed under Philip Ledger. In the new millennium that expansion has continued under John Wallace, with the creation of new studios for dance and drama beyond the Opera School and the M8 motorway in the canal-side development at Speirs Lock. This converted auto-spares warehouse is home to music theatre students as well as the technical and production courses and BA in modern ballet – all key ingredients in the latest name change. The new title was intended to reflect the broad range of creative, performance and arts education that the Conservatoire now offers.

Wallace, a trumpeter of international standing, who has his own Royal connection in having played at the wedding of Charles and Diana in 1981, became the first Scot to lead Scotland's premier performing arts academy in 100 years when he arrived at the start of the 21st century for a 12-year tenure. He was also unusual in being of working-class Fife stock. His father, grandfather and uncles had all played in the brass band at the Markinch paper mill where they worked. He himself joined the band aged eight and was educated at Buckhaven High School before gaining a scholarship to King's College, Cambridge, sitting the entrance exam in the stationery cupboard at Buckhaven High. From Cambridge he went to York University and London's Royal Academy of Music before becoming principal trumpet of the London Sinfonietta and Philharmonia Orchestra and leading his own brass ensemble, the Wallace Collection.

Having overseen the latest expansion and name change, a few months after his 65th birthday in 2014 Wallace handed over to an American pianist, Jeffrey Sharkey, much more the traditional type of leader for the institution. Although he grew up in Delaware and attended Manhattan School of Music as the first double major in piano and composition (on the recommendation of no less a figure than Aaron Copland), he then studied at Cambridge as a post-graduate

Above: The Queen Arcade from Renfrew Street, Glasgow, 1956.

Right, above: Construction work in progress, Royal Scottish Academy of Music and Drama, Glasgow. Designed early 1980s.

Right, below: The completed building.

before teaching at Wells Cathedral and Purcell Schools in England. His return across the Atlantic came after eight years as director of the Peabody Institute in Baltimore, and he is enthusiastic about the breadth of music that the Conservatoire now offers.

In the run-up to the most recent name change, distinctions between the various 'schools' – of music, drama and now dance – were dissolved and students were encouraged to take subjects across other disciplines to reflect the reality of life and work beyond education. As vice-principal Maggie Kinloch has said: 'There is always room for the virtuoso, but conservatoires need to be producing the kind of artist that can work in a multidisciplinary way, the artist who thinks about their place in the world and what they bring to it.'

As well as stressing the unique position of the Scottish Conservatoire in a nation with its own rich seam of traditional music, the new Principal also sees great merit in RCS students thinking outside their personal disciplines and drawing more inspiration from the world around them. He notes a particular contrast with the approach to teaching in his homeland. 'America is a nation of specialisms. If you are a pianist then you are not a composer. You have to declare your colours. Here it is much more holistic.'

Sharkey has not only expressed enthusiasm for the broadening of the education of individual students; he also has ambitions for the bricks and mortar of Glasgow's Conservatoire. Just as the Julliard School in New York has had a face-lift to make it more appealing as a place to visit for those not actually working and studying there, Sharkey has declared a dream to revamp the frontage of the Renfrew Street building with a view to enticing more of Glasgow's wider community into the concerts, plays and other performances going on throughout the year.

As well as being a key component of Glasgow's status as a UNESCO City of Music, the Royal Conservatoire of

Scotland is also one of the city's busiest arts centres. Performances of undergraduate, postgraduate and masters students take place alongside those of associate artists like pianist Steven Osborne, the Brodsky String Quartet, conductor Donald Runnicles and the Scottish National Jazz Orchestra. Since the opening of the Alexander Gibson Opera School, a close relationship has grown up between the Conservatoire and the national opera company, with Scottish Opera and the RCS collaborating on an opera most years and many students appearing in other productions.

Created by Glasgow's merchant classes in the middle of the 19th century, the Royal Conservatoire of Scotland has been an ever-developing organism at the heart of city life ever since — no matter what name is up in lights on the canopy over the entrance.

Left: The new signage of The Royal Conservatoire of Scotland (Gaelic).

Left: The Alexander Gibson Opera School, Cowcaddens Road, Glasgow.

THE SCOTIA BAR

To The Scotia we will go, will go

Ewan McVicar

The Scotia is at the bottom of Stockwell Street, just round the corner from the Broomielaw and the River Clyde. Draw a ring of a few hundred yards around it and you have encompassed the roots, the heyday and the enduring influence of Glasgow's folk revival.

There has been little structural alteration to the pub's interior – dark wood panelling, low ceilings – since the 1920s. It claims an establishment date of 1792, and the building that houses it is certainly that old, but its name derives from the adjacent Scotia Variety and Music Hall that opened in 1862. The bar was a watering hole for theatrical types and patrons until the Music Hall burned down in 1961, and in the early days when the Music Hall was a temperance establishment (coffee and tea being the hardest drinks on offer there) the pub next door would have been stowed out. Harry Lauder had his first professional gig at the Scotia, and the young Stan Laurel was assistant manager there to his father. All of Glasgow's best-known comic acts, including the Logan Family, trod the Scotia's stage.

The bar's musical heyday was the mid-1960s. The Scotia was the epicentre of the Glasgow folk scene, stuffed with electrifying characters, songs and stories. The pub boasted its own weekly newspaper called *Scotia Folk*, and many of its session stalwarts went on

Above: Scotia Variety Theatre programme, 1892.

Right: The Scotia Bar.

The Scotia Bar

Location	112 Stockwell Street, Glasgow G1 4LW
Capacity	150
Date opened	1792
Music	Folk, Rock, Blues
website	www.scotiabar.net

to achieve global fame. There was Billy Connolly and his fellow Humblebum, Tam Harvey – 'These bums are humble!' – and the fabled Glasgow folk singer and raconteur, Big Mick Broderick. The website of the Whistlebinkies, the group founded by Broderick, describes how 'the blend of humorous blethering, socialism, folk music and downright violent pacifism that carried the Scotia into the 1970s became legend.' As well as folk singers and folk fans, regular Scotia punters included the psychedelic blues band The Poets and various members of The Sensational Alex Harvey Band.

I myself first entered the pub in 1968. I bought a pint and took it into the Wee Back Room, a glassed-off enclave at the rear of the pub. There a rather wizened gnome of a man said to me in a soft Irish voice, 'You look like a man who could sing a song.' This proved to be the lyric writer, poet and playwright, Freddy Anderson. Freddy coedited *Scotia Folk*, in which he wrote about the pub's legendary characters and dashed off sharp lyrics on the hard news of the day. He was a long-time habitué of the Scotia, which he always told us had had better and worse days.

The roots of revival

I have a dear memory of going, in the late 1950s, to a matinee performance of the McPeake Family of Ulster at the Scotia Music Hall. Theirs was a rather unique line-up of two sets of Irish uilleann (elbow) pipes played by father, Frank, and son, 'Middle Francie', and a harp played by grandson, James. They played three numbers, as I recall, and later returned to accompany a pair of All-Ireland Champion Step Dancers. The dancers were so laden down by chestfuls of metal-clanking medals that the jigs they danced had to be played at half the usual speed – a quarter of the wild rate later popularised by Riverdance.

Above: A postcard photograph of Marie Loftus (1857–1940), one of Glasgow's greatest female music hall stars. She danced at the Scotia Music Hall there when she was a girl.

Right: The Scotia Bar, interior.

I had been sent along with two other young Glasgow singers to learn more about traditional music by hearing and talking with the McPeakes. I remember Middle Francie urging us to make sure to celebrate our own old 'big ballads' (our centuries-old majestic Scots ballads of warfare, disastrous wooings, fratricides, clan feuds, Borders ridings and cattle raidings) as well as the popular songs of the hard life of North East bothy farm workers.

The woman who had sent us was the future Glasgow MEP Janie Buchan, and one of the other young singers who came with me was Ray Fisher. When Ray's brother Archie, soon to be one of the architects of the Scottish folk revival, wanted to form a folk group with the fiddler, Bobby Campbell, on the model of the American group the Weavers, he consulted Janie Buchan's husband, Norrie Buchan. Norrie was then a school teacher and a highly influential writer on Scots song, but later he was to become an MP and Shadow Culture Minister. Norrie advised Archie and Bobby to recruit a girl singer to complete the group. Archie returned a few weeks later saying, 'I couldn't get a girl singer, so I had to get my sister." At the time Ray was a jazz singer who, dressed in a long white sheath, gave a stunning rendition of 'I Hate a Man Like You'.

Archie, Ray and Bobby became the Wayfarers and performed in bingo halls and other desultory venues, but soon Bobby decamped to become a London journalist. Ray and Archie became a duo. At the time, the Glaswegian singing duo Robin Hall and Jimmie MacGregor were among the regular performers featured on the BBC's nightly news magazine programme *Tonight*. STV wanted a folk duo for their own early evening news programme, and Ray and Archie found themselves launched as professional singers.

Robin Hall had encountered folk song in the 1950s as a pupil at Allan Glen's School, half a mile north of the Scotia. There he was inspired by Morris Blythman, one of two elder gurus for the flood of young folk musicians who began spilling in and out of Glasgow. Blythman started a lunchtime folk club in the school, the first such club in Scotland. The other guru was Norrie Buchan. His weekly song column in *The Scotsman* provided the beginnings of a repertoire of Scots song for enthusiastic youngsters, and led to him eventually editing the essential *101 Scottish Songs*, which was known as the 'Wee Red Book' of the Scottish revival. Buchan started a Ballad Club at Rutherglen Academy where he taught, and he and Blythman educated and inspired a whole generation of singers.

Above: Scotia Bar, smoke break.

Some youngsters were ensnared at schools. Others caught the singing bug from the Bridgeton-born Lonnie Donegan, whose skiffle message led by example: just strap on a guitar and get stuck in. Down in Liverpool, the Quarrymen skiffle band took a rock and roll route and became The Beatles. North of the border, after hearing old Scots songs at ceilidhs or around campfires, many young Scots skifflers ditched the mid-Atlantic twang and found their own native singing tongues. This was the beginnings of the folk revival, and in Scotland its first wave included Robin Hall and Jimmie MacGregor, Josh Macrae, Enoch Kent and Nigel Denver. In the second wave came Archie Fisher, Adam MacNaughtan, Hamish Imlach, Matt McGinn, Gordeanna MacCulloch and Ian Davison; riding the third wave were Billy Connolly, the Battlefield Band, Iona, Kentigern and the JSD Band.

A couple of hundred yards away from the Scotia Bar, round on the Broomielaw, was the Iona Community building. Ewan MacColl, a London-based actor and playwright with Scottish parents, came up for a few seminal concerts there. MacColl was reportedly appalled by the eclectic mix of American and Scots material favoured by local singers, whom he dubbed 'tartan cowboys'. Among these were Josh Macrae, Joe Gordon and Calum Sinclair. Joe and Calum were the nucleus of what was to be the Joe Gordon Folk Four, one of the first professional Scots folk groups, formed at the suggestion of the BBC to be house band on their long-running show *The White Heather Club*. Josh Macrae was a member of The Reivers, a band that had been assembled by Norrie Buchan to feature on STV's 1958 rival series *Jig Time*. Both groups were quickly snapped up and promoted by record companies who spotted a new tartanalia folk market.

In 1960 the Iona Community hosted informal Wednesday song sessions. One evening Janie Buchan brought in a hesitant wee fellow, just back from being a mature university student at Ruskin College, Oxford. Janie encouraged him to sing a composition of his own. To the tune of 'It's a Long way to Tipperary' he sang in trenchant tones, 'It's a long way to the Riviera, it's a long way to go – without your bankbook.' This assault on the idle rich who decamped to the Med each winter entranced us, and Matt McGinn became an accepted folk singer.

Heading 400 yards up Stockwell Street from the Scotia onto the Trongate (across from what is now the Tron Theatre), Glasgow's first official weekly folk club started in 1960 at the Corner House lunch counter. The resident singing group there was an anarchic assembly that called itself the Broomhill Bums, whose key members included Josh Macrae, Ray and Archie Fisher, Hamish Imlach, Jim McLean and myself. The group was named after a day-and-night party of song, booze and hilarity that went on for 19 months at Imlach's house in Broomhill in the West End. Imlach chronicled the party in his autobiographical song 'Cod Liver Oil and the Orange Juice'. It all began when his mother left him in charge of collecting rents from the family's large Broomhill House atop the hill. Hamish lived downhill in the big house's former laundry, a teenager with his own pad and his own money to buy alcohol. The party was at his place every single night until he went bankrupt.

Josh Macrae had by then become the most famous solo folk singer in Scotland, with three national Top Twenty hits including 'Messing About on the River'. Ray and Archie developed influential solo careers, as did Hamish Imlach. Jim McLean's best-known song is the elegiac 'Massacre of Glencoe', but he also collaborated with Morris Blythman on a series of anti-Polaris protest songs that fuelled mass demonstrations against the new nuclear submarine base in the Holy Loch. He then wrote and produced whole albums of songs with strong pro-independence themes for singer Alistair MacDonald. The Scotia repertoire had Red Clydeside running through its veins, with a strong core of songs with a left-wing message and a demand for Scottish independence.

Right: Notice on the exterior wall of The Scotia Bar.

Left: Theis Juul Langlands (left, on keyboard) and Michael Graubæk (right, on fiddle).

After two years the Glasgow Folk Club transmuted into the Glasgow Folk Centre, with a permanent base up a close in Montrose Street, behind the City Chambers and just 300 yards north-east of the Scotia. One resident performer was a local young guitar wizard called Iain McGeachy, who soon moved to London. There he couldn't get gigs with such an awkward name, so he changed it to John Martyn.

All of the emerging big names of the British folk revival performed at the Glasgow Folk Centre on Montrose Street. Young performers were cutting their teeth all around Scotland: Danny Kyle and the Tannahill Weavers in Paisley, Bert Jansch, The Corries, The McCalmans and Phil Cunningham in Edinburgh, Aly Bain, Barbara Dickson, Rab Noakes and Eric Bogle further afield. All of them came to the Folk Centre, and soon the new Scottish talent started spilling out across the UK, the Continent and North America. Scotland punched well above its weight in the UK-wide folk revival of the 1960s.

Enter the Scotia

The handy local pub for the Folk Centre was the Marland Bar, where local and visiting singers would gather before and after sessions. But around 1966 the Marland became unwelcoming, and scouts went out seeking a new friendly hostelry. News was spread by the Humblebums that they had found a welcoming tavern where it was quiet enough to play dominoes on the counter on a Saturday night. Enter the old Scotia Bar. At this time it was generally agreed that Billy Connolly's ever-extending funny introductions to traditional songs were so hilarious that he must be a comic genius, and it was a pity that he was too Glasgow of voice and style to ever take his humour outwith the city with any success.

Though the bye-laws of Glasgow allowed singing only in the lounge sections of bars, the Scotia's publican was friendly enough with the local polis not to have to worry about this. Soon 100 voices would be raised in harmony and dominoes became impossible on the bustling bar counter. The folkies kept to the left

side of the bar and entered by the left-hand door; the right side and right door belonged to the Blue Angels motorcycle gang, who tolerated us (we had to pass among them to use the toilets). The Scotia became the haunt of all visiting professional folk singers and groups as well as home-grown ones and wannabies. Alex Campbell and Matt McGinn held forth alongside Big Mick Broderick. Across the road from the Scotia a new group called Iona opened a shop and hosted their own record label, Iona Records.

Other clubs eventually came along. In 1992 I sat down with Hamish Imlach beside a tape recorder for a week and transcribed (minus my frequent cackles of laughter) the tales of his life. One tale was about Clive's Incredible Folk Club, where all-night sessions were 'housed in a dance premises in Sauchiehall Street that had lost their drinks licence, and allowed folkies in bearing cairryoots,' Imlach recounted. 'The police kept raiding that club. When I walked along Sauchiehall Street I'd look to see if there were police cars there. If so, I'd walk to a cafe and have a cup of coffee until they were gone. One night I saw the cops were there again, turned round to go to the cafe, and this American guy bumped into me. He saw the guitar case and asked for the club. "That's it there, where all the police are. If you wait ten minutes they'll be gone." That was Joe Boyd,' Imlach continued, 'who had come up from London to hear the Incredible String Band play there. He eventually signed them up and recorded them. Clive and I were residents getting a tenner each a night, and Robin Williamson and Mike Heron got a fiver each. The guy running the premises was taking three or four hundred quid on the door, plus coffee bar sales. We could have taken over the place for not much cash. Alex Campbell and others were keen that we run it as a cooperative, but I saw that I would have been doing all the work. I was already booking everybody, doing the paperwork, getting the money and paying it out, compering, trying to find out who was on next – they'd probably be out on the fire escape having a joint or gone out to buy a fish supper.' Clive's didn't last out the year.

Some 250 yards east from the Scotia takes you to Glasgow Green, the home of political meetings and protests for hundreds of years. Speeches there were enlivened by topical political song. In recent years the keynote political singer there on May Day has been Arthur Johnston, formerly singer with the Laggan group, who started and ran the Star Folk Club in the Communist Party building directly across the river from the Scotia. The Star Club is now the sole surviving folk club in Glasgow, relocated to a former church, St Andrew's in the Square, off the Saltmarket and a scant 300 yards from the Scotia.

In 1970 Jim McLean came back up to Glasgow, and with Big Mick Broderick and others recorded an LP of mostly traditional songs called *Scotia Folk*. The cover photo shows Alex Campbell semi-slumped on the road before the pub, cheered on by a crowd of regular drinkers. Also in the early 1970s, The Plague of Fiddlers arrived at the Scotia, playing an endless stream of Irish reels and jigs at such competitively fast paces that no-one could have step danced to them. Their relentless instrumental frenzy drowned out the singing – except during the singing-only session in the Wee Back Room, where 20 bodies could sit on top of, or pour beer over, each other.

No more fiddlers in the Wee Back Room

Then matters turned sour. The polis, convinced that the Wee Back Room was the location of drug-dealing, insisted that it be closed. All of the regulars knew that any dealing occurred off the premises, around the corner in front of the Chicken Factory. But protests were in vain. The folkies decamped to the Wee Man Bar across the road and put a picket on the left-hand door of the Scotia asking people not to cross the line. Regular punters took their turn for an hour in the cold, then were relieved from the Wee Man. (Of course, there was no picket put on the Blue Angels' door.) The WBR never reopened, and eventually its glass and wood partition was removed altogether and a formal little performance space was created. The folkies migrated to the Victoria Bar – the Viccy – one pub along from the Wee Man, and sang and played there.

By now, though, the bubble of the Scottish folk club boom was bursting. Some singers inhabited a stool in the corner of a pub, their renditions ignored by drinkers. Many more groups were created, concert venues used, and tours set up. The Whistlebinkies played to welcome Yehudi Menuhin at the Edinburgh International Festival in 1985. They, Hamish Imlach, Iain Mackintosh and Dougie Maclean were among many who followed the track blazed by Alex Campbell across Europe, and became itinerant performers in Germany and Scandinavia most of the year, only returning home to do a few Scottish gigs as a working holiday. Among them, The Battlefield Band, formed in that part of Glasgow's South Side, still survives. Folk clubs across Scotland and the rest of the UK were closing, their energy drawn off to folk festivals. For some years these festivals flourished, creating summers of nomadic folkies travelling out of the city each weekend with their tents and caravans.

Left: Gerry Rafferty performing with The Humblebums in Galashiels, 1969.

One Glasgow group stayed put. The Clutha was formed in a pub beside the Mitchell Library, where its members all worked as librarians. Singer Gordeanna MacCulloch joined; she eventually established the mighty Glasgow Socialist Women's Choir, named Eurydice because 'We're no the Orpheus'. Adam MacNaughtan, informal leader of the long-running collective of Glasgow traditional songsters called Stramash, eventually opened a second-hand book shop in Parnie Street, a spitting distance from the Scotia.

Nowadays the Scotia is a respected performance venue, utilising the small open performance space where the Wee Back Room once was for a mixed diet of folk-flavoured music and literary events including an annual short story competition. Back in the 1970s the folkies eventually straggled back after months of 'industrial action', but the almost febrile atmosphere of excited community was long gone, dissipated by frustration, changing times and changing tastes. The current spiritual home of Glasgow's folkies is Laurie's Acoustic Music Bar in King Street, 100 yards from the Scotia. Owner and noted traditional singer, Cy Laurie, cut his organisational teeth running floor-shaking ceilidhs in the Riverside Club, just west of the Scotia. It might have lost the special quality of its heyday, but the Scotia Bar's sphere of influence is a force to be reckoned with in global folk music history.

Opposite: Scotia Folk, album cover. The photograph for the album cover was taken by Alison Chapman McLean, the crowd set up for her by Billy Connolly.

THEATRE ROYAL

Conrad Wilson

Left: Theatre Royal, view of Auditorium roof.

Below: Theatre Royal programme 1935.

This is the story of a fine old Glasgow theatre, of an adventurous, ambitious young opera company, and of how, for better and sometimes worse, they converged in the year 1975 and contrived to stay together as successfully as they could in increasingly difficult circumstances.

The Theatre Royal – one of several auditoriums of that name to open in 19th-century Glasgow but now the sole survivor – had been unveiled as a Victorian variety theatre at the top of Hope Street in 1867, and twice went up in flames before being reopened in 1895. As a palace of entertainment with leanings towards opera and dance, it later formed part of the substantial Howard and Wyndham stable, consisting of theatres in Scotland and England. Among them were the King's Theatre in Glasgow (the young Scottish Opera's original base); the King's in Edinburgh (a vital and initially charming component of the *Edinburgh Festival*); the elegant His Majesty's Theatre in Aberdeen; and the inviting Theatre Royal in Newcastle, to which for a few happy years Scottish Opera paid regular visits. All of these buildings and a few others were invaluable to the company in its formative period, when it still had no permanent home of its own but made artful use of what was available.

At that time, as it happened, the one surviving Theatre Royal in Glasgow was not available to the company. A smallish but potentially useful auditorium with around 1,800 seats on four levels, it had been bought by Scottish Television and put to various modern uses as a studio, performance space, office block and other things, none of them particularly operatic. But earlier it had been a popular venue for drama, music, and harlequinade in a city that by the end of the 19th century was rivalling Edinburgh as Scotland's capital of culture.

Theatre Royal

Location: 282 Hope Street, Glasgow, G2 3QA
Architect: Charles Phipps (1867) Page & Park (2014)
Capacity: 1800
Date opened: 1867; renovated 2015
Music: Opera (Home of Scottish Opera)
website: www.atgtickets.com/venues/theatre-royal-glasgow/history/

Angelica Catalani, hailed by Stendhal for her 'prodigiously beautiful' bel canto voice and the first Susanna in Mozart's *Marriage of Figaro* in London, sang at the Queen Street Theatre Royal as early as 1808 – it burned down 20 years later. Jenny Lind starred in Bellini's *La Sonnambula* and Donizetti's *La Fille du Regiment* at the Caledonian Theatre in Dunlop Street in 1848. Sims Reeves, who had sung for Berlioz in *The Damnation of Faust* and been named by the composer as 'the god-tenor', appeared in Balfe's *Bohemian Girl* at the vast City Theatre, which burned down in its opening season (1848) after a performance of Weber's *Der Freischütz*. Later it was replaced by the similarly mammoth 4,000-seat Royal Colosseum Theatre, which soon became today's Theatre Royal in Hope Street.

Meanwhile, conforming with Glasgow's penchant for theatrical self-immolation (the same fate befell the illustrious St Andrew's Halls at Charing Cross after, of all things, a boxing match in 1962) the Colosseum also burned down, was rebuilt with 3,000 seats and again went on fire. But in its final reincarnation, reduced to fewer than 2,000 seats, it managed to endure, even if it was not invariably the place of choice for all the famous touring opera companies (the Carl Rosa, the Thomas Beecham and its flamboyant successor the British National, the Moody-Manners, the Wagnerian Denhof founded by a Scottish-domiciled Austrian) that were by then regularly descending on Glasgow. Meanwhile the city continued to lack a professional company of its own. By the middle of the 20th century most of these touring companies – including the hard-working Carl Rosa – had lost momentum or gone bankrupt, and it was Sadler's Wells Opera, replacing the Carl Rosa on an annual visit from London, that was left to keep things going at the King's Theatre in Bath Street, along with valiant appearances by Glasgow amateurs.

Of these heroic local groups, the deservedly admired Glasgow Grand Opera Society, which in the 1930s under Erik Chisholm's conductorship had given the British premieres of Mozart's *Idomeneo* and Berlioz's *The Trojans*. The pioneering Glasgow composer/conductor also took the British premiere of Bartok's *Bluebeard's Castle* on tour in 1956–57.

The King's Theatre, with 1,765 seats, had now established itself as Glasgow's nearest thing to an opera house, even if pantomime was its main activity. It was there, with Bath Street enclosed in one of the last pea-souper fogs I can recall encountering, that I reviewed, in my role as Scotland's only full-time music critic, Warwick Braithwaite conducting a tawdry old production of Saint-Saens's *Samson and Delilah* with the Sadler's Wells company and the Edinburgh-born Roderick Brydon (soon to become a staff conductor of Scottish Opera) clashing the cymbals.

Before it was transformed into English National Opera, Sadler's Wells was not always much of a company. But it was plucky, popular in Scotland and, with Alexander Gibson as its youngest-ever music director, showed new flair with a finely etched production of Tchaikovsky's *Eugene Onegin* that it brought to Glasgow along with a racy *Gianni Schicchi* and a dapper *Marriage of Figaro*. All had the Motherwell-born Gibson in the pit.

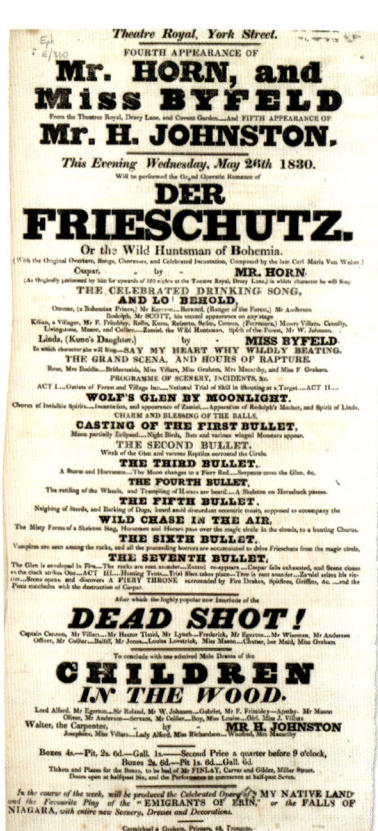

Right: Glasgow's first Theatre Royal, Queen Street, 1805.

Right, below: Remains of the theatre following its burning down, 1829.

Below: An 1830 playbill for performance of the opera *Der Freischütz*.

Meanwhile up in Hope Street, the Theatre Royal was enduring its conversion into STV's headquarters at the price of ceasing to be a theatrical presence in the city. Even as a base for STV, however, its days were numbered, because the television company was soon to build modern premises next door, thereby relegating the theatre to a lesser role – in the end it was little more than a storage unit.

Thus did things stand in 1974 when Scottish Opera stealthily entered the picture. Alexander Gibson and Peter Hemmings were at the height of their powers as conductor and administrator of a company that had recently filled the King's Theatre with its first *Ring* cycle followed by sensationally good productions of Strauss's *Der Rosenkavalier* and Wagner's *Tristan and Isolde*. Until then it had been building a national, indeed international, image of itself as a sort of urban Glyndebourne of the north, which made a festival out of everything it touched.

Its short spring season at the Glasgow King's, created each year from three or four carefully chosen operas, imaginatively cast and scrupulously rehearsed, had been setting Glasgow audiences agog before being toured to Edinburgh and Aberdeen. Every performance was an event, every event a particle of a festival that ran from May until the summer. Because these at the time were lean months for the Scottish National Orchestra (SNO), Gibson was able to employ the players, whose music director he was, in the pit in the same way as the Vienna Opera has the Vienna Philharmonic as one of its assets and Glyndebourne the London Philharmonic. The SNO added glamour to everything Scottish Opera performed and the sight of the players, spilling out of the King's Theatre's shallow pit and into the stalls and adjacent boxes, prompted one distinguished London critic to nudge me in the ribs and say, 'Whaur's oor Covent Garden noo?'

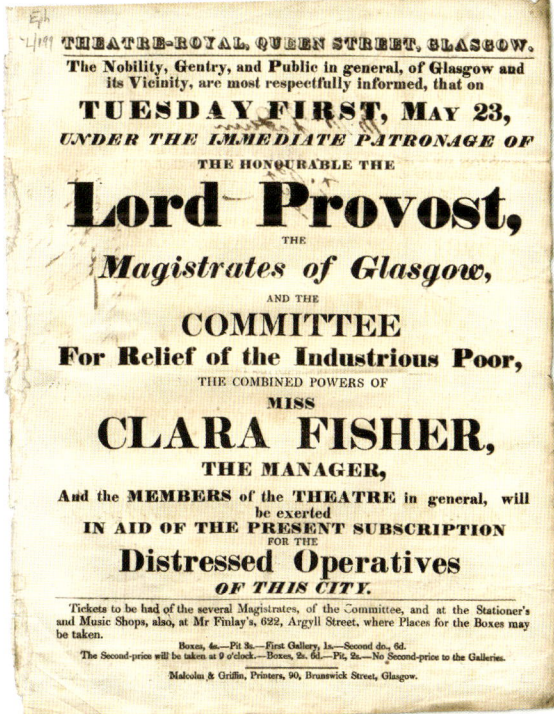

Inset, left: Engraving showing Theatre Royal, Dunlop Street, pre-1852.

Above: Theatre Royal, Dunlop Street, showing its redeveloped upper storey.

Left: Bill for benefit performance at Theatre Royal, Queen Street, Glasgow, 1826.

Above: View towards proscenium arch of the Theatre Royal in Hope Street.

The fact that opera in London, where Hemmings had been a manager with Sadler's Wells, was not operating at its highest level during Scottish Opera's first decade did the company nothing but good. London critics came regularly and saw for themselves what was being achieved up here. 'Tonight *Otello*' proclaimed the posters – an announcement that struck more effectively than 'Tonight *Traviata*' might have done. My own first experience of the company was in 1964, when it staged Gounod's *Faust* in conjunction with a revival of Verdi's *Otello* and a fascinatingly abstract production of *Don Giovanni* that employed large sliding panels between which the Don was ultimately crushed to death. 'Why Faust?' was the question that initially hung on my lips; why a hackneyed old warhorse that deserved no place in an ambitious new company's repertoire? Anthony Besch's astute production, not resorting to updating or other distortions, and Gibson's vivid conducting showed why. The result was thrilling.

For a further decade, as the company's principal chronicler, I tracked Scottish Opera's progress from season to season and city to city, writing in *The Scotsman* of its plans in an annual prediction entitled 'Scottish Opera and the Future'. In so doing I recognised that its aspirations were gradually changing, that the Howard and Wyndham theatres with their dependence on long periods of pantomime, were becoming obstacles to progress. Occasional add-ons to the spring season – a summer *Magic Flute* in honour of the 1970 Commonwealth Games, Christmas performances of *The Gondoliers* and a regular appearance at the *Edinburgh Festival* – were not enough. The spring season was becoming too confined. A full-scale season in the German or London manner was needed. 'We cannot go on being a semi-festival company,' declared Hemmings.

As a critic I was taken into the company's confidence. Negotiations had secretly begun with STV for the purchase of the Theatre Royal. Guaranteeing that I would not publish until permitted, I was kept abreast of what would be Scotland's biggest musical news story of modern times. Negotiations moved fast. A purchase price of £300,000 was settled upon for the almost derelict premises. Scottish Opera said it could raise the cash. But though it was agreed that the theatre was a gem, renovation costs involving the sinking of a big new orchestra pit, the construction of a new stage, the provision of a new backstage, a new front of house, new seating and new decor would all have to be paid for.

Amid all the private excitement, the guarantee I had received of an exclusive story somehow got lost. I was informed that a general announcement was going to be made on such and such a date. Breaking the embargo – how could I not? – I went ahead and splashed the story in *The Scotsman* a day early.

If anybody in the company was upset, I was never told – though other newspapers were displeased. My intervention simply speeded the process that was already racing ahead. The renovations were made. The decor, in different shades of coffee rather than traditional theatrical red, was subtle (though some years later it would be replaced by a more conventional colour scheme). Favourable comparisons were made with intimate Italian opera houses. The lofty proscenium arch, when open to its full height, looked splendid. A full-size portrait of Alexander Gibson in the new orchestra pit, painted by David Donaldson, was mounted above the scrubbed-stone staircase leading from the small

Left: Theatre Royal in Hope Street, undergoing redecoration.

Left: The main entrance on Hope Street.

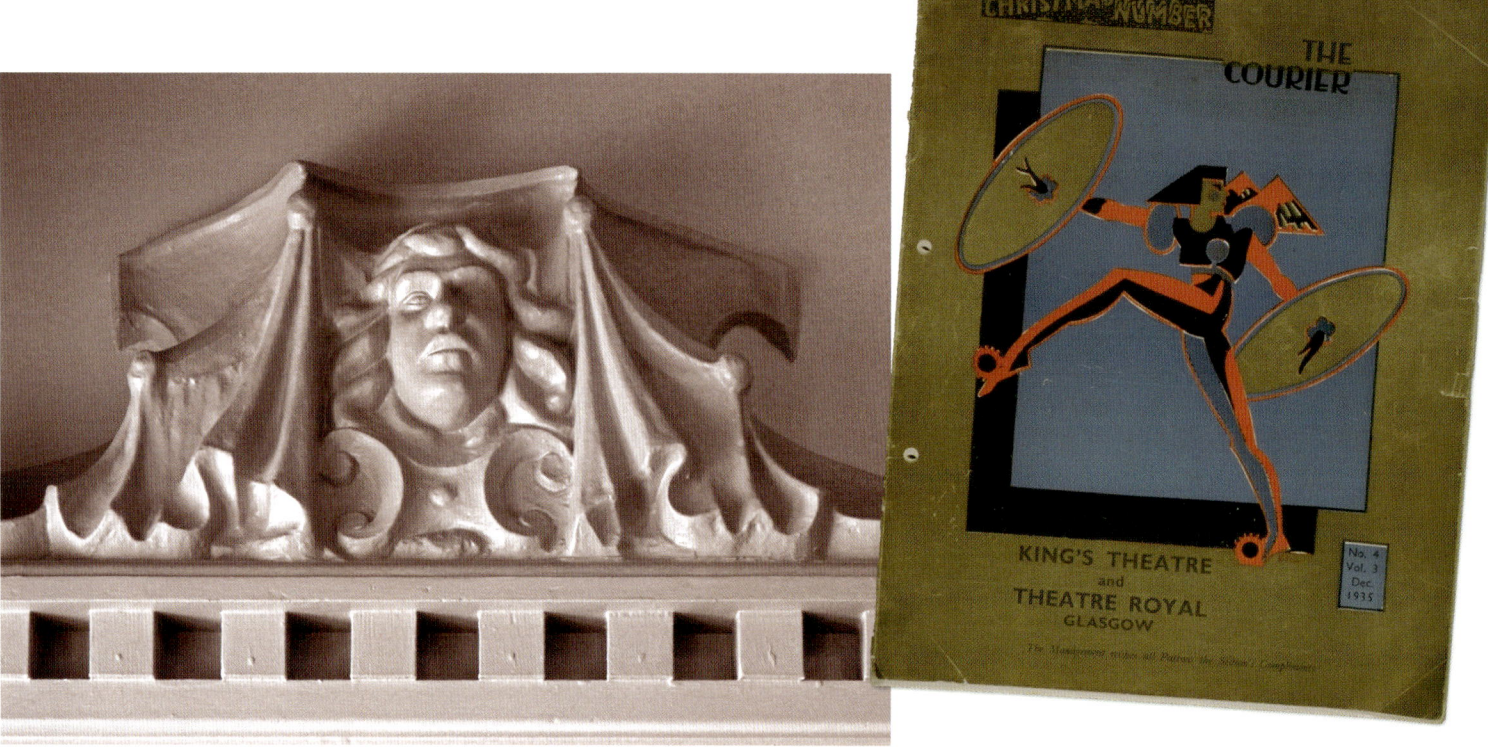

Above: Detail of decorative plasterwork from the theatre's interior.

Inset, right: December 1935 edition of *The Courier*, the in-house magazine for the King's Theatre and Theatre Royal.

Below: Scottish Opera Magazine, Winter 1967.

ground-floor foyer to the circle. Such was the euphoria that nobody except the players seemed to notice that the new orchestra pit, much of it beneath the stage, was unsatisfactory and would have to be redesigned before long.

Nor was it widely spotted, except by one observant London critic, Desmond Shawe-Taylor of the *Sunday Times*, that the SNO was no longer the company's orchestra. It had been replaced, by the symphony orchestra's own wishes, with an outfit called the Scottish Philharmonia, based on an expansion of the recently formed Scottish Chamber Orchestra. This would itself drop out later when a house orchestra was finally recruited.

In October 1975, the theatre triumphantly reopened as the first British city opera house outside London. Wisely, perhaps, no new Scottish opera was commissioned for the occasion – think of the poor fate of Samuel Barber's *Antony and Cleopatra* at the opening of the New Met in New York. Instead, two revivals launched the first season: David Pountney's deliciously eccentric staging of Johann Strauss's *Die Fledermaus*, televised live by STV, and the seasoned Anthony Besch production of Verdi's *Otello* on its steeply sloping ramp.

Gibson conducted both of them lovingly, and Strauss's central party scene was adjusted, as it sometimes is, to suit the occasion. Charles Craig, tenor star of many earlier Scottish Opera successes, sang Puccini's 'Nessun Dorma', William McCue forsook Wagner for 'Bonnie Strathyre', and Peter Ebert, the company's dedicated director of productions who had gained glory from *The Trojans* in 1969, stepped forward and announced, to long applause, 'Well, we've done it.'

But what had they done? Even now, nobody seems wholly sure. What was true was that nothing would ever be quite the same again. That Scottish Opera had increasingly needed a house of its own went without saying. That it has sometimes – perhaps too often – mishandled its opportunities has been equally evident. An agreement that Scottish Ballet would share the premises seemed sound, as did the decision that spoken drama would also be staged at the Theatre Royal. But Scottish Opera's new productions turned out too often to be glaringly less good than older ones. The long new seasons, running from autumn onwards, and their running costs, affected quality control. Gary Bertini, who had been principal guest conductor and would soon become music director at Frankfurt in Germany, was aghast at what he foresaw as a black hole in the company's finances.

Before long, declaring his mission to be accomplished, Peter Hemmings left for Australia. Perhaps he was right to go but he was instantly missed, not least by Gibson. Not long after, Gibson – now Sir Alexander Gibson – was clumsily replaced amid much local friction by the cool, somewhat passionless American

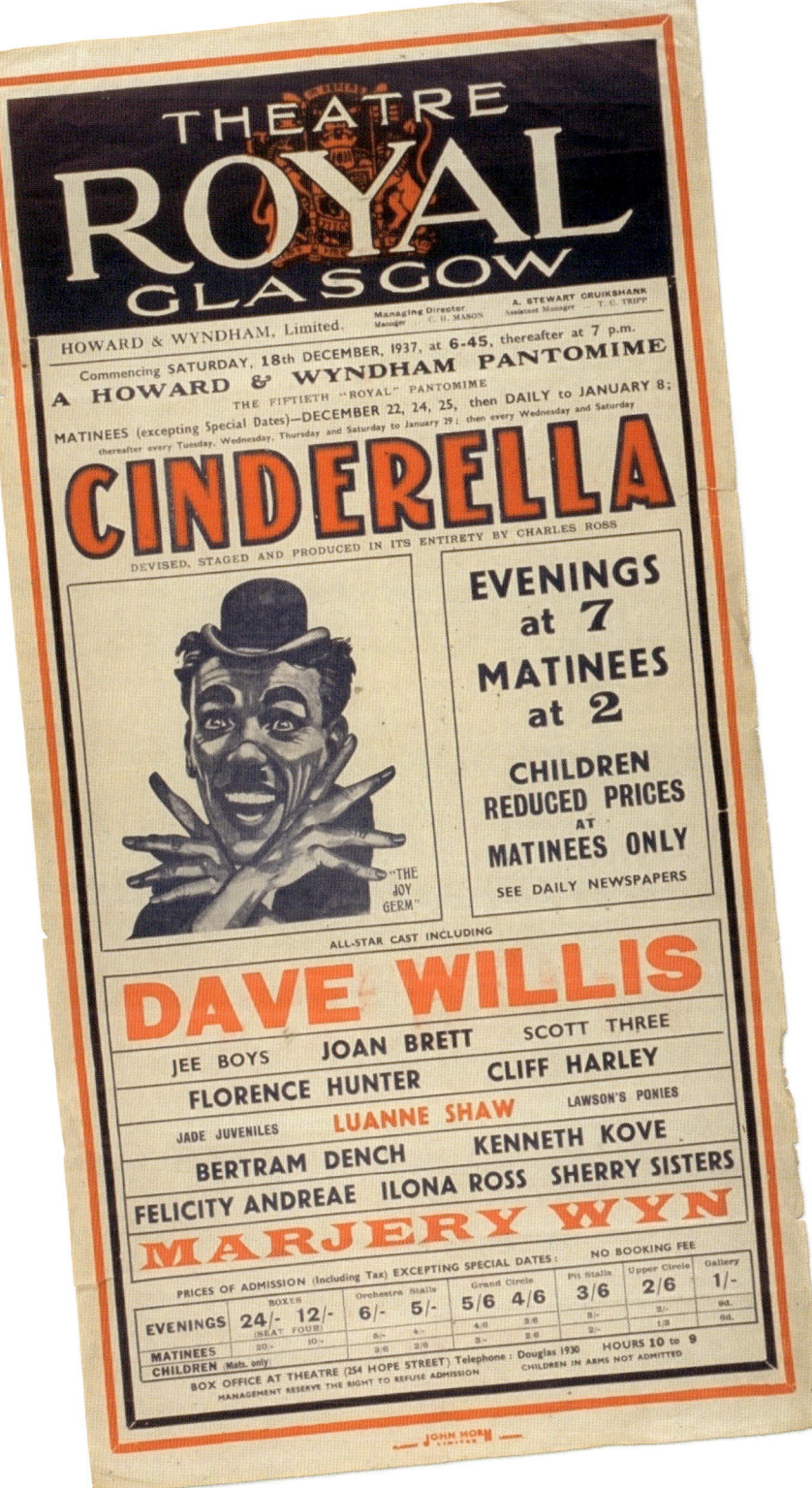

Above: Playbill for 'Cinderella', starring Dave Willis, 1930.

Above, left: Decorative stained glass on the window to the ticket office in the foyer.

Left: The foyer.

Right: American conductor John Mauceri pictured after taking over as musical director of Scottish Opera in April 1986.

Opposite, far right: Interior view to the right of the Proscenium.

Opposite, left, above: The new Theatre Royal extension, 2014.

Opposite, left, below: The impressive Sackler Staircase in the extension interior.

Below: Singer Pat Hoys, comedian/actor Billy Connolly and conductor Sir Alexander Gibson outside the Theatre Royal in Glasgow, where Connolly was to take part in the Scottish Opera production of *Die Fledermaus* in July 1978.

conductor, John Mauceri. A protégé of Leonard Bernstein, Mauceri's biggest achievement was an over-extended version of Bernstein's *Candide* – a work whose best music lies in its overture.

New administrators and conductors came and went, along with two further *Ring* cycles (one of them unfinished), leaving the impression that the company's ambitions for a ten-opera season were never to be satisfactorily fulfilled. Other British companies seemed to be operating more efficiently, particularly the long-established Welsh National and the upstart Opera North, forged out of the northern wing of English National Opera in Leeds. Gibson died suddenly in 1995, his achievements commemorated by the Royal Conservatoire of Scotland's Alexander Gibson Opera School on the other side of the street. Hemmings, after moving from Australia to America, died also. Both went before their time.

Today Scottish Opera prevails at the Theatre Royal, but it is a different company to Gibson and Henning's glitteringly ambitious upstart. It uses different and more controversial ways. Such things happen. A flashy new public annexe, with big foyers and a roof terrace, opened on the corner of Cowcaddens Road late in 2014, but at the time of writing the company has no music director, no permanent chorus, and only a part-time orchestra.

Scottish Opera's birth was a glorious moment, described by Lord Harewood, one-time director of the *Edinburgh Festival*, as a sublime confidence trick. Its formation was a brilliant sleight-of-hand performed with great panache in a land lacking real operatic roots. What is it now, and what will it become? We must wait and see. But since the theatre remains its principal asset, let us hope for the best and proclaim not only 'Long live Scottish Opera' but also 'Long live the Theatre Royal'.

EMPIRE THEATRE

Alison Kerr

Left: The stage of the Empire Theatre in Glasgow, 1963, as the curtain falls for the final time.

Below: March 1963 Variety Show programme.

The Empire Theatre is probably best known around Britain as the place where English comedians went to die. But for many Glaswegian music fans, it was the place where they had their chance to hear some of the 20th century's great names in popular music. In its heyday the Empire, at 31–35 Sauchiehall Street, was Glasgow's top variety theatre, a flagship outpost on the Moss Empires' chain of music halls that made it the Scottish equivalent of the London Palladium. Among the legends who graced its stage were Louis Armstrong, Frank Sinatra, Judy Garland and Nat 'King' Cole. These top-of-the-bill acts reflected international tastes in popular music of the day, and the fact that they often played the Empire exclusively in Scotland reflected Glasgow's passion for new musical fashions. Down in London, the central bookers knew the subtle variations in audience tastes up and down the country.

The Empire also attracted musical acts that defied categorisation. During the 1940s and 1950s it hosted an almost continuous stream of Hollywood talent whose acts were a blend of music and comedy patter. As in the case of Danny Kaye, one of the most phenomenally popular stars ever to appear at the Empire, these stars of the silver screen would usually bring along a pianist and/or a musical director and would be accompanied by the house orchestra.

When the Empire first opened its doors in 1874, it was as the Gaiety Theatre, a venue that staged 'legit' theatrical productions. These didn't prove commercially successful and the venue morphed into a music hall in 1883. Three years later it had become the Empire Palace, which opened in April 1897 and quickly attracted a noticeably more up-market clientele. But it wasn't until 1930, after being closed for internal reconstruction and extended up to the corner of Renfield

EMPIRE THEATRE

LOCATION: Formerly 31 Sauchiehall Street, Glasgow, G2 3AT (now replaced by Empire House)
ARCHITECT: Frank Matcham
CAPACITY: 2150
DATE OPENED: 1897 (demolished 1963)
MAIN GENRE OF MUSIC: Jazz, Variety
WEBSITE: More information at www.arthurlloyd.co.uk/Glasgow/Empire.htm

Street, that the Empire as it is now best remembered was established.

The reborn Empire had seating for 2,100 people and remained very much the archetypal variety theatre: the headliner invariably performed last on the bill (sometimes, as in the case of Nat 'King' Cole's 1954 residence, for as little as 30 minutes) after a range of acts that might include comedians, acrobats, dancers, and even animals. The music director was in charge of the music throughout the show, and it was to him that the responsibility fell of preserving the illusion of continuity when things went wrong. So on the night of young British singer-comedian Des O'Connor's famous fainting fit, when fear of the Glasgow audience got the better of him as he finished his act, it was music director, Bobby Dowds, who kept the orchestra playing as if nothing had happened.

In an interview for *Kings, Queens and People's Palaces*, Vivien Devlin's oral history of the Scottish variety theatre, Bobby Dowds's daughter recalls the many facets of her father's job. In addition to scoring the music for each week's show, he often had to orchestrate parts for a 15-piece band from the piano sheet music provided by whichever artist happened to be visiting. This should have earned him a decent fee from the performer in question, but invariably he would be handed a five pound note for an entire weekend's work.

A new show would open on a Monday, run through the week with two 'houses' (or sittings) each night then close on the Saturday night. Occasionally a show would stretch to a fortnight or even longer. The Empire's audience spanned generations and social classes, and its reputation for dealing harshly with acts it didn't like might have been something of an exaggeration. 'I'm not suggesting that Empire audiences were angels,' recalls the celebrated Glasgow journalist, Jack House, in his memoires. 'They could cut up rough if they didn't

Above: Stanley Baxter in The Five Past Eight Show at The Empire Theatre.

Right: The Empire Theatre, June 1930.

Below: Stan Laurel and Oliver Hardy at the Empire Theatre, April 1950.

Above: Singer Andy Stewart in his dressing room, 1957.

like the show on a Friday or a Saturday night, when you might find characters who had been on a pub crawl before they arrived at the second house … There was sometimes soundless criticism at the Empire. I recall a night when a soprano was doing her act. She was not in very good voice – possibly she had a cold. When she got to her second number I saw a gentleman in the stalls produce his evening paper and proceed to read it until the lady's act was finished. I can well imagine the dreadful effect this had on the unfortunate soprano.'

In the 1950s the Empire played host to a string of rock and roll greats, among them Gene Vincent and Eddie Cochran. Two decades earlier its stage hosted a raft of groundbreaking jazz musicians. Glasgow had a blossoming community of jazz aficionados, and when Moss Empires booked American jazz musicians, they were always sent up to the Empire. Indeed, by the mid-1930s the Empire had earned itself a reputation as a centre of 'hot jazz'. The *Evening News* reported in March 1934 that it was the singing bandleader Cab Calloway to whom 'fell the distinction of being the first person to book out both performances for a week at the Empire before he had even set foot in the city.' The dashing and charismatic 26-year-old Calloway was riding high on the success of his record 'Minnie the Moocher', the first jazz record to sell a million copies.

Calloway's opening night at the Empire was a sensation. One reviewer wrote that thousands of 'apparently sober Glaswegians almost "hi-de-hied" the roof off the Empire under the baton of Cab Calloway and to the inviting rhythm of the Cotton Club Orchestra. Cab took us over the whole history of Minnie the Moocher. We "hi-de-hied" Minnie into Chinatown and "hi-de-hoed" her through an opium party and a marriage where "she kicked the gong around".' The more cynical critics pointed out that the band played just as dynamically when Calloway wandered offstage, and that his writhing and wriggling style of cajoling his 13 musicians was all for effect. But the crowd loved it.

Two years earlier, the reaction had been mixed when the man now acknowledged as the single most important figure in jazz, Louis Armstrong, made his Scottish debut at the Empire – his only date north of the border in 1933. The mainstream Glasgow audience was clearly not ready for what the *Evening Citizen* termed "this new rhythm business". While some die-hard jazz fans were sent into ecstasies

Inset, above: The auditorium of The Empire Theatre, following its reopening, 1931.

Above: Variety at the Empire Programme, 1950.

Left: The Red Army ensemble of singers and dancers and musicians, 1959.

Below: The Empire Theatre, also known as The Empire Palace, was designed by Frank Matcham for Moss Empires and built on the site of the former Gaiety Theatre at the corner of West Nile Street and Sauchiehall Street. It opened in 1897 with Vesta Tilley topping the bill and quickly established itself as Glasgow's leading variety theatre.

by Armstrong's playing, others walked out. The press was equally divided. The *Evening News* described the man who effectively invented the jazz solo as a 'musical freak-contortionist' and described the music as 'Hot Rhythm run amok; Harlem madness'. Meanwhile the *Evening Times* reviewer acknowledged Armstrong's 'amazing' range but added: 'I refused to be thrilled.' The *Evening Citizen* critic described Armstrong's handling of his musicians as being akin to a lion tamer and declared himself a fan, adding; 'My only objection to the performance of the "world's greatest trumpeter" is that it is so short. Four tunes, I suggest, is totally inadequate for a top-line performer.'

Armstrong returned to the Empire in 1934 and between his two visits Duke Ellington, the other great jazz pioneer of the era, brought his famous orchestra to the theatre. Their landmark week-long engagement was generally viewed as another sensation. In a series of performances described as 'thrilling' by the press, Ellington's band – the line-up of which included all the great 'Ellingtonians' – performed recent compositions now regarded as masterpieces, including 'Rockin' in Rhythm', 'Mood Indigo' and 'Black and Tan Fantasy'.

Given their status as trailblazers of jazz, it was apt for Armstrong and Ellington to pave the way for the Empire's stream of important jazz acts over the next few years. During the 1930s the theatre's stage was graced by Coleman Hawkins, giant of the tenor sax, by gypsy guitar genius Django Reinhardt, piano wizard Fats Waller, song and dance star Josephine Baker and the close harmony singing sensations, the Boswell Sisters (at the time the most highly paid singers in the States). The Empire was undoubtedly the place where many Glaswegians had their first encounters with African American musicians and singers.

And from the late 1940s it was also where most Glaswegians would have their first encounters with Hollywood stars. Danny Kaye set the trend in 1949: his act was a mixture of comedy and song (he brought his pianist Sammy Prager with him from the States) and his arrival at Central Station drew an unprecedented crowd of 10,000 fans. He brought the house down by singing 'I Belong to Glasgow', with his new best friend, Harry Lauder, delightedly watching from the stalls.

Thereafter the traffic of singing stars from Hollywood continued for several years and spanned genres from the sultry Lena Horne to the high-octane comedy vocals of boisterous *Annie Get Your Gun* star, Betty Hutton. Her love interest in that musical, Howard Keel, also played at the Empire, as did the popular Italian opera-singer-turned-movie-star Mario Lanza just a year before his premature death in 1959. Dorothy Lamour often sang one or two songs in her movies with Bob Hope and Bing Crosby, but demonstrated that she didn't really have the talent to sustain a solo act when she played her only Scottish date at the Empire in May 1950.

More successful were two great singers who were down on their luck movie-wise but on the verge of major comebacks at the time of their historic Glasgow Empire appearances. When Judy Garland played the Empire in May 1951, her 'extreme nervousness' was noted by critics who described her twiddling her stockinged feet (she had taken off her shoes) as she sang, and observed that perspiration poured down her face as she walked offstage. She was fresh from a hugely successful four-week stint at the London Palladium, but Garland wasn't a seasoned live performer. She had recently been fired by MGM and was newly divorced from her second husband. At a press conference the day before her Glasgow debut, she confessed to reporters: 'Gee, I feel as nervous as a kitten. I hope I do well.'

She had nothing to worry about. The 28-year-old star immediately endeared herself to the packed house, introducing herself as 'only a minstrel girl' and opening with a specially written song about sporrans. During her 40-minute performance she sang many old favourites, among them 'Easter Parade', 'Over the Rainbow', 'You Made Me Love You', 'The Trolley Song', 'Just One of Those Things' and 'Get Happy', for which she sported a soft hat like the one she'd worn in the movie *Summer*

Stock. When she left Glasgow five days later, Garland was given a huge send-off. Traffic stopped on West Nile Street and a crowd of 500 cheered for her – so much so that, after waving to her fans from a window in the theatre, she had to be sneaked out of an emergency exit. 'They're just too wonderful,' she said. 'They've restored my faith in people. Now I know why other people always want to come back to Glasgow.'

Frank Sinatra – or 'The Voice', as the press liked to call him – did not have a 500-strong reception outside the Empire. Indeed, his publicist told the Sunday Mail that the star's usual routine was to walk into the theatre straight off the street and onto the stage in his lounge suit. But he did inspire roars of delight from packed houses through his week's residency in July 1953. At this point in his career Sinatra hadn't yet made his big comeback in Hollywood: the film that established him as a serious movie actor, From Here to Eternity, was only released in the United States a month later. On arriving in Glasgow, Sinatra told a press conference that he was considering concentrating more on light comedy than on singing.

That night, at his first house at the Empire, the thin, pale (perhaps he was pining for his wife Ava Gardner) 'Swoonatra' did indeed reveal his comedy skills with his mickey-take on 'Old Man (Bing) Crosby' and his ad-libbing (having sung the 'All of Me' line 'Take my arms' he paused and asked, 'My arms?!'). But it was his singing that drew the loudest squeals, yelps and whistles from the full house. Concentrating on songs from earlier in his career ('There have been no songs written in the past six months which are conducive to me,' he explained), he spent an hour of the show singing alone with his pianist, Bill Miller. Among the numbers were 'September Song', 'Old Man River', 'Nancy With the Laughing Face', 'Birth of the Blues' and 'Embraceable You'. He endeared himself to the crowd by taking a tea break, as Danny Kaye had done a few years earlier, just behind the footlights. 'It helps with the chords,' the crooner explained. Sinatra didn't return to Glasgow until 1990, by which time the Empire had long since disappeared.

In March 1963 the Empire closed its doors for the last time, a victim of the demise of variety theatre in the face of Saturday night television. Plenty of TV programmes adopted similar formats to the variety shows. Indeed, many of the biggest names to appear at the Empire during its last decade were familiar to audiences as a result of television shows – not that it guaranteed success. Liberace's disappointing box office returns for his three-week Empire stint in the summer of 1960 might well have been the final, diamond-studded nails in the theatre's coffin.

Above: The Glasgow Empire's 1956 Christmas Show 'We're Joking' was a new revue directed by Charles Henry, with music and lyrics by Ross Parker, choreography by Joan Davis, and featured Bobby Dowds and the Empire Orchestra. Santa Claus is depicted on the cover with his bag filled with artists.

Inset: Harry Lauder with fellow entertainers Bert Denver, Charlie Kemble, Dave Willis, Harry Gordon, Jack Radcliffe and Will Fyffe, c. 1945.

ST ANDREW'S HALLS

Hugh Macdonald

For anyone wishing to explore Glasgow's musical history there is nothing more poignant than a walk along Granville Street. There you may be taken aback by the impressive ionic-pillared façade framing what is now used as the main entrance to the Mitchell Library. You might well wonder why this Greek-inspired grandeur, with its caryatids and dramatic statuary, seems to have so little in common with the domed baroque architecture of the library's North Street façade at the other end of the block, assaulted as it is by a constant roar from the deep canyon of the motorway that yawns incongruously below. Then, looking up, you see five names etched into the stone: PURCELL – BACH – HANDEL – MOZART – BEETHOVEN. And you realise that this was once the entrance not to a temple of learning, but to an important concert hall.

St Andrew's Halls began its illustrious, 85-year contribution to Glasgow's musical history in 1877. The end came very suddenly early one morning in October 1962 when the building was gutted by fire, probably started by a smouldering cigarette carelessly dropped the previous night at an amateur boxing tournament held on the main floor of the hall. Scotland lost the tournament to Romania. Britain lost what was then its finest concert hall. For Glasgow and for Scotland it was a disaster.

By strange chance, the American architect and acoustics expert, Leo Beranek, had just published his authoritative book *Music Acoustics and Architecture* earlier that year. Based on a detailed study of the acoustical properties of more than 50 of the best concert halls from around the world, it placed St Andrew's Halls in the same exalted company as Vienna's Musikverein, Amsterdam's Concertgebouw and Boston's Symphony Hall. In fact, Beranek regarded it as one of the top five in the world, while Sir Thomas Beecham had gone further and declared it one of the best three. But Beranek's book was rendered out of date almost immediately. This most precious jewel in Glasgow's musical crown no longer existed.

Glasgow's extraordinarily rapid expansion through the 19th century gave it an unenviable reputation for overcrowded slum housing and poor public health. But internationally, the ever-burgeoning magnificence of its civic architecture proclaimed its status as one of the most advanced capitalist cities on earth and was the perfect visual metaphor for its role as 'Second City of the Empire'. Along with Glasgow's unbounded commercial ambition went a public appetite for the best cultural and entertainment experiences that life could offer, and a missionary belief by the city authorities in the improving qualities of art.

Since the 1840s, the City Hall had served the city well as its main concert venue, but by the 1870s it was increasingly seen by the city's mercantile elite as inadequate for the sort of large, prestigious events they wanted to see in Glasgow. An American visitor in the 1840s had

Left: The Great Hall.

Inset: Plate from the *American Architect and Building News* 06 March 1880, illustrating Campbell Douglas & Sellars' perspective drawing of the Granville Street facade of St Andrew's Halls, from the north-west.

Above: Exterior of St Andrew's Halls, showing the main enstrance, from Granville Street.

remarked that Glasgow was 'like one continuous building site'; by the 1870s and 1880s that ferment of construction had become a frenzy. Such enormous building projects as the University, Central Station and Hotel, the General Post Office, the Stock Exchange and the City Chambers all went up within a few years of each other. A new concert hall of suitable magnificence in the fast-growing west of the city was seen as the essential cultural and social accoutrement of a great commercial metropolis, and a private company was set up to finance and build it. Berwickshire-born John Cunningham, architect of Liverpool's original acoustically admired Philharmonic Hall (another sad loss to fire, in 1933) was asked to design the 'New Public Halls'. But he died when his ideas were still at the sketch stage, and the commission was taken over by James Sellars, a 29-year-old protégé of Alexander 'Greek' Thomson. How many of Cunningham's ideas survived in the final design is not known, but the basic shape of the Great Hall – a classic 'shoe box', or *gewandhaus*, with galleries on three sides – was similar to that of his Liverpool hall. More or less twice the size of the City Hall, St Andrew's Halls was Sellars's masterpiece with a capacity (over 3,000 in 1877, probably around 2,000 with modern fire regulations) big enough to accommodate an audience for the grandest musical events as well as the speeches of monarchs and prime ministers.

The very last music to be heard in the hall was conducted by one of the most influential figures in Scotland's musical history, Alexander Gibson. By Glasgow's great good fortune, the hall's opening celebrations in 1877 had coincided with the arrival of another highly influential musician: the most important conductor of the late 19th century, the German Hans von Bülow. A pupil and friend of Franz Liszt, a champion of Wagner and a close associate of Brahms and Tchaikovsky, Bülow was one of the musical wonders of the age – the first superstar conductor. He had a huge, charismatic personality and was famous for his ability to conduct complex new scores from memory and draw virtuoso performances from his players. He was also one of the finest pianists of his time, the first to perform all the sonatas of Beethoven as an integrated series.

Bülow had made the first of his momentous conducting appearances in Glasgow in 1875. A 'Glasgow Festival' committee had been formed. It was chaired by the influential music critic of *The Herald*, Thomas Logan Stillie, who with the directors of Glasgow Choral Union had resolved to establish an orchestra of some 50 players with the express purpose of mounting the city's first purely orchestral subscription concerts. The committee had a wider ambition, too, to create something resembling a 'national' orchestra that would tour across Scotland – not just to Edinburgh, but to Dundee, Stirling, Perth and several smaller towns. For the 1874–75 season they agreed that the choir's permanent conductor, Henry Lambeth, should conduct the orchestral programmes. But they managed to persuade Bülow (through contacts established from a prior Scottish engagement as a pianist) to conduct the

ST ANDREW'S HALLS

Location: Granville Street, Glasgow G3 7DR
Architect: James Sellars of Campbell, Douglas & Sellars
Capacity: 4500
Date opened: 1877 (destroyed by fire 1962)
(The Mitchell Library incorporates its only remaining façade, at the Mitchell Theatre entrance in Granville Street)
Music: Choral, Classical, Orchestral, Opera, Ballet

Below: Bruce Kennedy's drawing showing a section of The Great Hall.

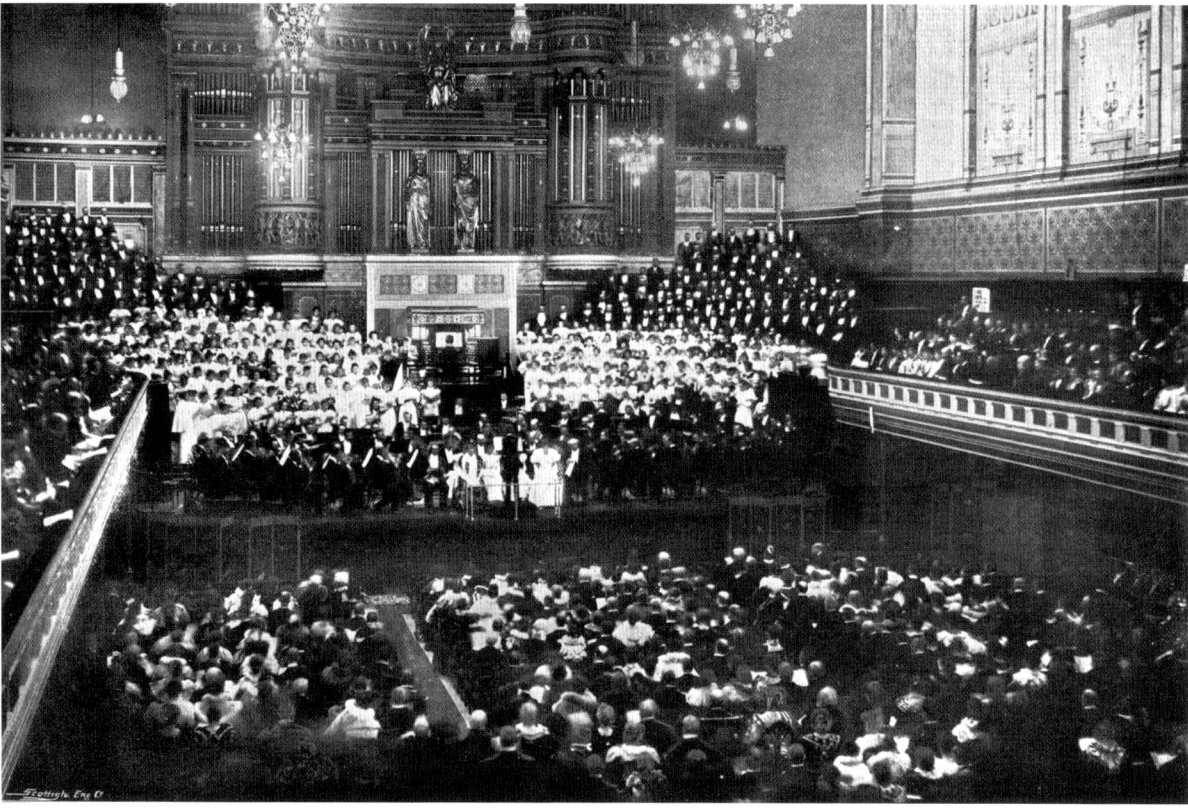

Right: Opening night concert at the new 'Glasgow Public Halls' (St Andrew's Halls) on 13 November 1877, showing original organ case. (The music performed was Handel's *Messiah*).

new orchestra at a single concert in the City Hall on 25 January 1875. Stillie, writing the next morning in *The Herald*, was ecstatic: '… we feel convinced that such a gorgeous concert of instrumental music was never before heard in Glasgow. This happy result we believe to arise in great part from the enthusiasm which Dr von Bülow feels for the works performed and the knack he has of imparting the same to his forces.' The minutes of the Choral Union recorded the board's feelings clearly enough: 'The orchestra has the ability to do well when it chooses, but it needs proper drilling … [they were] whipped up during his short stay with them … there was solidity of tone, brilliant colouring … .' In other words, Bülow's visit provided the revelation that, with the right man in charge, Glasgow's fledgling orchestra had the potential to rival the best in Britain.

The directors of the Choral Union already knew that Lambeth had no real talent for orchestral conducting, and they now had a clear vision for the way forward. To build an orchestra worthy of their city, they must recruit the best conductors they could find. Arthur Sullivan was invited to conduct the following two seasons (1875–77) and he did so with real distinction, introducing new works like Joachim Raff's three-year-old *Lenore Symphony* and some of his own music alongside symphonies by Beethoven, Mendelssohn and Schumann. But he was now being fêted in London with the success of *Trial by Jury*, his first operetta with WS Gilbert, and was unwilling to return for a third season. The committee decided to enquire whether Bülow might be persuaded to take over. He was more than happy to return to conduct all eight weeks of the 1877–78 orchestral season, but had already agreed to accept the post of music director in Hanover, so there was no question of him remaining in Glasgow. It's clear, though, that he had very much enjoyed his 1875 visit – enough to form a real affection for the city and its people: 'These Scots are ideal human beings,' he said, 'just as on the whole, this city appears to me infinitely homely, and homogenous.'

According to Bülow's biographer, Alan Walker, the relationship that he developed with the Choral Union and its orchestra (now being referred to in the press as the 'Glasgow Resident Orchestra') was 'one of the most collegial he ever enjoyed with any musical organisation'. He was, though, a notoriously prickly man, extremely demanding of orchestral players and always falling out with them – he was to last only two years in Hanover.

His infamous temper got the better of him during one rehearsal in Edinburgh: he was playing the solo part in a Rubinstein piano concerto while John Carrodus, the orchestra's leader, was making heavy weather of conducting it; stung by Bülow's angry complaints, Carrodus refused to continue, but luckily a substitute conductor was found and peace was restored.

That incident apart, Bülow's relationship with the new Glasgow orchestra seems to have been a happy one, as he reported with relish: 'The orchestra is now mine, all mine. A twitch of the thigh and they're off, hell for leather, in a veritable steeplechase of sound!' Subscriptions to the orchestral series had jumped by 84 per cent with the news that Bülow would conduct, and there were capacity audiences at all his concerts. He loved the new St Andrew's Halls, revelled in its richly responsive acoustic, and declared its four-manual organ, built by TC Lewis and inaugurated by the leading English organist, WT Best, to be finer in its range of colour and tone than any to be found in Germany. More importantly, he was delighted with the quality of the musicians, many of them from London, who had been engaged for the orchestra.

For the hall's grand opening, the Glasgow Choral Union under Henry Lambeth performed Handel's *Messiah*, the work for which they had been formed in 1844. Three days later, on 16 November 1877, the Choral Union's orchestra gave St Andrew's Halls' first orchestral concert, conducted by Bülow. The programme consisted entirely of Beethoven, beginning with the overture, *The Consecration of the House,* and ending with the *Choral Fantasia* with Bülow as piano soloist. Between these came the *Eighth Symphony*, the *King Stephen Overture*, some arias and pieces for solo piano. The impact of this concert, and the series that

Above: Architectural detail from *The Builder* magazine of 1880.

Left: Statues for the west frontage of St Andrew's Halls, being carved in Mossman's studio.

Bülow directed over the succeeding weeks, was enormous. Stillie hailed his performances as unprecedented in the city's musical life. Such was the commitment and discipline he instilled in his players that the sophisticated and much-travelled critic felt able to compare the orchestra to the finest in Europe by the time Bülow had finished with it.

And so musical Glasgow had quite quickly come to realise that almost anything might be possible. A real orchestra had been established in the best of possible circumstances, albeit one that functioned for less than a quarter of the year. But there was no going back; the progenitor of today's Royal Scottish National Orchestra had been born and the long, slow and sometimes fitful progress towards today's high orchestral standards had at last begun. Bülow returned to Germany in January 1878 with applause ringing in his ears. Among the wide range of repertoire he had introduced to his adoring Glasgow public during those two hectic months was the new *First Symphony* of his friend, Johannes Brahms. Having premiered it in Karlsruhe himself the previous year, Brahms had revised it over the summer, allowing Bülow to conduct the premiere of the definitive score in Hanover just four weeks before he brought it to Scotland.

Below: View of the Lounge (or Gallery) on the Ballroom floor.

Bülow's work with the Choral Union's orchestra had set the bar very high, and some of his successors would struggle to reach the same heights. But when, just a few weeks after Bülow's departure, Stillie was reviewing the first concert at St Andrew's Halls by Charles Hallé's orchestra, making its annual visit from Manchester, he made a point of thanking Hallé for 'furthering the cause of music' in the city. The previous year, when Hallé's orchestra had played in the City Hall, Stillie had thought that in some (though not all) respects it was better than Glasgow's new 'permanent orchestra'. Now, though, he felt that Glasgow's was superior, but was keen to praise Hallé's missionary work in the city over the years: 'More than 30 years ago he made his first appearance in Glasgow … [that] concert was, we believe, the first "classical concert", strictly so-called, in our city … since 1846 or 1847, from year to year, he has not failed to return, and in many capacities he has very materially aided in helping us to reach the prominent position in musical affairs to which our city now aspires.' By visiting so often Hallé had done more than anyone to develop Glasgow's desire for an orchestra of its own, and at last the dream had become a reality.

Over the next few seasons the Choral Union, no doubt aided by increased ticket income from the new larger hall, steadily expanded its orchestra so that by 1885 it was fielding 85 players. That in itself is remarkable considering the financial catastrophe that had overwhelmed the city when the City of Glasgow Bank had collapsed in 1878, less than a year after St Andrew's Halls' opening. In fact, Julius Tausch, successor to Schumann as music director in Düsseldorf and conductor for the 1878–79 Glasgow orchestral concerts, conducted a 'Grand Popular Night' on 16 November 'for the relief of the shareholders of the City of Glasgow Bank' – several of them, no doubt, directors of the Glasgow Choral Union. It was all hands to the pump, and Glasgow's musicians (as well as visiting celebrities like the actor, Henry Irving) were lining up to donate their services for benefit performances in the new hall.

The bank crash notwithstanding, the Choral Union's orchestral concerts continued to prosper. Increasingly plugged into the international touring circuit of star soloists, Glasgow audiences were beginning to experience hitherto unknown musical riches. For the 1879–80 season the orchestra was conducted by another German-born musician, August Manns, conductor of the famous Crystal Palace concerts in London, and considered to be the best orchestral trainer in Britain. 'Saturday Popular Concerts' had been an integral part of the orchestral season since the beginning and Manns launched his conductorship with a popular concert featuring the famous young Spanish violin virtuoso, Pablo Sarasate, as soloist. Sarasate returned the following week with Mendelssohn's *Violin Concerto* for the season's first subscription concert.

Clearly intent on educating as well as entertaining his audience, Manns programmed all nine Beethoven symphonies in chronological order, and such integrated planning across whole seasons was to be one

Above: The Great Hall, from the balcony, looking south, toward the platform.

of the hallmarks of his work in Glasgow over the next decade and more. The visiting procession of big international names continued: the great violinist, Joseph Joachim, friend of Brahms and dedicatee of his *Violin Concerto*, played with the orchestra for the first time in 1882; and the celebrated and highly eccentric pianist, Vladimir de Pachmann, played with them in 1883. By 1890 it was almost taken for granted that the orchestra should be able to bring two such world-famous artists as the violinist, Eugene Ysäye, and the Polish pianist, Ignacy Jan Paderewski, to Glasgow in the same season.

By the 1890–91 season, though, there were growing rumblings of discontent about the variable standard of the orchestra. In spite of Manns's efforts, there was something unsatisfactory about the orchestra's lack of permanence. Its freelance players were recruited annually from all over the UK for a season that was too short for them really to gel into the formidable force they had once promised to become. Public subsidy was far in the future, and without guarantees of substantial amounts of cash from wealthy individuals, the situation could not change. Then in 1891 a shipowner

Right: John Barbirolli (knighted Sir John in 1949), on the podium with the Scottish Orchestra, St Andrew's Halls, 1933.

named James Allan offered £20,000 to finance a new company capable of running a longer season. Known as the 'Scottish Orchestra', the new operation at first ran in competition with the Choral Union's orchestral concerts, splitting the audience and losing money for both companies. A bitter war ensued, with the Scottish Orchestra extending its season to 26 weeks to put the Choral Union's 10-week season in the shade. Eventually a truce was declared and the Glasgow Choral Union agreed to take the Scottish Orchestra under its banner. Later, in 1898, it renamed itself the Glasgow Choral and Orchestral Union. Manns had left by the end of the feud while George Henschel, yet another conductor of German origin (and another friend of Brahms at that!), had taken charge of the newly reconstituted orchestra that would eventually, in 1950, assume full-time status as the Scottish National Orchestra.

Henschel was a distinguished singer who had taken up conducting with some success, having been the first conductor of the Boston Symphony Orchestra. Though its 26-week season soon shrank to 20 weeks, the Scottish Orchestra was now able to move towards the 20th century with a sense of purpose, continually feeding its hungry Glasgow audience with new works such as the UK premieres of Dvorak's *Carnival Overture* and his *New World Symphony*, which Henschel introduced within months of its premiere in New York. Henschel's tenure of the Scottish Orchestra lasted only three seasons, but during that time he managed to take them to London's Queen's Hall to participate in his concert series there. He enjoyed his Scottish sojourn so much that he eventually retired, now a knight of the realm, to Inverness-shire. He and his wife were buried together in Aviemore.

In 1890, the Glasgow Public Halls Company had gone bankrupt and Glasgow City Corporation took ownership of St Andrew's Halls – which were indeed plural, since in addition to the large concert hall the building housed two smaller halls as well as a host of other rooms. The bigger of the two, the Berkeley Hall, was a popular venue for chamber music, solo recitals and public lectures. During the 1930s and 1940s the Glasgow and West of Scotland Pianoforte Society promoted many of its recitals there, with artists the calibre of Wilhelm Backhaus, Nicolai Medtner, Artur Rubinstein, Wanda Landowska, Josef Hofmann and (the society's very first booking) the legendary Moriz Rosenthal.

In 1933 a pianist of a rather different kind played there under the auspices of the extraordinary Active Society for the Propagation of Contemporary Music, formed by the young composer Erik Chisholm and some of his friends. Their aim was to bring as many of the world's leading composers to Glasgow as they could entice for the minuscule fees they could afford to pay. Stravinsky, predictably, proved too expensive, but Béla Bartók came twice, and in his 1933 Berkeley Hall recital he played his own gritty *1926 Sonata* to a large and enthusiastic audience with such percussive rhythmic intensity that Chisholm's wife thought that 'the legs of the piano seemed to be twitching in an effort to join in this animalistic, choreographic, Pan-worship rite'. Chisholm was himself no mean pianist, as he demonstrated in a 1940 Scottish Orchestra concert by playing the virtuosic solo part in his own *Piobaireachd Piano Concerto*.

The Active Society and the Piano Society were just two of the many voluntary organisations formed to promote music in the city in the days before public subsidy for the arts. Inevitably their fortunes rose and fell (the Active Society functioned for only five or six years in the early 1930s) as did those of the commercial promoters. But what is striking about all of them is the scale of their ambition and a common assumption that being in Glasgow should be no impediment to hearing the world's best. Over the years, St Andrew's Halls' main auditorium was regularly hired by several of Britain's leading impresarios, including the London agents Harold Holt and Ibbs and Tillett (promoters of the famous Max Mossel Concerts), who between them brought most of the leading classical artists of the day to the city. In the inter-war period it was part of an established touring circuit that also included Bristol's Colston Hall, Manchester's Free Trade Hall, Liverpool Philharmonic Hall, Newcastle's City Hall and the Usher Hall in Edinburgh.

Every season Harold Holt promoted a series of 'International Celebrity Subscription Concerts' at St Andrew's Halls with a list of artists that would nowadays take one's breath away. The 1936–37 Glasgow season, for example, included recitals by Jascha Heifitz, Vladimir Horowitz, Bronislaw Huberman with Artur Schnabel and Sergei Rachmaninov. The tradition of great composer-performers was still very much alive:

Rachmaninov played in Glasgow on no fewer than four occasions between 1929 and 1937; in 1926 Maurice Ravel played some of his piano music to a large St Andrew's Halls audience; while in 1937 Paul Hindemith appeared with the Scottish Orchestra and George Szell playing his new viola concerto, *Der Schwanendreher*. Other musical celebrities like Fritz Kreisler and the 'famous boy violinist, Yehudi Menuhin' were always guaranteed a full house at St Andrew's Halls. As for singers? Glasgow's penchant for great voices went back at least as far as Madame Albina and Adelina Patti, the world's highest paid singer, who first came in 1899. By the 1920s appearances in the city by such star vocalists as Elisabeth Schumann, John McCormick, Beniamino Gigli and Feodor Chaliapin were almost commonplace.

Of course, those were times when big-name classical artists habitually embarked on extensive recital tours to an extent they no longer do, and Glasgow was by no means alone among British cities in being able to attract them away from London. But *The Herald* critic who, in 1892, remarked on the 'glut' of classical concerts in the city – 'the stars in their courses are crowding one another sadly just now' – would have been amazed to find that it had grown even more by the 1920s. Countrywide orchestral tours were then more common in the UK than they are now, and in the early 20th century the London orchestras regularly came to Glasgow when visiting what they called 'the provinces'. St Andrews's Halls also occasionally played host to such celebrated foreign orchestras as the Berlin Philharmonic under Wilhelm Furtwängler before the Second World War. Perhaps surprisingly they returned immediately after the war. When their new Romanian conductor, Sergiu Celibidache, brought them in 1948 they demonstrated, *The Herald* critic declared, 'a new standard of orchestral values' – though he thought these were unfortunately wasted 'on the string of banalities which form Shostakovich's *Symphony No 9*.'

Unfamiliar new music wasn't always greeted so negatively in Glasgow. In fact, in the early 20th century St Andrew's Halls audience

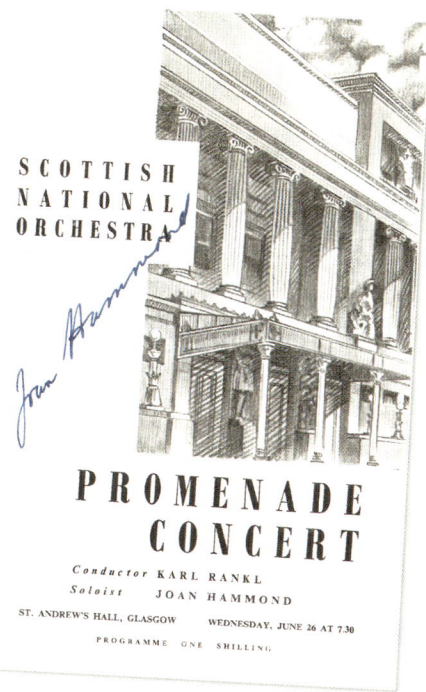

Above: A 1957 concert programme signed by performing soloist Joan Hammond.

Below: Architectural detail from *The Builder* magazine of 1880.

seems to have expected a constant flow of 'novelties' among the tried and tested masterpieces. The warm reception that greeted Bartók's recitals in 1932 and 1933, not to mention those of other composer-performers like Szymanowski and Hindemith who played for the Active Society, suggests a more open, curious attitude among Glasgow's music lovers than was sometimes found among its critics. Certainly new music cropped up from time to time in the programmes of the Scottish Orchestra and its predecessor, the Glasgow Resident Orchestra, from the earliest days: the Choral Union commissioned Sir George MacFarren's *Lady of the Lake* cantata for the hall's opening festival in 1877, and Bülow included a new overture by the young Scottish composer Alexander Mackenzie in one of his programmes. These were hardly cutting-edge, but when Richard Strauss – whose music was considered the most 'advanced' of its time – came in the Scottish Orchestra's 1902–03 and 1903–04 seasons to conduct the Scottish premieres of his *Don Juan*, *Death and Transfiguration*, *Till Eulenspiegel* and *Aus Italien*, he was rapturously received.

Much later, in 1937, when the extremely demanding Hungarian George Szell was conductor of the Scottish Orchestra, his planned performance of William Walton's new *Symphony No 1* was for some reason dropped from the schedule. But in the orchestra's annual 'plebiscite', the disappointed audience voted it as the piece they would most like to hear the following season. So it was reinstated and in January 1938, Szell conducted what *The Herald* called a 'great performance' of it. Later, in his long and distinguished partnership with the Cleveland Orchestra, Szell was to prove one of Walton's finest interpreters.

St Andrew's Halls was an orchestral venue par excellence. But as Glasgow's 'village hall' it was used for music of all sorts. Popular artists, from the Moore and Burgess Minstrels in the 1880s to Mario Lanza in the 1950s, drew enormous crowds. And while variety theatres like the Empire tended to be the venue of choice for artists like Frank Sinatra, Danny Kaye or Ella Fitzgerald, St Andrew's Halls was perfect for unamplified music. Burns Night and Hogmanay brought annual concerts of traditional Scottish music. Since the 1850s the Glasgow Abstainers' Union concerts of popular music – Scottish songs, well-known violin solos and the like – had been a feature of Glasgow musical life. Designed to entice Saturday night drinkers away from the pubs, this noble enterprise of the Victorian temperance movement was taken over in the 1920s by Glasgow Corporation, which moved it from the City Hall to St Andrew's Halls. The concerts seem to have been well attended, but how successful they were as a cultural alternative to the demon drink is not recorded.

Amateur music-making, too, had its niche in St Andrew's Halls – notably the Glasgow Orchestral Society (founded in 1870 and still going strong) and the Glasgow Music Festival, which since 1911 has run an annual fortnight of competitive performances in music, speech, drama and dance for amateurs of all ages. But no history of music in Glasgow would be complete without mentioning the extraordinary phenomenon that was the Glasgow Orpheus Choir. Formed in 1906 by the redoubtable Sir Hugh S Roberton, the choir quickly acquired a huge and devoted local and Scottish following. Roberton required total dedication from his 60 or so amateur choristers, and from them he created a choral sound that for its time was uniquely refined (even if to modern ears it seems over-smooth and often sentimental). He took them to London and other UK cities, then to the US and Canada. They sang in Carnegie Hall and regularly sold out the Royal Albert Hall. Their recordings of Roberton's own songs, such as 'All in the April Evening', and of his many arrangements, like 'Crimond' and 'An Eriskay Love Lilt', sold all over the world.

Every year the Orpheus gave a series of concerts in St Andrew's Halls that always sold out. Roberton believed in broadening the musical horizons of both his choristers and their audience, so in the 1920s, for example, the choir promoted its own annual week of international chamber music concerts in the McLellan Galleries. It was perhaps the only amateur choir in British history that had a mass international following as well as huge home support. Roberton's pacifist views led the BBC to ban the Orpheus Choir from the airwaves for a few months in 1940, but they were considered vital to the war effort. Questions were asked in the House of Commons and the ban was lifted.

When Roberton retired in 1951, the choir chose to disband rather than carry on under another conductor. They gave a long series of emotional farewell concerts – four of them in a packed St Andrew's Halls. After the last of those, appropriately on an April evening (the 11th) in 1951, *The Herald* reported: 'In acknowledging the applause, Sir Hugh described the audience as his 'very old and loyal friends', and speaking of the disbandment of the choir, said, 'I can say we are one – we are undivided. That is why we cannot lose a bit without losing all.' Roberton died the following year.

The Glasgow Orpheus Choir was one of the more spectacular products of the fervid Victorian belief in the morally and physically improving power of communal musical activity – exactly what St Andrew's Halls were built for. But the hall's story was first and foremost the story of orchestral music in Glasgow. The fortunes of the Scottish Orchestra, always (until 1950) under the banner of the Glasgow Choral and Orchestral Union, waxed and waned over the first half of the 20th century. By the First World War its season had slipped back to barely three months over the winter, ceasing altogether between 1916 and 1919. Conductors came and went, engaged for a season at a time, and the lack of continuity made it hard to maintain the highest standards. However, the most outstanding conductors could galvanise the orchestra into truly exciting performances. In 1923, the flamboyant Russian, Serge Koussevitsky, took the helm, thrilling his audience with such over-the-top Russian repertoire as Scriabin's *Poem of Ecstasy*. He was later to reach the height of his fame at the Boston Symphony Orchestra, where he commissioned a whole raft of important new pieces, from Bartók's *Concerto for Orchestra* to Stravinsky's *Symphony of Psalms*.

Other Scottish Orchestra conductors at that time included Adrian Boult and the distinguished Austrian, Felix Weingartner. But the Choral and Orchestral Union's finances between the wars fluctuated from moderately healthy to dire, and it lacked the wherewithal to persuade these conductors to stay for more than a season or two. The Czech, Vaclav Talich, who

subsequently made the Czech Philharmonic into one of the world's finest orchestras, was another of those world-class musicians that the orchestra's, and perhaps the hall's, reputation were able to attract, but again he stayed for only one season in 1926.

Orchestras, nonetheless, were a Glaswegian passion. A little-known period in the pre-history of the BBC Scottish Symphony Orchestra (founded in 1935) centres on Glasgow's first radio station, 5SC, which began broadcasting locally for the British Broadcasting Company in 1923. By 1925 it had, like several of its sister stations in other cities, its own little 'station orchestra', a freelance group of only 17 players that broadcast live music almost every day. But 5SC's station director, Herbert Carruthers, was also its energetic and ambitious director of music and the conductor of its orchestral programmes. In the 1926–27 season, demonstrating the kind of chutzpah that in anywhere other than Glasgow might seem like sheer madness, he decided to mount a series of six full-scale symphony concerts in St Andrew's Halls with what he called the 'Station Symphony Orchestra' – his studio band augmented to over 70 musicians. One of those concerts included the first complete Scottish performance of Gustav Holst's *Planets Suite*, conducted by the

Above: Salvaged instruments following the fire at St Andrew's Halls.

Opposite, top: Boxing in St Andrew's Halls.

Opposite, middle: Firemen tackle the blaze.

Opposite, bottom: West frontage of the Halls following the 1962 fire.

This spread: Statuary from the St Andrew's Halls' frontage.

This page, top: Music, including Apollo.

This page, bottom: Literature, represented by Shakespeare, Homer and Dante.

Opposite, top: Art, represented by Michelangelo, Raphael and Leonardo.

Opposite, bottom: Architecture, including Pallas Athene.

composer himself. Carruthers also boldly programmed a Beethoven symphony cycle that season, and the Scottish premiere of Honegger's *Pacific 231*. But in 1926, 5SC was absorbed into the new British Broadcasting Corporation, and in 1929 its station orchestra was reduced to an octet.

In 1933, the Scottish Orchestra's management committee, once again demonstrating its canny eye for talent, secured the services of a rising star among young conductors who had appeared as a guest during the previous two seasons. John Barbirolli's short conducting career had, up to that point, been spent more in the opera pit than with symphony orchestras – indeed, he had visited Glasgow as a staff conductor with the British National Opera Company in the 1920s. Three memorable seasons as the Scottish Orchestra's chief conductor from 1933 to 1936, his first proper orchestral job, at last gave the orchestra real stability under a musician capable of inspiring superb playing. The audience loved him and ticket sales went up. But siren voices were already beginning to call from more glamorous quarters, and Barbirolli was seduced across the Atlantic to fill Toscanini's shoes at the New York Philharmonic. In the end, that appointment was relatively short-lived, and Barbirolli was back in Britain in 1943, relishing the challenge of rebuilding almost from scratch a much depleted and demoralised Hallé Orchestra in Manchester. Perhaps, if the Scottish Orchestra's management committee had been quicker off the mark, they could have got in before the Hallé. But Barbirolli had become frustrated, before his departure for New York, by the huge number of concerts that the Scottish Orchestra was expected to cram into a short season of less than four months. Things would probably have had to change radically in Glasgow for him to have been tempted back.

Radical change came, but not until after the Second World War, by which time public and critical clamour for a full-time, salaried orchestra had become deafening. It took until 1950 for a newly constituted governing body, to be known as the Scottish National Orchestra Society, to emerge and its orchestra to start operations full-time. The Czech-born, Walter Susskind, had been appointed conductor of the Scottish Orchestra in 1946 and he continued until 1952 when he was succeeded by two Viennese conductors, first Karl Rankl and then Hans Swarowsky. By 1959, as the undistinguished tenure of Swarowsky was running out of steam, the Scottish National Orchestra (SNO) was in serious need of a new broom. This time the orchestra's management took a risk but made the right call, recruiting the orchestra's first Scottish conductor and instantly transforming its fortunes. The arrival of Alexander Gibson – young, dynamic, full of ideas and most importantly, utterly committed – marked a watershed in Glasgow's and Scotland's musical life. Listening to a recorded broadcast of Gibson conducting the SNO in Brahms's *First Symphony* at St Andrew's Halls in 1962, one is struck not just by the generous richness of the hall's acoustic, but also by the powerful sense of orchestra and conductor completely united in musical focus and intent.

Gibson was the first of the orchestra's conductors to become a national figure. In his first season he chose to programme all seven symphonies of Jean Sibelius, regarded by Scottish concert-goers almost as one of their own. It was a project that neatly symbolised the break with the mostly Austro-German repertoire of his two predecessors, who would never have dreamed of conducting the music of the great Finn. Even more significantly, he persuaded the management to let him start a contemporary music festival, *Musica Viva* (later to become *Musica Nova*), through which he could introduce new pieces and important mid-20th century European music still awaiting a hearing in Scotland. Undoubtedly the most important of several premieres he conducted was the first UK performance, in 1961, of *Gruppen* for three orchestras by the fiercest young turk of the avant-garde, Karlheinz Stockhausen. It was a mammoth undertaking, requiring 120 players divided into three groups under three conductors. The BBC Scottish Orchestra, also experiencing the bracing energy of a new, radically minded conductor, Norman Del Mar, was invited to collaborate. John Carewe was the third conductor. The stalls seats of St Andrew's Halls were cleared away so that the huge orchestra could occupy the whole of the floor, with the capacity audience filling the galleries and the stage.

Gruppen was a triumph, and a rare enough event to tempt the cream of London's music critics to journey north to Glasgow. Both audience and press were fervently divided. In *The Observer*, Edmund Tracey found it strange that 'with so much apparatus, Stockhausen has apparently so little to say to us.' One audience member shouted 'Rubbish!' in the brief moment of silence before the applause began, but, the *Daily Telegraph*'s critic Donald Mitchell remarked, '… lone cries of indignation bounce off Stockhausen's brilliance like peas off armour plate. There may be much to be said against *Gruppen*, but "rubbish" the work is not.' As a powerful statement of intent on the part of the SNO's principal conductor, *Gruppen* signalled a new openness to everything the musical world outside Scotland had to offer. It was a watershed in Scotland's musical life, and the last really important event in the history of St Andrew's Halls.

In January 1962, the great violinist, Yehudi Menuhin, arrived to rehearse there with Alexander Gibson and the Scottish National Orchestra. To his consternation he found that a boxing ring had been erected in the main hall and that his rehearsal had been moved to the Berkeley Hall. He let his views be known to the press, and the *Glasgow Citizen* reported his shock at seeing a concert hall being used for boxing. 'The two don't mix,' he said. 'This is a great concert hall, and the hall carries with it the echoes of what has happened in the past. I am amazed. I imagined this was a hall for music!'

Had someone taken note of Menuhin's prescience, St Andrew's Halls might well still be with us now. Nine months later, all that a Glasgow Corporation official could offer on the bleak morning of 26 October, after St Andrew's Halls had been almost totally destroyed by fire, was that 'No Smoking' signs had been displayed widely but a ban was never 'rigidly enforced'. 'It was left to the discretion of the people,' he said. The press and official reaction to such a terrible loss seems muted by today's standards. No calls for a public enquiry, little sense of outrage that fire precautions should be so carelessly ignored. The Scottish vice-chairman of the actors' union even went so far as to say that it offered a 'wonderful chance' to build a new arts centre that might include a new home for the Citizens Theatre. The Lord Provost, Dame Jean Roberts, called for the hall to be rebuilt – after all, Germany had rebuilt many of its bombed-out opera houses after the war. But the city's librarians were covetously eyeing the useful new space that the fire had opened up behind the Mitchell Library. Local architects began to dream of an improbably vast new 'cultural centre' elsewhere in the city, along the lines of the Lincoln Center in New York. Long years of financial and political wrangling and of makeshift concert halls being hastily fashioned from redundant cinemas began, while the sad shell of a once-majestic building stood forlorn and abandoned. And as Glasgow's baleful era of 1960s and 1970s city 'planning' unfolded, the climate moved decisively away from preserving and rebuilding towards tearing down and throwing up.

A few weeks after the fire, Alexander Gibson wrote in the *Radio Times* of his grief at the loss of 'this wonderful old hall. For me it is like losing a close friend.' It was not that it was an especially comfortable hall to sit in, he explained, with its antique heating system and balcony seats that gave you a crick in the neck. But the acoustic was irreplaceable. 'This is the tragedy: that when good concert halls are scarcer than Stradivarius violins we should lose one of the finest.' From its very first days, when the great Hans von Bülow gave the downbeat for Beethoven's *Consecration of the House*, St Andrew's Halls had been the key that for Glasgow's people opened the door to the art of music's greatest experiences. Six days before that key was lost, Alexander Gibson and the Scottish National Orchestra ended their Saturday concert with Sibelius's *Second Symphony*. The thrilling, brass-dominated finale is a paean of triumphal defiance. It was the last music ever heard in St Andrew's Halls.

Left: Composers' names carved into the frontage: Purcell, Bach, Handel, Mozart and Beethoven.

ROTTENROW
Singing in the Streets

Ewan McVicar

Left: Townhead Primary School, on Rottenrow East.

*There is a happy land, doon in Duke Street Jail,
Where aa the convicts stand, tied tae a nail.
Ham an eggs ye never see, dirty watter fur yer tea,
There they live in misery, God Save The Queen.*

The weans who sang this parody of the hymn 'There is a happy land far far away' lived in the Drygate beside Duke Street Jail, just down from Glasgow Cathedral and overlooked by the imposing tombs of the Necropolis (the City of the Dead). Some of their fathers would have worked in the Jail, some of their fathers may have been been inmates. The kids would have crossed over High Street to Rottenrow to go to school at Townhead Primary or Rottenrow Primary. The meaning of 'Drygate' is clear enough: it identified the higher dry road, the one not prone to flooding by the Clyde. The provenance of 'Rottenrow' is argued over. Was it the Gaelic Rathan Righ ('The Road of the King') because it leads up to Glasgow Cathedral? Or was it where a row of rotten, rat-infested hovels once stood?

Adults too often believe that children no longer sing songs or chant rhymes that they learn from each other without grown-up mediation. Teachers, too, often confirm this belief. But if you know how to ask, you will find in any primary school in the land a few of the old rhymes, a few old ones remade and a few brand new ones chanted across the playground. I found a flood of such rhymes when I started talking to the classes visiting Glasgow's Scotland Street Museum in the early 1990s, and hundreds more up until 1997. In 2006 I

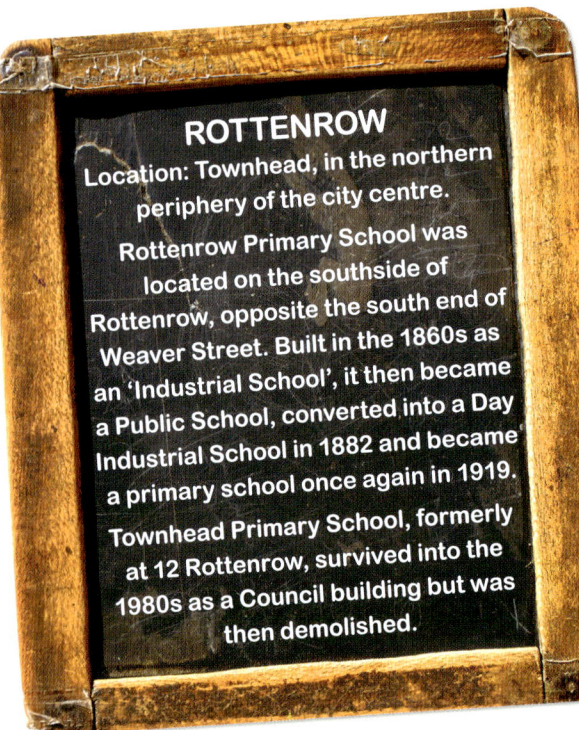

ROTTENROW

Location: Townhead, in the northern periphery of the city centre.

Rottenrow Primary School was located on the southside of Rottenrow, opposite the south end of Weaver Street. Built in the 1860s as an 'Industrial School', it then became a Public School, converted into a Day Industrial School in 1882 and became a primary school once again in 1919.

Townhead Primary School, formerly at 12 Rottenrow, survived into the 1980s as a Council building but was then demolished.

collected more than 120 rhymes that are still in use in Moray schools, and when I was putting together a book on the subject in 2007 a last-minute dip into a few West Lothian classes gathered a rich harvest.

Such songs and rhymes are now generally learned in the school playground, but they are still referred to as 'street songs': songs deployed by kids playing in streets before roaring automobile beasts began to dominate them and chased the chasing, skipping, ball-bouncing children away. Some of the rhymes and songs are known throughout the land, though the words and tunes are often remade as they travel. Others hold the distinctive language, social norms and societal references of Glesga.

> *Last night there was a murder in the chipshop,*
> *A wee dog stole a haddie bone,*
> *A big dog tried tae take it aff him,*
> *So ah hit it wi a tattie scone.*
> *Ah went roon tae see ma Aunty Sarah,*
> *Bit ma Aunty Sarah wisnae in,*
> *So ah keeked through a hole in the windae,*
> *An ah shouted 'Aunty Sarah, are ye in?'*
> *Her false teeth were lyin on the table,*
> *Her curly wig wis lyin on the bed,*
> *An ah laughed an ah laughed till ma heid fell aff,*
> *When ah saw her screwin aff her wudden leg.*

In the late 1960s, Ian Davison, now well known as a singer-songwriter who has celebrated Glasgow in many of his songs, was a new teacher and folk singer. He decided to collect from his pupils what they had learned at play with other children. Davison found Rottenrow Primary to be particularly hoaching with songs, and proceeded to collect more than 150 separate items from that one school. Most of them were used to accompany physical play. Some were for 'the game of language' and most had an element of humour, often surreal. Some were notably subversive in tone:

> *Santa Claus cam doon the lum*
> *Wi toys for oor wee Minnie;*
> *He stole ma mammy's best fur coat*
> *And noo he's in Barlinnie.*

Others were sentimental, used for guising around the closes of the Drygate at Halloween:

> *I once had a dear old mother, she was all the world to me,*
> *And when I was in trouble she sat me on her knee.*
> *One night as I lay sleeping upon my feather bed,*
> *An angel came from Heaven and told me Mum was dead.*

Some were frankly rude; some featured famous names; a few did both:

> *As I was walking doon the street*
> *I thought I smelt some kippers*
> *I asked a lady what it was*
> *She said it was her knickers.*

Right: Rottenrow Primary School.

And:

*Rabbie Burns got sixty days
For lookin up a wumman's claes.*

Some contained threats of bloody gang violence offered up by what Davison called 'nice wee boys'. Glasgow gangs weren't like the gun-toting, drug-running gangs of American TV. In general they were, and are, loose territorial groupings of teenagers who assert control over other teenagers passing through their area. They occasionally had confrontations using make-shift weaponry at a mutually recognised border, and even more occasionally used knives to settle disagreements or perceived slights. Davison's 'nice wee boys' sang the gang songs to state their allegiance to whatever local crew their older brothers and neighbours ran with. The tune for the then-popular American ballad 'Sixteen Tons' was used for the following verse, though the second line of the original has fallen away and the 'nice wee boys' had clearly never considered how a bayonet might actually be used.

*You take a trolley to the Calton, you're into the town;
We don't carry razors, we don't carry chains,
We only carry bayonets to bash in your brains.*

Football, of course, figured in plenty of rhymes. The army anthem 'Bless 'Em All' transmuted into:

*A big bus was leaving from Hampden Park,
The Rangers had just won the cup, the cup,
The Celtic were greetin because they were beaten,
A big bus was leaving from Hampden Park.*

Religious intolerance featured, too:

*Hail hail, the Pope's in jail
He wipes his bum on the Sunday Mail.*

Parodies of popular songs or old favourites abound. 'It's a Long Way to Tipperary' is used for the following sad verse:

*It's a long way to the pawnshop, where all our mothers go,
Goodbye to my jacket, farewell my watch and chain,*

If I don't hang on tae ma troosers they'll be gone the same.

The pawnshop features more antagonistically here:

*Old Mother Riley at the pawn shop door,
Her baby in her arms and her bundle on the floor,
She asked for ten bob, she only got four,
An she nearly pullt the hinges aff the pawnshop door.*

Above: Balmano Brae was another name for Balmano Street which linked George Street with Rottenrow to the north. The street is now covered by university buildings.

Below: Outdoor activities at Kennyhill Special School in 1916.

Above: Skipping.

Below: Finger games.

Most of these songs are short and very sharp but now and then longer pieces crop up. There are five sad and sentimental verses to this ballad-like rhyme:

I once knew a Borstal boy, he sure broke my heart.
He told me a story about his sweetheart.

The tune of the then-popular 'Putting on the Style' is employed for a 24-line solemn account of seduction and unwanted pregnancy that begins: 'It happened doon at Barrowland' and ends with advice to 'all you hairies' to take the new wean when older 'up to Barrowland and show it how to dance'.

Many of the songs collected from Rottenrow ex-pupils were widely known in other Glasgow schools. They were used for similar purposes: to accompany ball-bouncing or skipping, to choose who would be 'it' in chasing games, for guising at Halloween, for formal ring games, each with their own choreography, to assert geographical allegiance to a local gang or football team, and for the sheer enjoyment of uttering aloud the absurd or rude words in the verse.

So in playgrounds across Glasgow, the timing of rope-jumping or ball-catching was aided by rhythmic chants about grannies catching fleas, chants ridiculing 'the polis' or the feared factor who collected rents, parodies of songs learned in classrooms and assertions about superior ball skills such as: 'Ladies in the tight skirts can't do this'. Counting out who was to be 'it' in a game was served by many rhymes. For example:

Green, white and blue,
The cat's got the flu,
The dog's got the chicken pox
And so have you.

The guising songs were lugubriously sentimental, often featuring dead or dying parents, children or soldiers: 'Dear Old Mother', 'Don't Go Down the Mine Dad' and 'The Night Was Dark The Battle Over' were likely Halloween fare.

Some of these songs would also be sung in back court concerts. These ad-hoc gatherings thrived in the days when families were crowded into rows of tenemented streets, each group of six or eight flats sharing a common back area railed off from the next tenement close. Rubbish bins nested together and there was usually a communal wash house that billowed steam every Monday. There was also an open space that was just right for children's games. Some of these had two or three long steps where in summer the smaller kids of the neighbourhood could be gathered up and seated together by older girls already sharpening their maternal skills. Adults would lean out of their kitchen windows to be entertained by a mixture of community song, exhibitions of dance steps, and solo 'party pieces' delivered by the organising girls and any medium-sized lad they could forcibly recruit to join in. If the adults liked what they heard, they might just toss down a coin.

Glasgow geography was learned through verse, too. There was 'Down In Duke Street Jail', 'The Big Mansion Hoose Ca'd Barlinnie Hotel', or the lines:

Rabbie Burns was born in Ayr,
Noo he's doon in George's Square.

Glasgow references could lose sense when exported outside of the city. Before the statue of William of Orange was moved up to near the Cathedral from its Glasgow Cross location, the song said:

If you want to see a hero, take a tramcar tae the Cross,
There you'll see a noble sodger ridin on a big white horse.

In rural Argyllshire around 1900, however, they sang:

If you want to see King William, take your trumpet to the Cross,
There you'll see a noble lady riding on a big black horse.

The kids singing the songs tended to favour a limited selection of tunes. Simple American melodies such as 'Redwing' were much used, and 'Katie Bairdie Had a Coo' and 'Knees Up Mother Brown' featured heavily for old favourites such as this one:

One two three, ma grannie caught a flea,
She salted it an peppered it an had it for her tea.
She didny like it so she gave it tae her son,
He didny like it so he threw it up the lum.

A lot of the lyrics had Glasgow-specific versions (Billy Connolly recalls singing the carol 'A wean in a manger') and old rhymes were amended to become topical for the times:

Down in Liverpool,
The Beatles go to school,
Ringo canny do his sums
But he can do his drums.

Some of the longer pieces became widely sung during the Scottish folk revival. In 1970, Robin Hall and Jimmie MacGregor recorded an LP called Glasgow Street Songs, but most of what Ian Davison collected from the children of Rottenrow still sits silent in his card index. Duke Street Jail and the old Drygate housing were flattened by Glasgow Corporation, as were Rottenrow and Townhead Primaries. Rottenrow Primary stood to the south of Rottenrow (East), opposite the south end of Weaver Street (as was). But a remnant of the other school for Drygate kids remains. On the corner of Rottenrow and the High Street sits the Barony Parish Church building (University Of Strathclyde Barony Hall). Behind it in Rottenrow is a carpark, where stood Townhead Primary, an imposing square-faced edifice. To enter it from Rottenrow you must walk under a stone arch topped by the 'Infants' sign that once told the wee wans which door to enter school by. The stone lintel for the 'Boys' entrance is embedded within the carpark. No echoing children's voices now, the roar of the motor vehicle has conquered here too. But in the playgrounds of any of the primary schools nearby, the careful enquirer will find in use not the 150 items that Davison recorded at Rottenrow, but still 20 to 40 rhymes and verses old and new.

Above: Bools.

Below: One Two Three a-Leerie.

THE PAVILION
Glasgow Belongs To Me
Ewan McVicar

The only survivor of music-hall days still running in Glasgow is the Pavilion, up at the top of Renfield Street on the corner with Renfrew Street. At one time there were said to be 30 halls of variety and music in Glasgow. Now there is only one.

Music halls flourished from the 1850s for about 100 years until driven out by film and television. Early music-hall fare consisted of popular song and comedy, performed for patrons who sat at tables, drank alcohol, smoked, chatted to pals, joined in raucously with the choruses they liked and booed or pelted off the unfortunate performers who failed to impress them. This vigorous, semi-competitive atmosphere exactly fitted the taste of Glasgow's working classes, out for fun and frolic and intolerant of having to be patient with, or kind to, an unassertive performer.

Through the 19th century the music halls gradually melded into the mould of variety theatres. Tables and chairs became rows of seating, alcohol was banished to the foyer (though

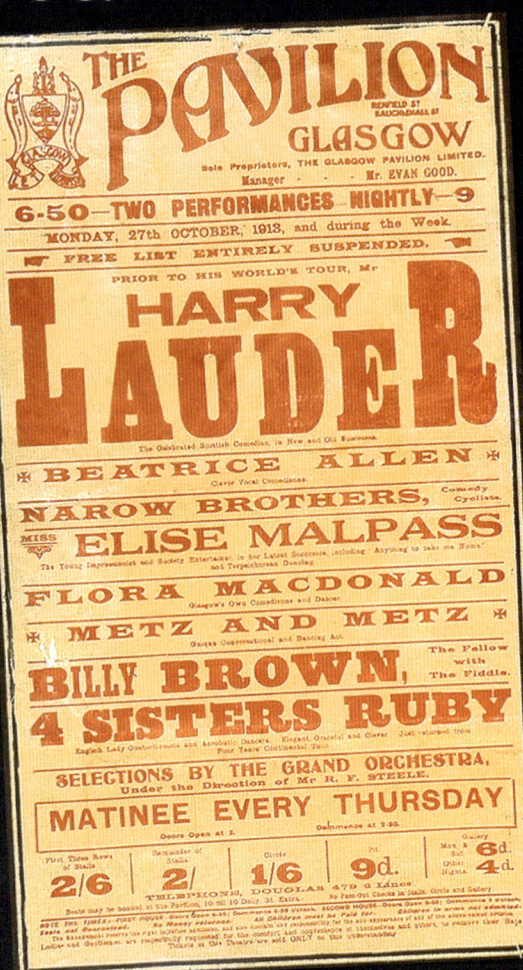

Right: Exterior of the Pavilion theatre in Glasgow, by night, January 1981.

Left: A playbill from 1913 announcing one of Harry Lauder's last Scottish performances before he set off on his latest world tour.

THE PAVILION.

Above: Renfrew Street signage of The Pavilion.

The Pavilion
Location: 121 Renfield Street, Glasgow G2 3AX
Architect: Bertie Crewe for Thomas Barrasford
Date Opened: 1904
Performances: Mainly variety, melodrama and pantomime
Capacity: 1449

the ashtrays remained), and comics and singers were joined by speciality acts. Ventriloquists, acrobats, performing animals, magicians, mime artists, comic pianists, harmonica bands and more bounced on stage in a speedy sequence with no coherent theme or continuity – just variety. A continuing taste for strong meat in comedy and song kept up the music-hall atmosphere of fierce challenge and the demand to be amused, *or else*. Comics visiting from the south almost feared for their lives when facing a drunken Friday night Glasgow audience.

Some other halls, the Metropole in Stockwell Street for example, were built much earlier than the Pavilion. Some, like the Empire, specialised in visiting acts from England and famous recording stars from America. The Alhambra in Waterloo Street went upmarket to bring a more cultured and polite middle-class audience the sophistication of the themed and literate *Half Past Eight* shows. But the Pavilion has always held onto a core gritty, urban identity that celebrates Glasgow's own speech, witty patter and song.

The audience then, as now, expected to interact with their performers, offering knowing laughter at local references and full-throated joining-in with choruses. There tended to be a generous consumption of alcohol before the show and during the intervals, but the Pavilion was considered a 'family' theatre so the jokes were never too blue nor the dancers too underdressed. The front stalls and the circle seats were thought to be the best and as a result were the most expensive. The rear stalls were dimly claustrophobic and up in the 'gods' (the top gallery) you felt in danger of tumbling down towards the distant stage. Those in the dear seats wore their Sunday best and behaved themselves, while the denizens of the dark rear stalls or the gods would arrive still in their workaday clothes and be vocal in their assessment of the acts they craned their necks to view.

The Pavilion was built in 1904. Inside there was seating in rows and a unique feature in its electrically operated sliding roof. The terracotta facade and Rococo plasterwork decor was described as 'pure Louis XV'. It was called 'The Pavilion Theatre of Varieties' and not officially a music hall, but song and music were always integral to its variety shows, pantomimes and concerts. Every headlining comic had to include in his act songs specially written for and associated with him, with a supporting bill of several solo singers, an instrumental musical act or two, speciality dancers and a chorus line.

In the early days it was Scots legends of the boards, like Harry Lauder and Will Fyffe, or visiting songstresses, like Marie Lloyd and Florrie Forde, who would grip the audience by its collective throat and get them to join in their choruses. American acts were mainly

Right: Pavilion programme for The Lex McLean Show.

Pavilion Theatre Glasgow
The Lex McLean Show

of the blackface minstrel variety: white performers who blacked their faces with burnt cork and sang, danced and cracked jokes in parodic imitation of Afro-American culture. Back then they were highly popular but nowadays such performers would be booed off-stage as offensively racist and pursued to the nearest police station.

In the 1930s Glasgow's Dave Willis and Aberdeen's Harry Gordon, with his songs of the fictional community of Inversneckie, starred in the Pavilion pantomimes. In the 1940s and 1950s, the pantomimes ran on for 16 weeks, and Tommy Morgan was the star of lengthy music-hall summer shows. By the 1960s the variety shows had been in part supplanted by concert formats featuring new Scots singing stars like Lulu, Lena Martell and Sheena Easton. Folk performers were also included, and Glasgow's own Billy Connolly lengthened his song introductions into a new genre of comic monologue. Young fiddler Aly Bain came down from Shetland to visit his brother in Glasgow and was bemused to find himself quickly dressed up in a trim red jacket and shoved onstage as a Pavilion variety turn.

More recently, rock concerts have packed the 1,449 Pavilion seats, featuring stars like local ex-folkie-boy-turned-wild-rocker John Martyn. When the rock guitarist, John McLaughlin, wrote and performed an orchestral piece for the *Glasgow International Jazz Festival*, half of the orchestra had to be accommodated in the wings because the Pavilion stage was too small for them. Nowadays the Pavilion still resounds to much music and laughter, and the occasional bout of wrestling both onstage and in the audience.

The music halls were preceded by 'the penny geggies' (temporary theatres of wood and cloth) at the annual Summer Fair on Glasgow Green. In July 1864 their bill included short magic acts, tumbling, 'melo-dramatic performances', magic lantern slides, and dubious oddities of human or animal life. Some of the music, from bagpipes, drums and brass instruments, happened out on the square in front of the South Prison. One contemporary account reads: 'The medley of tunes torn and twisted out of these instruments by men and boys, almost black in the face, is positively sufficient to drive a sensitive person mad.' For the rest of the year, the singers and dancers would keep themselves busy at talent shows in Temperance Halls, church socials, 'free and easies', and 'singing saloons'.

Singing saloons were the back rooms of pubs, where a nervous singer would mount a low stage and hope to overcome the roar of his audience. One of the first of these to call itself a music hall was Sloan's Oddfellows Music Hall off Argyle Street; today one can still enter Sloan's to get food and alcohol or step it out at the Friday ceilidh upstairs in the Grand Ballroom. Another early music hall was the Scotia in Stockwell Street, built in 1862. Fifty years later the owner had made his thin young son assistant manager; one night that son took time off 'to go to a party' and instead made his debut on stage at the nearby Panopticon in Argyle Street. The lad's name was Stan Laurel.

The Scotia features in another fabled début. The singer and songmaker, Harry Lauder, was born in Hamilton and worked as a coal miner, but he was determined to 'tread the boards'. His first professional engagement as an entertainer was a week at the Scotia, and when he went to collect his salary the then owner, Mrs Bayliss, said to him in a kind voice, 'There ye are laddie. Noo awa hame an practise.'

In the heyday of the Glasgow music halls, the Pavilion, the Scotia and the Alhambra all ran extended seasons of shows with one of the great triumvirate of

Above: Poster for the Pavilion. Designed by Bertie Crewe for Thomas Barrasford, the Pavilion Theatre opened its doors at the corner of Renfield Street and Renfrew Street in 1904. It was regarded as luxurious for its time with its decor being described by the owners as "pure Louis XV". An electrically operated sliding roof ensured good ventilation

Performances in the early days were mainly variety, melodrama and pantomime. Many of the leading music hall artistes of the period appeared at the Pavilion, including Marie Lloyd, Harry Lauder, Florrie Forde, Will Fyffe, Sarah Bernhardt and a then unknown Charlie Chaplin.

Left: Exterior stonework detail.

Right: Danish-born comedian/pianist Victor Borge, 1975.

Right: The Wooltoun Jazz Band on stage.

Lauder, Will Fyffe and Harry Gordon as the headliner. All were singer-songwriters who sang comic and sentimental songs and interleaved the verses with comic rehearsed patter. Fyffe was a Dundonian. One night in Glasgow's Central Station he was accosted by a well-oiled local. Fyffe asked sociably, 'And do you belong to Glasgow?' The response, so the story goes, was, 'At the moment, Glasgow belongs to me'. The phrase rang in Fyffe's head until he made a song out of it and took it along to the Alhambra to offer to Harry Lauder. The nervous young songwriter was graciously received, but Lauder rejected it, saying 'I never sing songs in praise of drink.' (When a startled Fyffe asked about Lauder's song, 'A Wee Deoch an Doris', Lauder said he always emphasised the word 'wee' as a warning.) Fyffe started performing 'I belong to Glasgow' himself, playing a drunk man trying to convince the audience he was sober, and it was his first big hit in London. He would go on to pen another Glasgow music-hall anthem, 'Sailing up the Clyde'.

After Fyffe and Lauder, the stars of the music-hall stage tended to be comics rather than singers, but like all comics of the time they also sang and came with their own specially composed songs. When out-of-town comic Dave Bruce arrived at the Royal Princess's Theatre in the Gorbals for pantomime discussions, the owner, Harry McKelvie, said, 'Right! Where are your songs, comic?' Bruce offered a couple of published song sheets. McKelvie was aghast, and despatched Bruce to find a songsmith to scribble a few comic songs especially for his use.

At this time another Bruce, the writer, Frank Bruce, comments that in the late 19th century 'Glasgow and the West of Scotland seems to have been something of a song-writing centre for the United Kingdom in general, supporting two long-running song magazines.' These archived 'what must be tens of thousands of songs over the decades' and not just Scots songs, but Irish, emigrant, patriotic, 'minstrel', 'masher' songs about fashionable young men, and football songs. The best known football song, 'Fitba Crazy', was written by James Curran, the 'Parody

King' of Glasgow, who by 1890 had written around 1,200 songs and parodies.

The best-remembered Glasgow comics of the inter-war years are Tommy Lorne, who was brought up on New City Road, Dave Willis of Cowcaddens, and Tommy Morgan, born in Bridgeton. Lorne, Willis and Morgan each ruled the Pavilion stage for lengthy summer or pantomime seasons. Lorne was famous for his knobbly knees under a too-short kilt and Morgan's ashes were scattered on the Pavilion's roof. Morgan even starred in a playground rhyme from Rottenrow Primary School:

Tommy Morgan played the organ,
And his father played the drum,
And his sister had a blister
In the middle of her bum.

Dave Willis was more noted than the others for his songs. When Mahatma Gandhi was visiting London garbed in a dhoti (a traditional men's garment worn in India that is wrapped around the waist and the legs and knotted at the waist), Willis sang, questionably:

Ye look a galoot in your wee dish cloot.
Ye'd look far better in a plus-four suit.

His best known song was 'In Ma Wee Gas Mask'. As 'the nicest lookin' warden in the ARP', he warned of the possible approach of enemy aircraft:

Whenever there's a raid oan,
listen tae ma cry,
An airyplane, an airyplane, a way way up a kye.

Other music-hall songs survive without a performer's name attached, such as 'Ah'm Lizzie MacDougal frae Auchenshuggle, the caur conducteress' and another song about tramcars, praising low ticket costs, 'Noo Lachy MacKinnon

Above: A colourful programme cover.

Left: Exterior, 1979.

Right: Poster for George Mozart in the revue *Following the Band* on 17th November 1913. Also on that bill were M. Gaston Chevalier and Mdlle. Etoll Le Noir & Coy, which although they sound like a French act actually performed a Western Ranch sketch and *The Mexican Rebel Dance*.

is keepin us winnin wi Glasgow's Tuppenny Tram'.

And who, I wonder, wrote and who sang this song?

Ah'm Dan McCann the mountie, ma horse is only wee,
Ah've ran and ah've swam tae get ma man frae Govan tae Saskatchewan.
An aa the wee ladies o ninety, they aa run aifter me,
Sayin 'Dan, Dan, if ye get yer man, gonny get wan fur me?'

Glasgow pantomimes used to run until the spring weather arrived. The American actor, Cary Grant, appeared as a young man in a 1920s Alhambra pantomime, and before that in variety and music halls across Scotland as a dancing stilt-walker. Songs always featured strongly in pantomimes, and often in the big finale a large sheet was unfurled bearing the words of a song, with the chief comic wielding a huge pointer to aid audience participation. I myself recall one 1950s pantomime starring Jimmy Logan, when the big new chorus song was:

Have a slice of Loganberry Pie, munch it, crunch it, you'll discover why
Boys and girls enjoy it when they try a great big slice of Loganberry Pie.

Music for speciality acts required no special new compositions and the dancing girls (Young Ladies or Dancing Belles) used stock arrangements of old and current favourites to suit whatever genre of dance they were emulating: acrobatic, ballet, tap, Highland or hornpipe. Comics sang their comic songs but they weren't considered singers. Actual singers had truer and sweeter voices and although they might introduce their songs this didn't involve any comic patter. Most singers sang the hits of the day or songs that had become associated with them rather than having

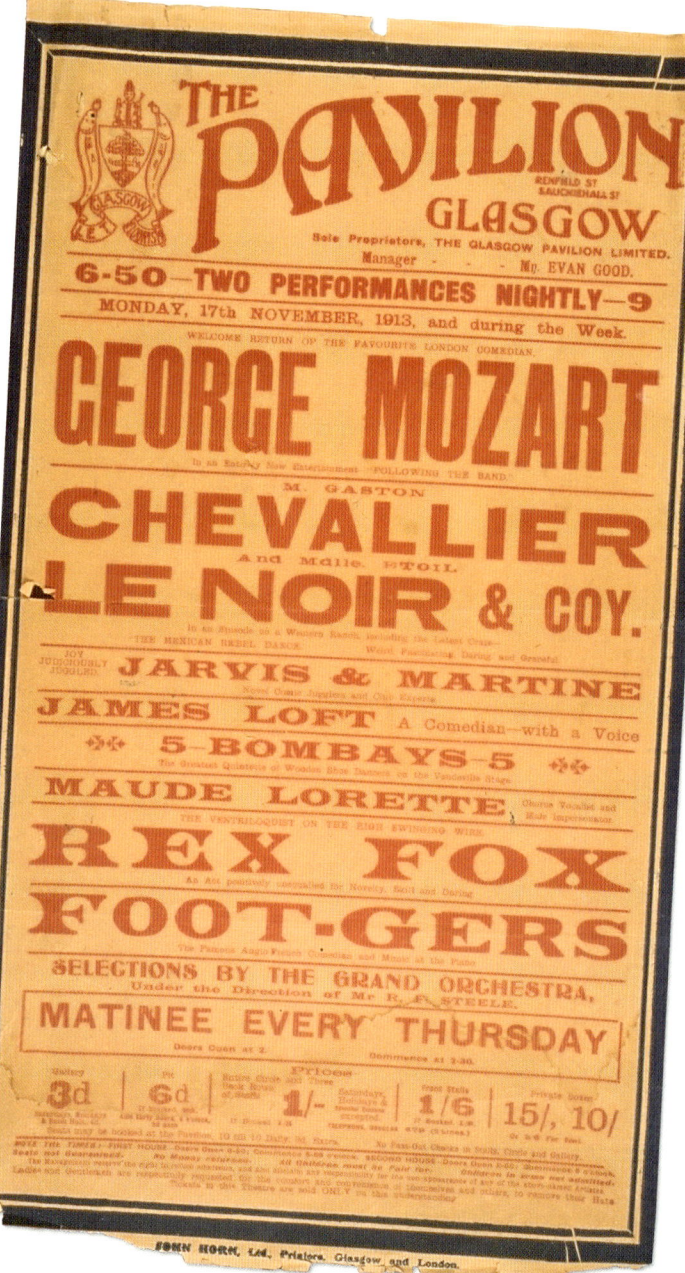

Below: Scottish entertainer Johnnie Beattie and Maidie Murray launch her late husband's biography *The Chic Murray Story: The Best Way to Walk* at the Pavilion theatre in Glasgow, September 1989.

songs specially composed for them. Tartan-clad Robert Wilson from Cambuslang sang 'Down in the Glen', while Lulu from Dennistoun sang 'Shout'. Lulu broke Pavilion box office receipt records in 1975.

The Empire usually featured international acts, like singers Howard Keel and Slim Whitman, but it was in an Empire dressing room in the early 1950s that Scots writer and journalist Cliff Hanley offered his lyrics for 'Scotland the Brave' (the lyrics commonly sung today) set to an old pipe tune to Robert Wilson, who needed a song to close his act in a musical show being performed at the Empire. Andy Stewart 'got his chance' as a youngster at the Scotia, by then renamed the Metropole. Then he revitalised the last months of the dying Empire in 1962 with his smash-hit *Andy Stewart Show*. Other Glasgow variety theatres, of course, featured much music but in Glasgow rather than of Glasgow. The Alhambra and the King's had their sophisticated *Half Past Eight* and the later *Five Past Eight* shows. The King's imported Gilbert and Sullivan musicals and modern shows like *Can Can*.

In 1964, when nearly all the music halls and variety theatres had been swept away by the power of television, a late brave attempt was made by Jimmy Logan to renew old ways. He bought over the New Metropole at St George's Cross, formerly the Empress Playhouse, and ran twice-nightly variety interspersed with visiting musicals like *Hair*. Jimmy was the best-known member of Scottish variety's Royal Family. His parents were 'Pa and Ma Logan' (though his father's given name was Jack Short); his aunt, Ella Logan, starred in *Finian's Rainbow* on Broadway, and his sister Annie Ross made it big in America as a jazz singer in the trio Lambert, Hendricks and Ross. The Logan variety shows toured the halls of Scotland and various family members helped to run the New Metropole, keeping the final curtain from falling and the shutters from going up until 1972.

Late and long-running celebrants of Glasgow's music-hall patter songs were Francie and Josie, a double act delivered by comedians Jack Milroy and Rikki Fulton from 1958 into the 1990s. They took their act all around Scotland and, of course, often to the Pavilion. Francie and Josie and their 'Glasgow Underground' hit song are gone now, but the Pavilion still rattles along, with concerts, touring musicals, new-generation comedians, Premier British Wrestling, nostalgia shows, tribute bands – and true Glesga pantomime.

Left: Detail of the Pavilion foyer's mosaic floor.

BARROWLAND BALLROOM

Graeme Virtue

Left: A huge crowd of young people are in the Barrowlands dance hall in 1960.

Below: The Barrowlands was refurbished after a disastrous fire and reopened in 1960. The 160ft neon sign above the Barrowland Ballroom remains one of the city's best known landmarks.

Usually the magic doesn't really begin until you are inside a music venue. Exteriors are often crumbling, kitsch or plain nondescript: a happenstance container for the experience rather than an integral part of the gig itself. However, at the Barrowland Ballroom — known, almost universally, as 'the Barras' — excitement begins brewing on the outside.

The street-facing side of the five-storey building is dominated by an enormous neon sign, the word 'Barrowland' announced in snazzy red neon with a rakish curve and a constellation of animated stars. It's part Hollywood, part gaudy Las Vegas. The massive neon layout costs around £10 an hour to run and, since this is thrifty Scotland, it's only switched on when a gig is actually scheduled. The distinctive glow from the Gallowgate in Glasgow's historically down-at-heel East End can be glimpsed from the Trongate at the edge of the city centre. Passers-by would be right to suspect they're in danger of missing something: there have been more legendary gigs at the Barrowland than at any other venue in Scotland.

The sign was erected in 1960 but the history of the Barrowland stretches back a further three decades. The first incarnation of the venue was financed by the formidable Margaret McIver, who these days would be called an entrepreneur. As young Margaret Russell she ran a successful fruit stall in Parkhead before marrying a local businessman called James McIver. In 1921 the couple began renting out barrows (stalls) to independent traders, creating a bustling weekly marketplace. By 1931 this ad-hoc market was completely enclosed by a formal structure that allowed Margaret McIver to begin construction on a second storey, nominally as a venue for the annual Christmas party that she hosted

Above: Enter Shikari at Barrowlands, 2011.

Right: Simple Minds at Barrowlands, 2012.

for her loyal market tenants. The Barrowland Ballroom opened on 24 December 1934, named in honour of the rented stalls that had enabled McIver to underwrite it.

This was at the beginning of the golden era of UK dance bands and orchestras, and after initially renting out the ballroom to local group Billy Blue and the Bluebirds, McIver realised she was neglecting a potentially lucrative revenue stream. She recruited Bluebirds drummer Billy McGregor and put together her own house band called The Gaybirds. Glasgow's dance hall scene was expanding rapidly, with venues like the Dennistoun Palais, the southside Plaza and the Locarno on Sauchiehall Street all competing to attract patrons to 'the dancing'. The Barrowland, while not the biggest venue, was one of the most popular from the outset.

Even in the 1930s the shrewd McIver understood that advertising was important. The original building

featured a neon sign of a trader pushing a barrow. On Friday and Saturday nights, couples socialised, waltzed and boogied, and later absorbed the US-influenced jive and jitterbug. No alcohol was sold on site (although, this being Glasgow, drink might well have been taken by patrons before arriving at the venue). The ballroom proved so popular that in 1948 the capacity was almost doubled to 2000. Often the end of the night would be signalled by the band striking up Manning Sherwin's 'Who's Taking You Home Tonight?' – a song popularised by Vera Lynn.

Margaret McIver passed away in June 1958 and the original ballroom was destroyed by fire in November of the same year. Just two years later, construction on a redesigned Barrowland was complete and it opened on Christmas Eve 1960. The new ballroom boasted a dance floor made of imported Canadian maple hardwood, and to help cushion the impact of up to 4,000 stomping feet the floor was 'sprung', an effect achieved by hundreds of tennis balls sliced in half, or so the story went. The high ceiling was carefully curved to create sympathetic acoustics for the non-amplified acts who took the stage. The roof was also stippled with decorative stars of assorted sizes, some of which are still there more than 50 years later. The Gaybirds came home to roost as the house band, still led by Billy McGregor, who had slipped into the habit of calling himself 'King Showman'. The brass section of the band sat behind formal music stands that identified each member and each band member was expected to deliver a short comic turn if required.

Swinging musical numbers were interspersed with stunts and games, including a 'Take Your Pick' challenge modelled on the popular TV show in which competitors could win anything from £100 to a rotten egg. (The nearby People's Palace museum on Glasgow Green has a permanent exhibit dedicated to the history of the Barrowland, with a miniature replica of the famous sign and a recreation of the 'Take Your Pick' experience – though without any rotten eggs.) Throughout the 1960s the venue remained alcohol-free,

Barrowland Ballroom
Location: 244 Gallowgate, Glasgow G4 0TS
Capacity: 2000
Date opened: 1934 (rebuilt after 1958 fire – reopened in 1960)
Music: Rock, Pop, Dance, Folk, Irish
Website: www.glasgow-barrowland.com

Left: The original –, Gallowgate, photographed in 1935. The sign over the door, of a man pushing a barrow, was taken down during the Second World War after it was referred to in German propaganda broadcasts by the notorious "Lord Haw-Haw".

and door staff would politely but insistently look into the handbags of female patrons to check for smuggled booze.

The bands and dancers at the Barrowland adapted to new pop culture crazes like the Twist and in 1964 the venue hosted a rare Scottish appearance from rock and roll pioneers Bill Haley & His Comets. A less happy historical association came from the notorious 'Bible John' murders, when three young women were strangled and robbed after nights out at the venue, ostensibly by the same tall, scripture-quoting man who had met them at the dancing. The murders took place between 1968 and 1969 and remain unsolved to this day. At the time, the police made pleas from the Barrowland stage between musical numbers for potential witnesses to come forward.

The decade from 1970 to 1980 was a difficult one for the Barrowland. Its shows had to compete with the growing entertainment monopoly wielded by television and a general cultural dissatisfaction that would eventually manifest itself as punk rock. The venue belatedly became licensed in 1973, but even the prospect of alcohol couldn't halt a steep decline in attendance. By 1976 the Barras was mothballed as a ballroom while the ground floor marketplace remained vibrantly busy every weekend.

But just as jive and the jitterbug had migrated over the Atlantic in the 1930s, so the pulse of New York disco eventually reached the East End of Glasgow. In 1980 there were tentative plans to turn the venue into a huge Studio 54-style discotheque. Instead the venue was leased in April 1981 by a company who rebranded it the 'Fantazia Triskate Centre'. The ballroom was transformed into a child-friendly roller disco. The Fantazia turned out to be mercifully short-lived, but this willingness to adapt to even the most fleeting of trends meant the Barrowland outlasted all of its former ballroom rivals.

The third and arguably most significant evolution in the life of the Barrowland came in 1982 when Regular Music, an Edinburgh-based concerts promoter, approached the venue with a proposal. They wanted to stage a brace of gigs by Simple Minds, then a Glasgow band on the cusp of breaking through to international success. Preparing for the shows involved redesigning the stage to accommodate the considerably larger PA system required by a rock band (in their pomp), but the other characteristics of the venue – the grand ballroom floor, the star-flecked ceiling – were deliberately left untouched.

Left: The dance hall pictured in 1935.

Left: Brownbear rehearsals, for The Libertines support, 2014.

Opposite, top: A view of the fire-gutted ballroom, 1958.

Opposte, bottom: Firemen examine the wreckage of the building.

Above: Barrowlands in lights.

Right: Barraloadasoul 'Alldayer' event, May 2014.

Below: Barrowlands today.

increasingly influential Scottish band, scheduled a concert for New Year's Eve 1983, as a welcome homecoming after a gruelling three-month tour of the US. Demand for this Hogmanay gig was so great that they ended up playing an additional matinee show. 'The excitement going on in the room that night was really a Scottish thing,' recalled guitarist Bruce Watson years later. 'We tried to make it a huge party.' The Barrowland had essentially been reborn as a rock venue, and the ballroom's reputation began to spread.

In 1984 the Barras played host to The Clash, The Cure and The Smiths. Simple Minds, now international superstars, remained loyal to the venue that they had helped revive and returned to play four nights in succession. U2, teetering on global success with their album *The Unforgettable Fire*, played to a crammed crowd with hundreds more fans packing the Gallowgate streets outside. According to a glowing review in heavy rock magazine *Kerrang!*, Bono seemed particularly taken with the performance.

Surfing a wave of enthusiasm for their fifth album *New Gold Dream*, Simple Minds sold out the 1,900-capacity venue across back-to-back nights in December 1982, and returned the following year for two more over-subscribed dates. Big Country, another waited a long time for this,' he announced from the stage. 'I won't forget tonight, and I hope you won't.'

There have been events made unforgettable for other reasons. In 1987 the Barrowland hosted the first UK headline tour by the Beastie Boys, who caused tabloid outrage with their crass lyrics, sexualised stage props and habit of sequestering female fans into dancing cages. In 1994 at a gig by LA rapper, Ice Cube, a 27-year-old man died after being stabbed. Metal detectors were installed at the doors soon after and have remained ever since.

The post-grunge rise of Britpop in the mid-1990s brought a new wave of bands to the venue, with the Fred Perry-clad triumvirate of Blur, Oasis and Pulp playing memorable concerts to youthful crowds newly excited by home-grown music. These sweaty punters would often emerge into the Glasgow chill to discover an impromptu bazaar set up on the pavement outside. In this shadowy echo of the Barras market, sellers of questionable legitimacy hawked poorly-printed T-shirts featuring the night's musical act. The turn of the millennium saw pop reclaiming ground lost to guitar bands in the UK charts and the Barrowland still pulling in substantial crowds. In March 2001, Ocean Colour Scene sold out for five consecutive nights; when illness forced them to cancel two of the dates, they came back the next month to do another three.

In 2005 the Barrowland was voted the best venue in the UK in a comprehensive poll of more than 60 bands conducted by BBC Radio 1, but it was also being squeezed by increased competition in the live music scene in Glasgow. The Academy venue opened south of the Clyde river in 2003 with a restored art deco interior and a split-level capacity of 2500. Just two years later, a converted cinema on Sauchiehall Street reopened as the ABC, hosting gigs and student-friendly club nights for crowds of up to 1300. In 2007 the Academy and the ABC became part of a national chain of venues, attractive to both domestic and foreign acts looking for a one-stop solution to booking entire UK tours. The Barrowland, while still being used by a wide range of promoters, remained fiercely independent, but the impression was that fewer major gigs were being booked in the East End.

Luckily, few venues in the world have inspired such loyalty from bands and fans. For example, Irish punks Stiff Little Fingers have played the Barrowland on 17 March – St Patrick's Day – every year since 1992. Undoubtedly the loyalty has something to do with the venue's atmosphere. The Barras might look a bit run-down, but the paint-peeling shabbiness also makes it somehow timeless, a place so saturated in musical history that you can literally smell it. For up-and-coming bands, playing the Barrowland means treading the very same boards as their heroes, be they REM, Bob

Left: Belle & Sebastian at Barrowlands, 2010.

Dylan, Metallica, David Bowie, Grace Jones, Radiohead or the Arctic Monkeys. Justin Timberlake played a special late-night Barrowland show in 2004 after selling out the 10,000-capacity Scottish Exhibition and Conference Centre. The most recent wave of successful Scottish artists, from Biffy Clyro to Admiral Fallow and Frightened Rabbit, have made a point of headlining their own shows at the Barras, their tangible excitement at playing on the revered stage reflected back by enthusiastic fans. The success of these young acts will hopefully inspire another generation of bands to dream of playing the ballroom.

The Barrowland's status as Scotland's favourite

Below: Inside the dressing room at Barrowlands.

Right: Amy Macdonald, 2010.

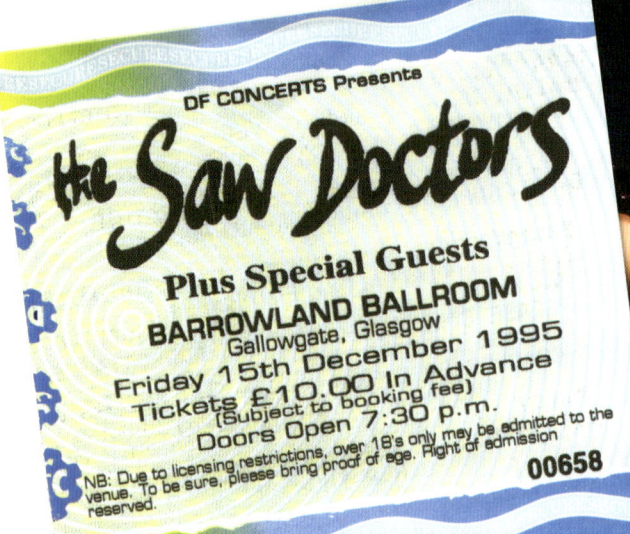

Below: Carrie MacNeil, The Vatersay Boys, 2013.

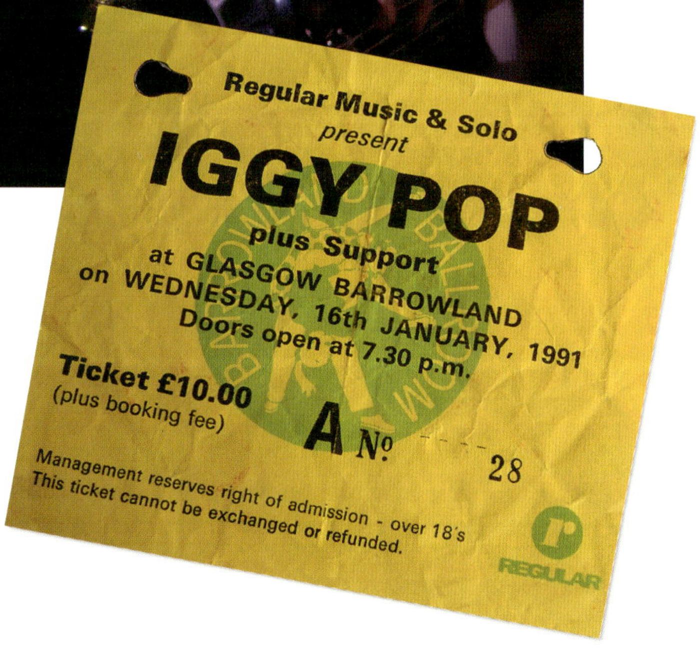

venue might remain unofficial, but it has already carved a permanent niche in the cultural imagination of the nation. It has also demonstrably served as a muse. While still a teenager, local singer/songwriter Amy Macdonald wrote a song called 'Barrowland Ballroom', a love letter to the venue that featured on her best-selling 2007 debut album. Inevitably, it begins with a description of the neon sign. Macdonald has gone on to play the venue multiple times.

Final word goes to the Irish troubadour Christy Moore who wrote his heartfelt ballad 'Barrowland' with the Scottish songwriter and kindred spirit Wally Page. For Moore the ballroom remains somewhere enlivening and unique, a place where bonny lads and lassies mingle with benevolent spirits from the past. 'Hear Mags McIver and the ghost of the Gaybirds calling,' goes the chorus. 'Come all you dreamers to Barrowland.'

Left: A plaque by Glasgow Landmarks commemorates the architects who designed the rebuilt Barrowland Ballroom.

Below: Twin Atlantic, 2011.

BBC SCOTLAND

John Purser

In 1923 the BBC's first Scottish broadcasting station was set up under the code name 5SC in an attic room at 202 Bath Street. Before the end of that decade, the station would move twice – first to Blythswood Square, then to West George Street – to accommodate its expanding activities. In 1935 came the shift that would see it into the 21st century with an iconic home at North Park House on Queen Margaret Drive in Glasgow's leafy West End.

Until the advent of tape recording on a viable scale, virtually all broadcasting was live, and for the first 50-odd years of the Scottish Home Service (now BBC Scotland) *live* meant *radio*. For this, if for no other reason, the BBC employed musicians and set up its own semi-permanent ensembles that developed into the BBC Scottish (later Symphony) Orchestra, the Scottish Radio Orchestra and the BBC Scottish Singers. Of the three, the BBC Scottish Symphony Orchestra is the sole survivor. In the early days there was also a house pianist on the staff, whose duties included accompanying all manner of invited artists.

At first the Scottish Home Service employed a group of 12 musicians, rising to 27 in 1928 and cut back to an octet in 1929, but the BBC had also been relaying live concerts, including opera, from the very start. Members of what would eventually become the BBC Scottish Symphony Orchestra were recruited on a permanent basis in 1935 and initially consisted of just 35 musicians. It was only in 1967 that the then part-time studio orchestra was expanded to symphonic status.

From 1935 the orchestra's home was the custom-built Studio 1 at North Park House in Queen Margaret Drive – a huge cube of space without any windows

Right: BBC Broadcasting House, Queen Margaret Drive, stairwell and vaulted ceiling.

Right: North Park House, BBC Scotland HQ, 1980, from Queen Margaret Drive.

BBC SCOTLAND BROADCASTING HOUSE

Location:	20 Queen Margaret Drive, Glasgow, G20 8PD
Architect:	As North Park House (private home), John T Rochead 1869, (completed by John Honeyman); adapted to be Queen Margaret College with a new Medical Hall by John Keppie & Charles Rennie Mackintosh of Honeyman, Keppie & Mackintosh, 1895. Adapted to be BBC Scotland headquarters by James Millar 1936-38
Date opened:	1869 / 1936-38
Date closed:	2007 (due to relocation of BBC)
Music:	Multi; home of BBC Scottish Symphony Orchestra

BBC SCOTLAND HEADQUARTERS

Location:	Pacific Quay, Glasgow, G51 1DA
Architect:	David Chipperfield Architects
Date opened:	2007
Music:	Multi
Website:	www.davidchipperfield.co.uk/project/bbc_scotland_at_pacific_quay

and, in anticipation of the Second World War, sound-proofed against the possibility of enemy gunfire being heard during live broadcasts. One sound engineer, doubling as a lookout during the war, fell off a ladder on the roof as he watched a blast mine parachuting in above his head. It missed the studio but blew up the flats across the River Kelvin, killing several people. The engineer never fully recovered. On a more positive note, the orchestra would frequently accompany the redoubtable Harry Lauder singing Churchill's favourite song, 'Keep Right On To The End of The Road'. The prime minister would apparently listen to the song whenever things looked black, which they frequently did.

Despite the calibre of the orchestra, the BBC attempted to disband it on three occasions, and nearly succeeded in 1980 – just two years after the creation of Radio Scotland as an independent station rather than an opt-out from the BBC Home Service. A UK-wide Musicians' Union strike and international protest averted disaster, but the price of the BBC Scottish Symphony Orchestra's survival was the disbandment of the Scottish Radio (formerly Variety) Orchestra. This left a permanent hole in the provision of light music across a wide variety of genres from dance music to jazz, and also meant that the station had no house band to accompany singers such as Lulu, Kenneth McKellar, Ella Fitzgerald and Shirley Bassey.

Perhaps shamed by such decisions, a new management team restored North Park House to its former glory as a centre for the orchestra and upgraded Studio 1 to be used for live concerts. Tickets for these concerts were free and audiences were treated not only to wonderful music but often to events of historical significance. One such event was the first performance of the surviving movements of a suite called *Behind the Lines* composed by Cecil Coles, a Kirkudbright-born composer who was killed on active service during the First World War. His music was found on his body then

left in a cupboard in his former school; there it would have remained had his daughter, Penny, not rescued it, and it was BBC Scotland that brought this deeply moving music to life and gave Penny the chance to hear it herself for the first time. By then in her eighties, almost blind, her voice a mere whisper, Penny sat dignified and in wonder as, through his music, she learnt a little more about the character of the father she never knew.

Other moments of musical history took place within the intense privacy of the BBC's recording sessions. The great Czech pianist, Rudolf Firkusny, came to Glasgow to record Bohuslav Martinu's *Second Piano Concerto*, a work composed especially for him back in the 1930s. Conducting the orchestra was a much younger Czech, Jiri Starek, who had never met Firkusny, now an elderly but wonderfully vigorous musician. For the two of them this was as happy a musical collaboration as the music itself. The walls of North Park House also witnessed moments of quiet educational value. One young conductor, taking his first rehearsal in the studio, was so excited that sweat was pouring off him. During the tea break the principal viola, a quiet Scot, approached him with 'a word of advice in your ear. In Scotland we only make love once a day.' Or so the story goes.

The orchestra centre was superbly refurbished in the 1980s but the Queen Margaret Drive site included two architecturally significant buildings that could not be altered: North Park House, once the home of the owners of the famous Bell's Pottery and now occupied by BBC Scotland; and a medical school for Glasgow University's female students that was designed by John Keppie and Charles Rennie Mackintosh. Poorly integrated with these was a soulless and inefficient extension consisting of offices and a canteen in which it was easy to get lost. The BBC's move to new premises was inevitable. In 2007, they took occupancy of a new, glassy and glitzy purpose-built building next to the Science Centre at Pacific Quay on the Clyde. One of the last musical events in Studio 1 at Queen Margaret Drive occurred after it had already been emptied of everything except for a few packing cases and a grand piano. Sitting beside the piano was the Indian singer, Prakriti Dutta, whose sensuous and exotic songs left a lasting echo for Studio 1 to store in its memory.

With the move from Queen Margaret Drive to Pacific Quay, the BBC Scottish Symphony Orchestra was relocated to a splendid new home at Glasgow's refurbished City Halls. The downside has been that the orchestra has become somewhat detached from

Left, both: BBC Broadcasting House, Queen Margaret Drive, ground floor, entrance hall.

Below: BBC Broadcasting House, Queen Margaret Drive, Mackintosh courtyard.

BBC Scotland itself. The comings and goings of more than 60 classical musicians through the corridors and the canteen brought their interests and skills into the rich mix of talent that the BBC has fostered over the years, and that potential casual interaction has now sadly been lost. The new BBC headquarters at Pacific Quay are more likely to host traditional and pop musicians nowadays. Live concerts are occasionally staged in its foyer, but the building has the potential for many more musical events than it currently hosts. Beyond its glass box exterior the River Clyde ebbs and flows, tide against river, river against tide.

BBC Scotland's charter obliges it to reflect the nation's culture, and for nearly a century that obligation has been largely met across a broad musical spectrum. Traditional music was served by live broadcasts from dance halls across the country, notably in the BBC's longest-running programme *Take the Floor* (in the 1930s it was called *Scottish Dance Music*) with Robbie Shepherd its long-time presenter. With the advent of television came programmes such as *The White Heather Club* that kept musicians in semi-permanent employment. *The White Heather Club* featured some of the great names of yesteryear, such as Robert Wilson, Andy Stewart, Robin Hall and Jimmie MacGregor, Jimmy Shand, Ian Powrie, Jimmy Logan and Stanley Baxter. Although it is now fashionable to laugh at its insistent tartanalia, the programme was a great success in its day and it would take a brave person to question the musical skills of those who appeared on it.

Piping tended to be given a slot of its own, especially when Alasdair Milne was station controller in the late 1960s. Pipers being what they are, and broadcasting generally being averse to risk, a discreet list was drawn up with a briefing on individual pipers and their needs. It went something like this: Piper A was to be met at the train station or bus and taken at once to the studio to avoid any deviation to the pub; Piper B, on the other hand, was incapable of playing without at least three stiff drams that should be administered at a judicious time before the live broadcast; Piper C was to be given a single dram in the studio. The current weekly piping programme is called *Pipeline* and it continues to reflect all styles of piping from pìobaireachd (the classical music of the Highland bagpipes) through slow airs, marches, reels, strathspeys, pipe bands and drumming.

On the pop and rock music front, the two most significant programmes are introduced by Vic Galloway and Ricky Ross. Vic, who penned two of this book's

Opposite: Junior Kirkintilloch Choir sing for BBC Radio's 'Children's Hour' in 1946.

Left: Jimmy Shand and his band in May 1956 recording 'The Kilt is my Delight' for BBC.

chapters, primarily features young Scottish bands, while Ricky's perennially popular *Another Country* burns the flame for Americana and alternative country music. Each of these shows has a two-hour weekly slot and both reflect a recent broadcasting trend to rely heavily upon the recording industry for content, live acts simply being more expensive to broadcast.

Recently there have been other worrying developments at BBC Scotland. Funds for location broadcasting and commissioning have been steadily eroded, making it hard for producers to reflect Scotland's changing musical scene, never mind stimulate it. Popular radio programmes such as *The Reel Blend* and *Global Gathering* have disappeared from the airwaves and have as yet to be replaced. Among the few programmes representing Scottish traditional music not to have been axed are *Pipeline* and *Travelling Folk*, a programme long presented by the folk singer, Archie Fisher, that draws on connections with the vast Scottish traditional diaspora.

Much the same applies to classical music programming at Radio Scotland. Once a week, *Classics Unwrapped* takes an approach that reflects its light-weight title. It is the only slot in the schedule that offers any regular representation of classical music in the whole of Scottish broadcasting, both radio and television. There was a time when programmes such as *The Musician* in Scotland and *The Music Makars* broadcast live chamber music and new commissions while the BBC Scottish Orchestra would broadcast weekly for the Scottish Home Service.

That said, BBC Scotland still records at festivals such as the *Edinburgh International Festival*, the *St Magnus Festival* and *Celtic Connections*, including televised and specially commissioned programmes. The present writer's own radio series *Scotland's Music* involved many special recordings, and the programmes were spread over a whole year of broadcasting and accompanied by a book. It was commissioned twice and the second series was paralleled by an eponymous television series hosted by Phil Cunningham. These were major commitments, but such ventures are rarely, if ever, repeated, are not available commercially and are not part of the regular schedule.

Outside the specific remit of the BBC's music

Right: Lonnie Donegan appearing in the film 'Six Five Special' in 1957.

Far left: Lulu, singer, performing at Celtic Park, 1990, recorded by the BBC.

Left: Mr Peter Mooney, conductor of the Glasgow Phoenix Choir, accepts the BBC Rose Bowl from Mr Andrew Stewart.

departments there are opportunities for the commissioning and broadcasting of music. Not directly organised by the music department, but with an emphasis on singing, is the Sunday Service, and also of musical importance is the Gaelic Sunday Service with its spine-tingling singing of the psalms in Gaelic, recordings of which constitute a priceless archive of traditional religious singing now threatened by increasing secularism but still available on *Radio nan Gaidheal*.

The presence of the radio station *Radio nan Gaidheal* and the establishment of a dedicated Gaelic television channel, *BBC Alba*, together reflect an increasing awareness of the value and significance of Gaelic language and culture, in which live music plays an important part. Launched in 2008, *BBC Alba* is a young station still stretching its muscles, but it has the potential to become a very significant cultural force not just for Gaelic speakers, but for a national and international public. Also outwith the music department, television and radio drama are potentially important employers of composers and performers. Were Scotland to have its own full-time television channels, such opportunities would expand. In order to retain musicians of calibre in Scotland there must be a critical mass of available work, and without adequately funded and intelligently motivated broadcasting stations, that critical mass is less easily achieved. Among the various powers not devolved to the Scottish Parliament is broadcasting, which is 'reserved' for the UK Government.

The BBC at every level is the one national institution that can reach into every household without being driven by commercial requirements. It is a precious asset, envied across the globe, but too often undervalued at a national level. This situation is further confused by the fact that much that is made in Scotland for the BBC is destined for the BBC UK-wide. This is, of course, a splendid opportunity for Scotland to export its own approach to music, but there is also a danger of it being dominated by UK schedules and priorities, with major editing decisions being taken in London. After the 2014 independence referendum, the structures and remits of our major institutions, of which the BBC is a leading example, cannot simply remain as they were. There is now a great opportunity for the BBC to renew its commitment over the years, not just to reflect the nation's musical culture, but to stimulate it.

Below: New BBC Headquarters at Pacific Quay.

THE NATIONAL PIPING CENTRE AND THE COLLEGE OF PIPING

Competition According to Tradition

John Purser

Left: The National Piping Centre pictured from the top of Hope Street.

The Highland bagpipes are Scotland's national instrument. Some fiddlers might wish to argue the toss, but the world is full of fiddles all of the same design as the ones played by Scots, whereas the Highland pipes are a Scottish development, and that should be an end to the matter.

One might expect this fabulous musical asset – internationally recognised and internationally used in public expressions of triumph and grief – to have been the object of profound study for centuries. In fact, the first comprehensive Scottish study of the organology of the instrument was only made in the late 20th century by Hugh Cheape for the National Museums of Scotland in Edinburgh. Scotland's two main centres of piping tuition are both in Glasgow: Glasgow has always had a strong presence of native Gaels, and the bagpipe is their native instrument. That said, the Army School of Piping is based at Edinburgh Castle, and there is a long history of bagpipe manufacture in Edinburgh. Two rival dynasties of Glen bagpipe-makers were born there of an irreconcilable difference of opinion between the

THE COLLEGE OF PIPING
Location: 16 Otago Street, Glasgow G12 8JH
Date opened: 1944
Music: Piping
website: www.collegeofpiping.org/

THE NATIONAL PIPING CENTRE
Location: 30-34 McPhater Street, Glasgow G4 0HW
Architect: Campbell Douglas & Sellers (1872) originally Cowcaddens Free Church And Hall; conversion to The National Piping Centre by Gerry Grams of McGurn, Logan, Duncan & Opfer (1993/96)
Capacity: 150
Date opened: 1996
Music: Piping
website: www.thepipingcentre.co.uk/

brothers Alexander and Thomas Glen over whether to use yellow or black hemp on their bagpipe fittings.

Let us return to Glasgow, though, where the College of Piping was founded by Seumas MacNeill and Thomas Pearston in 1944. It was originally housed in Pitt Street, eventually moving to the Red Hackle Whisky premises in Otago Street and subsequently to its present location across the same street. There is history behind that location, for the Red Hackle Whisky Company was set up to provide employment for retired soldiers of the Black Watch Regiment, who wore (and still wear) a red hackle on their headgear. One of the Red Hackle whisky labels shows a piper of the Black Watch striding forth, and the company spawned its own very fine band, the Red Hackle Pipes and Drums. The College of Piping gives instruction in all aspects of piping, provides recently improved facilities for teaching and recitals, and publishes tuition books. It also publishes the *Piping Times*, which was initiated and edited by Seamus MacNeill for 48 years.

The National Piping Centre, off Cowcaddens Road, duplicates the College's facilities – these include a museum, a library, teaching rooms, a concert hall and a shop – but also has its own restaurant and hotel. The Centre also enjoys close links with the universities of Glasgow, Edinburgh and St Andrews, and in particular with the Royal Conservatoire of Scotland, just across the road, whose BA in Scottish Music is partly taught there. The Centre publishes tutors and produces the magazine, *Piping Today*, rival to the College's *Piping Times*. It is also an important venue for concerts during the *Piping Live* and *Celtic Connections* festivals, being more centrally located than the College.

It might well seem strange to some coming from outside of Scotland – and indeed it is very strange to many

Right: Seamus MacNeill.

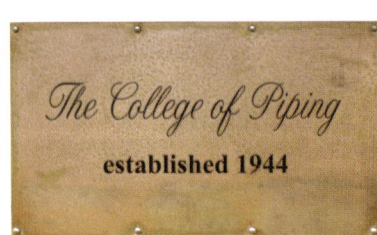

Above: Brass plate from the front door.

Right: The College of Piping, in Otago Street.

within Scotland – that there should be two such institutions within walking distance of each other, each publishing its own magazine and tutors, each offering lessons and other facilities, each with museums of the instrument and performance venues, and mutually failing to cooperate or – heaven forbid – amalgamate. But there are distinctions.

Put simply, the College of Piping, which is by far the older institution, tends to propagate a more conservative take on piping. Some would say it is old-fashioned; others, more extreme, might say it is stultifying, but that would be unfair. Rather, it reflects a certain approach to the tradition that favours regularity and adherence to precept. In an oral tradition, this approach could be said to be fundamental. On the other hand, the National Piping Centre is the younger but larger and probably more influential institution, enjoying the patronage of HRH The Prince of Wales, Duke of Rothesay. The Centre might be seen as more ready to embrace innovation; in this case, 'innovation' often means searching for even more traditional ways of playing, responding to recent scholarly research and maintaining that the oral tradition was never laid down in a rule book.

So how did all this come about? When the opportunity arose for rehousing the College in what is now the Centre's premises, a clash of personalities developed into an irreconcilable rift. MacNeill had always understood that the College was to move to the new premises and that he, its long-standing principal, would continue in that role. When it transpired that that wasn't a possibility, he withdrew his involvement. It is truly sad to read in the *Piping Times* of April 1996 an entry marked 'End of a dream'. It was the end of a dream for MacNeill and the College, but not, of course, for the Centre and the College still survives, though with rather less financial security than it once had. Fortunately, Highland piping as a whole is in a state of rude health and does not overly suffer from this divided rule. In fact, based upon long traditions of competitiveness in piping, one could easily give a more positive twist to this competitive situation.

At the heart of the piping tradition is pìobaireachd (pibroch in English). The word simply means 'pipe music' but is applied to a specific form of variations on a theme or ùrlar (ground). These variations become increasingly virtuosic in their demands on the piper's finger dexterity, before returning to the opening theme. Pìobaireachd is only played by solo pipes, is always played by memory, and requires great concentration and musicality if it's to be done well. Mostly, pipers play pìobaireachd in competition – the music is often felt to be too demanding for use at ceilidhs or other social gatherings – which is a pity. The

Below: Roddy MacLeod performs a lunchtime recital in the Piping Centre.

Above: Display case in the museum of The National Piping Centre.

Opposite, top: Drummers at The World Pipe Band Championships at Glasgow Green.

Right: Pipers at The World Pipe Band Championships at Glasgow Green.

fact that competitive pìobaireachd playing is the norm means that there are judges who can impose their own ideals on the pipers, for whom winning a gold medal in the piping competitions at the Highland Games in Oban or the Northern Meeting in Inverness can be life defining. MacNeill was a regular judge.

The fact is that piping seems to have been a competitive business from early days. It is certainly legitimate to envisage the battle in 1582 between the Campbells and MacDougalls near Taynuilt as being in part driven by the competitive playing of their clan pìobaireachd: their respective pipers would have challenged each other from the tops of two hills, one of which is known to this day as *Tom a phìobaire* (the piper's hillock). On the other hand, there is the well-documented occasion of 1745 when a famous piper, Donald Bàn MacCrimmon, Clan McLeod's chief piper, was captured by the Jacobite army; so well-respected a player was he that the Jacobite pipers refused to play until their leaders released him, which was duly done.

Another example enshrined in music lore took place in 1651 at the Battle of Worcester. There was a competition among the pipers, and when the Duke of Sutherland's piper, John MacGyurmen, was voted the best, he stood proud without removing his bonnet. Charles I went over to see who he was and gave MacGyurmen a kiss of his hand – hence the famous pìobaireachd, '*Thug Mi Pòg bho Làimh an Rìgh*' (I Got a Kiss of the King's Hand). The piper, then, was not averse to competing with his own monarch for the right to keep his cap on.

Piping disputes have on occasion found their way into the courts of law. A claim of plagiarism was once levelled in the High Court and only withdrawn at the last minute. And lest this be thought to represent a peculiarly Highland bagpipers' approach to music-making, let it be noted that practitioners of the Sardinian launeddas (a kind of triple pipe) never bothered with the courts but resorted to violence straight away: on one occasion musical jealousy and revenge led to a murder on the island. In the Scottish past, too, there were certainly serious antagonisms between harp players and fiddlers. In 1594 one Ogilby, a fiddler, was executed for the murder of Caldell, a harper; in 1638 the Laird of Grant's agent explained the failure of his clarsair (harper) to return from the Lowlands by recounting how there had been a drunken fight with a violer and that one of them ended up with severe head injuries.

So perhaps the competition between the National Piping Centre and the College of Piping merely reflects an aspect of tradition. Fortunately, when, in 1994, Seamus MacNeill famously derided the playing of some of Scotland's finest young pipers, the response didn't end quite so bloodily. The story goes like this: MacNeill – controversial and combative to the last – declared that 'if that's piping, I'm off to learn the fiddle'; Gordon Duncan, a stunning player, soon after released an album called *Just for Seamus*, whose wonderfully impudent final track blends djembe drum, drum corps, electric bass, guitar, congas and pipes in a virtuosic display of fingering over which floats part of the pìobaireachd 'The Lament for Mary MacLeod'. In terms of Highland piping, it was an act not dissimilar to painting a moustache on the *Mona Lisa*. But there was to be no comeback from MacNeill who, elderly and frail, died in 1996. He left a remarkable legacy, including a useful booklet on pìobaireachd in which he outlines a fascinating theory on the scale of the bagpipe.

The current director of the College of Piping is Robert Wallace and of the National Piping Centre is Roddy MacLeod. It would be a grand sight indeed to see them face each other from the summits of two hills, each playing their own clan pìobaireachd. Who knows, one day they might even play each other's.

Above: Façade of The National Piping Centre.

THE APOLLO

Graeme Virtue

If you were writing a rock ballad that had to encompass the entire cultural history of Glasgow, focusing on a period of just 12 years might seem a little short-sighted. Such a brief chronological blip might yield enough material for half a verse, maybe, or might at least help prop up a middle-eight *[(the third contrasting eight-bar section of a 32-bar pop song) ??]*. Yet within that relatively short time frame, one venue in Glasgow exemplified an aspect of the city's relationship with music that has resonated long after the actual building was razed to the ground.

In its key operational years from 1973 to 1985, the Glasgow Apollo was famous for being a volatile cauldron determined to inflame the bands who performed there for good or for ill, but the sprawling structure – initially breathtakingly grand, latterly busted-up and mouldering – somehow helped Scotland's second city identify and celebrate its musical soul. In that fictional ballad about Glasgow culture, the 12-year sovereignty of the Apollo resonates so powerfully that it must be the chorus.

Left: Mick Jagger performing with the Rolling Stones at the Apollo Theatre, 1976.

Below: Ticket stub from the pictured concert.

Before it became the Apollo in 1973, the building started life as Green's Playhouse, the jewel in the crown of a family-run chain of Scottish cinemas. When it opened at the top of the city centre's Renfield Street in 1927, Green's Playhouse was demonstrably the largest cinema in Europe, with a main auditorium capable of seating 4,368 patrons. The multi-level building included a double-height ballroom and, in the first few years, an ambitious putting green on the roof; altogether it claimed to have the capacity for 10,000 customers – a capacity comparable to Glasgow's 21st-century custom-built music venue, The Hydro. A seven-storey marvel with Corinthian columns, a projection booth incorporated into the dress circle and theatre-style boxes, the Playhouse was designed by Glaswegian architect John Fairweather. Fairweather had been sponsored by the Green family to tour the US in the early 1920s to assimilate the look of the sprawling, multi-purpose 'movie palaces' that were in vogue then. Fairweather would go on to design a different Playhouse in Edinburgh in 1929; it, too, began life as a cinema, but unlike its Glasgow counterpart survives as a theatrical and musical venue to this day.

The silent film adverts that screened at the time of the opening of Green's Playhouse proudly proclaimed the Glasgow venue as the UK's premier ballroom with a particular emphasis on the important criteria of 'floor, catering, music, general comfort and environment'. Every level of the building had distinctive green carpets customised with the memorable slogan, 'It's Good – It's Green's'. The venue enjoyed three decades of success but by the 1960s the national obsession with ballroom dancing had begun to wane. The auditorium was occasionally reconfigured to stage one-off concerts for which the enormous cinema screen retracted to reveal a notably raised stage. In one of his earliest and most unsuccessful incarnations, David Bowie played Glasgow in 1966 with his newly formed band The Buzz. In June 1967, an extended UK package tour finished up at Green's with two gigs in one day that consisted of a phenomenal crammed bill featuring Jimi Hendrix, Pink Floyd, The Move and DJ Pete Drummond.

Gigs at Green's ramped up in the 1970s, with bands like Black Sabbath, The Who and Emerson, Lake & Palmer returning for multiple engagements. Music bookings were rare enough that Green's was still primarily thought of as a cinema, albeit one unable to compete with nationwide chains in securing first-run films. Instead it found a niche screening X-certificate

APOLLO

LOCATION: Formerly on the corner of Renfrew Street and Nile Street, now the site of Cineworld (the world's Europe's tallest cinema) Glasgow, G2 3AB

ARCHITECT: John Fairweather

CAPACITY: (as Green's) 4000+

DATE OPENED: 1927 (Green's Playhouse); 1973 (Apollo)

DATE CLOSED: 1985 (partially demolished 1987; fire damaged 1988, remaining building demolished 1989)

CAUSE OF DESTRUCTION: Fire

Main genre of music: Rock, Pop

WEBSITE: More information at http://www.glasgowapollo.com/

movies, from disreputable horror flicks to sex comedies like the 1970 hit, *Naughty Knickers*. The once-venerable Green's Playhouse closed its doors for the last time in July, 1973.

However, the doors didn't stay closed for long. After a period of nominal refurbishment, the building reopened under new management as the Apollo in September of the same year. The new name was apparently inspired by the legendary venue in New York City's Harlem district, a stage synonymous with James Brown, Ella Fitzgerald and Marvin Gaye. The transformation came with much trumpeting in the local press. 'The building has been redecorated throughout from back to front, recarpeted, rewired, and rethought' ran an advertorial in Glasgow's *Evening Times*. Perhaps 'recarpeted' was an overstatement – the original carpets had been dyed purple, which wasn't quite enough to obscure the original Green's branding – but the new décor still inspired a long-standing nickname for the venue, 'the Purple Palace'.

The Apollo's official opening concert was on 5 September 1973, when Johnny Cash played the first of a two-night engagement. The 'Man in Black' also became the first to receive the Apollo's plastic commemorative trophy awarded to artists who sold out the now 3000-capacity auditorium. It was the start of a long-standing tradition, though Cash reputedly binned the memento in his dressing room. In that first September alone, the Apollo played host to Lou Reed, Diana Ross and Status Quo, and the Rolling Stones played on two sell-out dates. The legend of the Apollo was up and running.

Of all the venue's distinctive and sometimes crumbling features, the one that seemed to stick in the minds of both performers and punters was the notably high stage. Situated a full 12 feet above the venue floor, it was enough to discourage the (officially seated) fans from attempting a stage invasion and keep any flamboyant performers relatively penned in. Of course, what looked like a stage to some bands could feel like a raised sacrificial altar to others – the enthusiasm and spontaneity of 3,000 Glaswegians, even spread over three levels, could sometimes be mistaken for volatile aggression. Nostalgic hyperbole notwithstanding, the Apollo crowd soon became as notorious as a creature from ancient Greek mythology. As well as bellicose heckling, they were prone to unpredictable singing en masse and some bands took to calling them 'the Glasgow Choir'. In a best case scenario, the Choir could thoroughly augment a band's planned set list and provide their own hilarious curlicues. But at their worst, they could hijack a gig with an irreverent litany

Above: Jack Bruce, bass player and singer of Cream, performing at The Apollo.

Inset: Aerial shot of The Apollo, previously Green's Playhouse.

of catcalls and/or preferred songs. The venue might have been unlicensed for alcohol, but among the crowd there remained little evidence of temperance.

As with any legend, it can be difficult to separate hard facts from the romantic fiction. Was Freddie Mercury dragged off that vertiginous stage by hysterical fans? Did AC/DC's Bon Scott really take a wrong turn backstage and end up out on the street, only to be refused re-entry by stony-faced bouncers? Was the general manager once used as a battering ram by impatient fans to break open the front doors? As the music industry sleepwalks towards digitisation, these analogue tales of rock and roll misbehaviour have a pleasingly hands-on feel, whether or not tinged with nostalgic hyperbole. That the stewards could occasionally be a little heavy-handed, though, is a matter of record: in his book *Apollo Memories*, Martin Kielty describes the security arrangements as a 'micro-police state'. Notoriously, a gig by The Clash on 4 July 1978 ended in chaos after repeated

Above: Programme for Billy Connolly, Apollo Theatre, 1975.

Left: Billboard advertising Billy Connolly, Apollo Theatre, Glasgow

Right: Golden Earring live in concert 1974 at The Apollo Theatre, 126 Renfield Street, Glasgow.

Opposite: Various tickets from famous Apollo gigs though the years.

skirmishes between bouncers and the crowd, to the vocalised annoyance of the band. Joe Strummer and Paul Simonon were lifted by police after the gig and subsequently charged with breach of the peace.

In the wake of that volatile Clash gig, the Apollo looked set to close for good. Tickets for a gig on 5 July by Christian (the stage name of popular local singer Chris McClure) were marketed as 'The Last Show At The Apollo'; it was also the first and only gig at the venue to be granted an alcohol license. The bingo giant Mecca announced plans to re-purpose the building, but public pressure – and a petition that managed to accrue 100,000 signatures including those of Eric Clapton, members of Wings and Georgie Fame – meant that the Apollo reopened four months later under new management.

Later that same year, AC/DC released their first live album, *If You Want Blood You Got It*, which has been recorded at the Apollo in April 1978. Midway through their song 'The Jack', Bon Scott wonders aloud whether there are 'any virgins in Glasgow?' – the response from the Apollo crowd is typically boisterous. It was not the first live album to be recorded at the Apollo – Status Quo had released *Quo Live!* in 1976, a record drawn from three sell-out shows in Glasgow – but *If You Want Blood* remains the bestseller. The enthusiastic and unpredictable sound of the Glasgow Choir enhanced and otherwise embellished many other live recordings, both official and bootlegged, including memorable releases from Alice Cooper and Rush. A Wings-enhanced live version of Paul McCartney's song 'Coming Up' was used as the B-side to its single release in 1980; American radio stations seemed to prefer the Apollo version, which helped the single reach number one in the US.

Inevitably, the Apollo was most strongly associated with rockers like AC/DC, Status Quo, Deep Purple, Thin Lizzy and T Rex, as well as The Sensational Alex Harvey Band, who played a series of raucous Apollo Christmas shows, but the Bay City Rollers also played sell-out gigs there, as did Cliff Richard and Leo Sayer. Billy Connolly monopolised the venue for a celebrated two-week run in 1975. There were other outlier acts, too, from performers like Max Bygraves, David Soul, Barbara Dickson and Miles Davis. On New Year's Eve in 1979, Blondie played a gig that was broadcast live on BBC2's 'The Old Grey Whistle Test', a Hogmanay show that finally answered the eternal question: what would 'Sunday Girl' sound like played on the bagpipes?

In the 1980s, pop music got shinier and more polished – reflected by tour stops from Toyah, Kim Wilde and Wham! – but the Apollo building was settling into decrepitude. Some gigs had to be postponed due to flooding and by the mid-1980s it was time for the curtain to come down for good. The official final Apollo gig was on Sunday 16 June 1985, when Paul Weller's Style Council played a 24-song set that closed with a cover of Curtis Mayfield's 'Move On Up'. The shutters came down, the building was left to rot and – after

being damaged by fire just as it was under consideration to become a listed site of historical interest – the Apollo was finally demolished in 1987. A pile of rubble remained in place for a few more years until the Renfield Street site was eventually fully redeveloped.

It is inevitable that fans will excitedly recollect the sights and sounds of a legendary venue that is no more, but while sifting through accounts of the Apollo, it is notable how many of them acknowledge a unique and pungent smell as a key part of this particular venue's legend – perhaps proof that olfactory memory can the most evocative of all. For over a decade, a vibrant online community at www.glasgowapollo.com has collated hits, myths and trivia about the venue, assembling a near-exhaustive list of the acts who played there and gathering appreciations from bands past and present, many of whom received that wee plastic trophy for selling the place out.

The venue even inspired its own musical, entitled *I Was There: The Story Of The Glasgow Apollo*. Initially staged at the nearby Pavilion Theatre in 2009, the show was successfully revived a year later at the SECC to mark the 25th anniversary of the Apollo's closure. Unsurprisingly, this story of two fans and their formative experiences at gigs featured a rock-solid soundtrack of songs by Apollo regulars from AC/DC and Kiss to David Bowie and Tangerine Dream.

The Apollo started life as a cinema and the site now houses a cinema once again. While the footprint of Green's Playhouse was broad, the current occupant at the top of Renfield Street is tall – in fact, the 18-screen Cineworld multiplex is the tallest cinema in Europe. There is neither plaque nor memorial to the Apollo but standing on perpendicular Renfrew Street you do occasionally get a pungent whiff of ... *something*. And the gallus spirit of the venue does live on in the devotion, eagerness and occasional profanity of Glasgow audiences, flourishing in other venues from the cramped intimacy of King Tut's Wah Wah Hut to the bouncing ballroom floor of the Barrowland and the sweaty, hedonistic throng of The Arches. The Apollo might not have invented that spirit, but it did epitomise it for a time.

Left: Demolition progresses, February 1989.

Opposite: The roof of the ballroom continues to smoulder after the fire, October 1988.

Left: Demolition underway at The Apollo, October 1987.

GLASGOW'S GRAND OLE OPRY

Martin Cloonan

Glasgow's Grand Ole Opry is essentially a country and western music club that each weekend hosts live bands and various Americana-related activities. Except it's not quite that simple. For many, the Opry is so much more than just a country and western club – it's a way of life.

Let's begin with a few facts about the building that houses the Grand Ole Opry on 2–4 Govan Road in the south side of Glasgow. It has been variously used as a post office, a carriage-hirers and an undertakers (the walls of the former mortuary still form part of the structure), but enter the building today and its most obvious pre-history is as a cinema. This incarnation dates back to 1921 when William Beresford Inglis converted the place into the Imperial Picture Hall, a film theatre able to accommodate 1,100 people. Following a fire in 1952, the cinema reopened as the Ritz before finally closing its doors in 1959. After a brief stint as an Irish dancing club, 2–4 Govan Road finally morphed into its current guise as home to the Grand Ole Opry.

Alex Fleming opened the Grand Ole Opry as a country and western club in 1974, naming his venue after the world-famous Nashville institution that remains dedicated to honouring country music and its history to this day. The feel of the 1920s silver screen remains: immediately inside the entrance is a ticket booth typical of cinemas before the age of the multiplex, and while there aren't any actual cinema seats left, the layout of ground floor and upper circle will be familiar to movie-goers of a certain age. These days the ground floor is where the action happens in terms of bands and dancing, while the area that housed the projectors is still visible above the bar. The upper floor features old-style seating and a snack bar (the lovingly named Chuck Wagon), both of which provide welcome breathing space from what can be a hectic evening.

The Grand Ole Opry was an instant success when it opened, and the club reports having 2,000 members in the 1970s. Non-members were always welcome to attend, although they generally paid a higher price for admission. The 1980s saw the arrival of the Glasgow Gunslingers. Founded in 1981, this group of Western enthusiasts is dedicated to preserving the First Draw and Western Re-enactment tradition in Scotland. In 2007, the Glasgow Gunslingers amalgamated with the Scottish First Draw Association (founded 1975), retaining the name of the former. The Gunslingers' antics include mock gunfights at the Opry's regular weekend shows. They form an essential part of the contemporary Opry experience.

Nowadays the Opry can seat around 450 people over the three levels of the old cinema. It's an ideal size of crowd, creating an atmosphere but retaining a sense of intimacy. The membership scheme is still in place, with members getting a pound off the entry fee to regular weekend shows. During the week the venue hosts a

Inset: Alex Fleming.

Right: A lonesome cowboy at the entrance to Glasgow's Grand Ole Opry.

GRAND OLE OPRY

Location: 2-4 Govan Road, Glasgow, G51 1HS
Architect: William Beresford Inglis (rebuilt older building as a cinema in 1921)
Capacity: 350
Date opened: 1974
Music: Country & Western
website: www.glasgowsgrandoleopry.co.uk/

Below: Exterior of the Opry in 1983.

variety of events such as line dancing, jiving and mock gunfight training, but the club's main focus remains its Friday and Saturday night country and western gigs. To go to the Opry on these nights is to step into a world of Americana that goes way beyond the music: the venue is furnished with scenes of the American West; a shop in the corner sells all manner of Americana tat; cowboys and girls strut by; Stetsons are worn and toy guns tooted; Confederate and Union flags are flown and images of native Americans adorn the walls. Govan might be a long way from Galveston, but the spirit of the latter haunts this small corner of the former. The line dancers who fill the floor wouldn't look out of place on the dance floors of America's deep south.

Friday and Saturday night entertainment at the Opry generally follows a regular routine: the featured band plays three sets interspersed with bingo; mock gunfights take place between club members; and a raffle is held. The end of the band's last set – usually around 11.30 pm – is followed by the club's regular DJ, Rowdy A, keeping the line dancers going until the early hours. The evening climaxes with the flag troop lowering the Union and Confederate flags to the sound of 'American Trilogy' as sung by Elvis Presley. (The regular presence of the 'king of rock and roll' at a country music event serves as a reminder that as well as being a key cultural form in its own right, country music has made a major contribution to other genres of American music.) 'If it ain't country, it ain't music' declares the sign behind the bar – a statement of pure affection, not politics.

Country and western music is the music of ordinary folk and it's no surprise that a city like Glasgow, with its vibrant industrial history, has long had a love of it. The origin of country music lies in the US with its roots in Western music and the folk music of mostly white, working-class Americans who had blended a number of musical forms, including the folk music brought to America by Scottish immigrants, to create their own American folk music. The themes of country music historically have always reflected the lives of the working classes: working and the escape from it; love and its ups and downs; booze and its highs and lows; religion and its hope. In the UK this has meant that a love of country music has been rooted in the nation's proletariat. Other post-industrial British cities, such as Liverpool, share Glasgow's love of country music and its penchant for telling it like it is while also hoping for better times.

On 16 November 1891, *Buffalo Bill's Wild West Show* began a three-month residency in Glasgow, the sole Scottish venue chosen for this tour. The show ran until 27 February 1892 at the East End Exhibition Buildings in Dennistoun. In 2006 a statue of Buffalo Bill was unveiled on the site of the show. The Andrew Hook Centre for American Studies at the University of Glasgow furthers the city's interest in all things American, while visits by US country and western stars, such as Dolly Parton and Kenny Rogers, regularly sell out major Glasgow venues like the SECC. The Grand Ole Opry is able to build on and perpetuate a long-held and still vibrant Glaswegian passion for Americana.

On the Glasgow music scene, there is nothing quite like a night out at the Opry – and probably not many like it elsewhere, either. The genuine enthusiasm of the Opry regulars for their music is a sight to behold. The bands themselves come both from the city and across the globe, and while attendances might nowadays be generally lower than in the club's early days – the regular Friday and Saturday night shows attract crowds of around 200 – the club is still hugely popular. This popularity is doubtless buoyed by modest entry prices (generally no more than a fiver) and some of the cheapest bar prices in the city. Like country music itself, the Opry remains the domain of the man and woman in the street. It has no airs or graces, but knows how to enjoy itself; it takes people as they are and expects the same in return. It can dress up, with many of its regulars donning Western costumes, but is relaxed about dressing down; cowboys and cowgirls rub shoulders with those in jeans and T-shirts and any dressing up is

Above: Interior detail.

Left: Linedancing at the *Calamity Jane* event at Grand Ole Opry, 2013.

Left: Barley Scotch of Hayseed Dixie, 2010.

done with affection rather than pretension. Identity at the Grand Ole Opry is based on musical passion and a wider interest in America, not on how you look.

For Alex Fleming, the simplicity of the club has been a key element in its success. 'There are no hassles about dress code,' he said, 'and you can listen, sing and dance to country music. What more can you ask?' The club hosts a number of charity events across the year, raising money for various good causes, and members of the audience are regularly invited onto the stage to sing with the band. 'Southern Star' (Mrs Sandra Anderson of Clarkston) is a regular attender who outlined the appeal of the Opry as follows: 'It's the most easy-going company you will get anywhere. It's for whole families or for singles. But the main thing is, it's for happy nights, and there's never any trouble.'

The wider affection many Glaswegians have for country music has been reflected in its music scene. The Parsonage Choir, for example, named after the country icon, Gram Parsons, specialises in covering popular music; many of its members have a background in indie music. And while the Opry's focus is emphatically country, it has also hosted a range of shows from other genres over the years. Any Glasgow band with the slightest penchant for Americana is sooner or later

drawn to the club, and among the luminaries of the local indie scene who have played the Opry stage are Mogwai, Franz Ferdinand, Sons and Daughters, Lloyd Cole and Teenage Fanclub. Former Belle and Sebastian manager John Williamson, who promoted the Teenage Fanclub gig at the Opry, recalls that, in keeping with regular practice, the band was asked to remind the audience of the food available at the Chuck Wagon; lead singer Norman Blake took great delight in the very un-rock and roll act of informing the crowd that 'pie and chips were on special offer'.

In February 2012, the Opry hosted former Oasis main man Noel Gallagher with his new band, High Flying Birds. The show was open to competition winners only and subsequently shown on YouTube by In:Demand Scotland. Sadly the customary Opry scenes of the American prairie had been covered up by a starry, black backdrop; it might have been the Opry, but for all viewers knew it could have been anywhere. I can't help thinking that it was Gallagher's loss. He didn't even mention the Chuck Wagon; perhaps the pie and chips were off that night.

Another example of the links between indie bands

Above: Taking it easy the *Calamity Jane* event at Grand Ole Opry, 2013.

Right: The Moonshiners perform, 2013.

Below: Local boys Franz Ferdinand prove that The Opry isn't restricted to Country & Western.

and the Opry was provided by Franz Ferdinand on 4 and 5 June 2007. On the latter date the headliners were supported by the Royal We, about whom there was a fair amount of industry buzz at the time. There was something wonderfully incongruous about Franz's crowd of hipster kids and music industry slickers heading off to a country and western club which is generally the domain of an older demographic. A nervous uncertainty among fans was palpable. Some appeared a little unsure about quite how to behave. Can one go to the Chuck Wagon and still be cool? Indeed, can one even be seen in a country and western club and still be cool? Possibly not, but the Opry experience depends on embracing it as it is.

I've been enjoying regular weekend shows at the Opry for around a decade now, and my simple advice is to get yourselves along to one of the regular Friday or Saturday nights there. Take it for what it is; join in the fun; celebrate Glasgow's connections across the Big Pond. That said, keep an eye out for the one-off gigs, the unlikelies, and the incongruous anomalies. They can occasionally be even more special than the regular nights. 'If it ain't country, it ain't music' – that's one way of looking at it, but this wonderful venue has a big enough heart to host all sorts of music.

Above: Exterior of The Opry at Paisley Toll.

Left, inset: Glaswegian gunslingers Norrie Morris, Josephine Bryce, Charlie Bryce and John Johnstone, May 1989.

Below: Linedancing at the *Calamity Jane* event at Grand Ole Opry, 2013.

POSTCARD RECORDS
The Original Indie Sound

Vic Galloway

183 West Princes Street: a small, rented flat at in the West End of Glasgow. It might not sound like the birthplace of a musical breakthrough, but the global terms 'indie-pop' and 'post-punk' can be traced back to this address – and to the man who lived there.

The untamed expression, unbridled joy and independent spirit of rock and roll can, of course, be traced further back: to the cultural explosion of the 1950s; to the beat boom and psychedelia of the 1960s; to the glam-rock and punk of the 1970s. Over decades and generations, three chords and an uncompromising stance have changed lives. But the short-lived story of Postcard Records makes for a major chapter in pop music history.

It probably didn't seem like it at the time. In 1979 the dying embers of the punk explosion were fizzling out, and they left something that was arguably more important in their ashes. Having been empowered by punk's DIY ethos and unquenchable desire to challenge the norm, young men and women across the UK sought something beyond the trad-rock formulas and well-trodden paths of major-label stardom and manufactured pop. The Buzzcocks released their iconic *Spiral Scratch* EP on their own New Hormones label and the notion of setting up an independent label became a real option. Indie labels sprang up all over the place, especially in the working-class areas of the UK's biggest cities. London had Rough Trade, Manchester had Factory, Liverpool had Zoo and Glasgow – well, Glasgow had Postcard.

Strangely enough, while Glasgow was (and still is) broadly seen as Scotland's music Mecca and innovative hub, Edinburgh was already out of the starting blocks with its own hugely influential and forward-thinking label, Fast Product. Its founders Bob Last and Hilary Morrison had shown that a cottage outfit could take on the UK music industry and subvert it into new ways of working. Their 'difficult fun' and 'mutant pop' helped to reshape the post-punk landscape and gave rise to ground-breaking releases by The Gang of Four, Human League and Edinburgh's own Scars. Fast Product isn't celebrated or mythologised in the same way that Postcard is today, but its initial impact was just as important.

Fast must have been a major influence on a certain young botany student from Saltcoats called Alan Horne and on the way that he would go about setting up Postcard Records. Crucially, Fast

Right: 183 West Princes Street.

Inset: Detail from album cover.

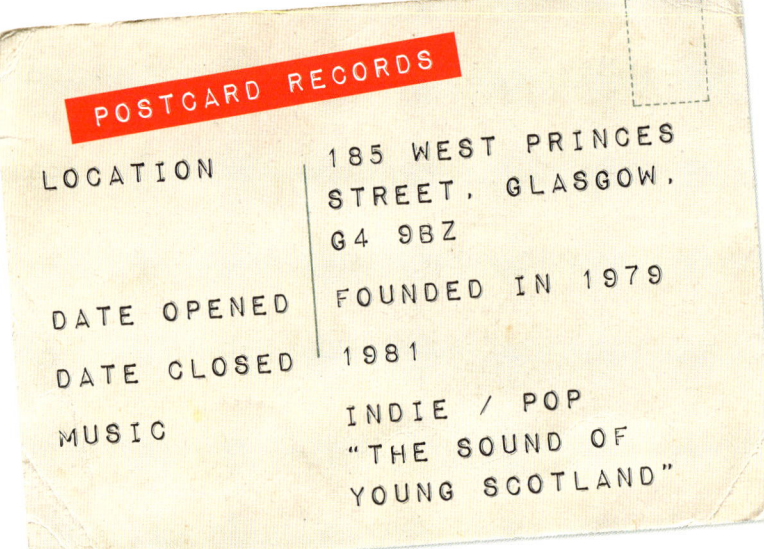

POSTCARD RECORDS

LOCATION: 185 WEST PRINCES STREET, GLASGOW, G4 9BZ
DATE OPENED: FOUNDED IN 1979
DATE CLOSED: 1981
MUSIC: INDIE / POP "THE SOUND OF YOUNG SCOTLAND"

Below: 'Poor Old Soul', by Orange Juice, 7″ vinyl.

showed that running a Scottish label with a punk spirit was possible.

In the mid-1970s, Glasgow had a hardman reputation for drinking, fighting and working-class blues-rock. After the cultural year-zero mentality of punk, anything was possible for bold young artists – as long as it wasn't a hoary old cliché. Women were encouraged to make music, scream loudly and express themselves in a less-than-ladylike manner. On the flipside, men could be something other than beer-swilling, football-chanting meatheads; they were allowed to be witty, erudite and fey and to explore their femininity. The scene was set for Postcard to encompass a new kind of independent pop music.

As for young Alan Horne? He was spurred on by huge personal ambition, and also by any obvious obstacles. In fact, obstacles were what fuelled his fire. Even after punk's broad levelling of the music industry, Scotland was either ignored by the London media and music industry or considered (if considered at all) an uncultured outpost. Horne was determined to prove London wrong. He decided to start a record label and to operate it out of the wardrobe in his flat – his 'West Princes Street of Dreams', as he called it. But what kind of sounds could this angry entrepreneur commit to wax?

Cue a Bearsden group formerly known as The Nu-Sonics and fronted by a doe-eyed soon-to-be-pin-up called Edwyn Collins. Renaming themselves Orange Juice and sporting flowery shirts and fringes, here was a band that took influence from Northern soul, disco and funk to the benchmark Velvet Underground, Bowie and punk favourites Subway Sect. Orange Juice's trebly guitars, sweet, buoyant melodies and life-affirming approach eschewed Glasgow's hardman attitude and the bootboy mentality of punk.

Orange Juice was the perfect vehicle for Horne's fledgling label and he threw his all into promoting the band. Their imagination matched his conceptual idealism. Postcard Records was officially set up to release the band's material before it branched out as a fully-fledged label. Horne, Collins and Orange Juice bassist David McClymont pooled their meagre resources of £400 and pressed 1,000 copies of their debut single 'Falling and Laughing'.

As much a necessity as an artistic choice, the sleeves for the single were handcrafted then delivered to Scottish record shops in the boot of Horne's car. A few copies were sent to tastemakers around the UK in April 1980, and the more discerning of these immediately recognised the single for what it was. The hugely influential but polarising *New Musical Express* (*NME*) magazine declared the vinyl a prestigious 'Single of the Week', and it wouldn't be long until young Edwyn was gracing the magazine's front cover. The follow-up, 'Blue Boy', was the next release in a run of five Orange Juice singles on Postcard.

Many, including pop historian Simon Reynolds, attribute Orange Juice's speedy jettison into public consciousness to the general mood in the UK at the time. After the blast and fury of punk, then the gloomy post-punk of Joy Division and Ian Curtis's subsequent suicide, listeners were ready for a lighter touch. Orange Juice still had the attitude, the lean, punchy arrangements, the minimal production and the general cynicism that the early 80s audience wanted. But they also had a sense of fun that was missing from a lot of contemporary furrow-browed groups. There was a romanticism and sensitivity to their music and lyrics, all delivered with an eyebrow raised to the world – especially when it came to marketing and manufacture.

Postcard made its name using a tongue-in-cheek tagline: 'The Sound of Young Scotland' was a tribute to Motown's motto 'The Sound of Young America'. The logo was a cat banging a drum and there was plenty of kitsch tartan-tat and country-and-western iconography to go with the fairly ironic name 'Postcard' itself. Together, the band and the label honed a jangly new image and sound that would go on to influence a wave of bands including The Smiths and The Wedding Present, who coined the term 'indie'.

With an unmitigated success on his hands, Horne set about fleshing out the label. He needed other bands. Edinburgh's scene was more vibrant and developed at the time, thanks largely to the Fast Product and Pop Aural labels, so Horne looked east for his next signing. He had met Malcolm Ross at a gig and was intrigued by the dark, caustic, wiry sounds of Ross's band, Josef K. The name came from Franz Kafka's protagonist in his play, *The Trial*, which somewhat set the tone for a group of serious, austere young men who had been influenced by Joy Division and the off-kilter art-rock of American bands like Pere Ubu and Television.

Josef K was the second group to be released and championed by Postcard, and they fitted perfectly into the label's new sonic palette. They loved disco-informed rhythms and took an anti-macho, anti-rockist stance. Allegedly the band's intense and sensitive frontman, Paul Haig, didn't always see eye-to-eye with Horne and claimed the label boss had little time for the band's music and demeanour. Whether or not that is true, Horne had another critical and artistic success on his hands. The music press wholeheartedly embraced the four singles that Josef K released on Postcard, and the band's debut album was also issued out of West Princes Street. After that the band and the label parted ways, and the band split up not long after.

Another two groups were soon added to the Postcard fold. Horne had encountered an Australian band called The Go-Betweens in London and thought that their whole manner and disposition would suit his label down to the ground. With their undisguised debt to Talking Heads, Jonathan Richman and the Velvet Underground, as well as their naive knack for simple melody, The Go-Betweens decamped briefly to Glasgow and employed the services of Orange Juice drummer Steven Daly for their one and only Postcard single. Once again Horne had struck gold – as far as independent charts were concerned, anyway.

Finally an East Kilbride outfit came along, intriguingly named Aztec Camera and led by teenage guitar virtuoso Roddy Frame. The band made two singles for Postcard and showed huge promise; purportedly a debut album was recorded, too, but never issued. Roddy and his band went on to have major success after leaving Postcard, including a bonafide hit single called 'Somewhere in My Heart'.

It should be noted at this point that all of this flurry of activity took place within an extremely short time period. Postcard's first release was in April 1980; its last was in August 1981. Those 16 months flew by in a blur of ideas and manifestos, a collection of unique-sounding singles and an album. But the pace proved impossible to sustain. For a start, Horne's ambition was too great. He wasn't satisfied at being lauded solely by the underground and independent sectors of the music business. He wanted more than his much-loved but niche operation could afford. He behaved increasingly like an Andy Warhol figure, sneering and mocking the UK scene, local groups and even peers around him. He had an innate desire to change things, to subvert the pop machine from within and to entirely upset the apple cart. To Horne, at the time, anyway, it seemed increasingly that Postcard wasn't the vehicle to do this.

Ironically, that's exactly what Postcard's real legacy would become in the years to come: the motivation for musicians to mistrust the norm and do it themselves. But in the early 1980s, as soon as Postcard's roster of bands and, more specifically, Orange Juice began to turn heads and gather momentum, so the UK music industry rather predictably came calling. Rather than courting London on their terms and on their turf,

Below: Postcard's drumming kitten – nicknamed Felicity.

suddenly labels and journalists were jumping on trains and heading north. Soon Glasgow was awash with hungry A&R (artists and repertoire) men signing any group whose members sported clean-cut mops or quiffs, who wore stripey hooped tops and Ray-Bans and whose guitars jangled accordingly. For these bands the lure of decent money, serious promotion and potential pop success was strong. Altered Images went on record saying they couldn't possibly sign to Postcard when a major label was offering them a deal and the promise of proper pop stardom. Postcard soon crumbled, eventually going bankrupt.

Orange Juice's debut album *You've Got to Hide Your Love Away* was released via a major label (Polydor) in collaboration with Postcard. Aztec Camera moved to Rough Trade then Warner Brothers and The Go-Betweens returned to Australia, embarking on a lengthy, well-respected career throughout the 1980s and beyond. Apparently The Bluebells were the last band to be signed to Postcard, waiting in the wings but unable to release anything as the label fell apart. Horne himself ended up taking a job at London Records.

Capitalising on this new-found interest in the Glasgow music scene, a whole host of copycats emerged from the woodwork and diluted the original, viscerally raw sound

Inset: Cover and inner sleeve from Josef K's only album for Postcard – *The Only Fun in Town*.

Below (set): Josef K performing in 1981.

that had been so appealing in Postcard's bands. These new bands added the kind of stadium-rock sheen that had worked profitably for Glasgow's most successful sons, Simple Minds, and in the following years a slick and radio-friendly collection of Scottish groups – Del Amitri, Deacon Blue, Hipsway, Wet Wet Wet, Love and Money – would move into the limelight, sign to major labels and make real money. Of course there's nothing wrong with that *per se*, but the instigators who had started the ball rolling weren't rewarded in the same way.

Orange Juice did in due course have an official hit single in the form of the groove-laden classic 'Rip It Up', but the band eventually split. Edwyn Collins has since found a modicum of success as a solo act, label boss and producer. The influx of attention on Glasgow is now seen as part of Scotland's cultural rebirth, and Scotland's independent music scene has flourished through successive generations ever since. The mainstream 'blue-eyed soul' groups of the 1980s notched up huge short-term success on the back of it.

Postcard's influence, however, manifested itself in more underground culture. Formal proof of that influence came soon enough in the *C81* and *C86* compilation cassette tapes released by *NME* magazine in 1981 and 1986. These tapes were a veritable who's who of indie music; three of Postcard's bands (Orange Juice, Josef K and Aztec Camera) were included on *C81*, and on *C86* the label's effect could be heard across the entire album. Postcard might not have existed any longer, but no fewer than six groups from Scotland – Primal Scream, The Soup Dragons, The Pastels, The Shop Assistants, Close Lobsters and The Mackenzies – were included on the album. Postcard's trademark minimal, scratchy aesthetic was etched into all of them.

The Jesus and Mary Chain – nihilistic East Kilbride feedback-lovers and NME darlings – definitely took notice of Postcard's bearing in the early 1980s before storming the barricades down south. And before long a scene would emerge based primarily in the Bellshill area, south-east of Glasgow: the Boy Hairdressers, BMX Bandits, The Vaselines, Captain America and eventually Teenage Fanclub would go on to tour the world and release records that would connect with millions thanks to the 'grunge' phenomenon in the late 1980s and early 1990s. Wave after wave of Scottish indie bands have since come to the fore, with acts such as Belle and Sebastian and Camera Obscura all beating a trail back to Postcard and its DIY ethos. Alex Kapranos, frontman of Scotland's most globally successful recent indie band, Franz Ferdinand, has talked freely about his love for Postcard, Orange Juice and Josef K. He and members of Teenage Fanclub have all doffed their caps and played onstage with Edwyn Collins in recent years; Collins himself is making a slow but steady recovery from a stroke and a brain haemorrhage.

As well as the musicians themselves, Postcard made an indelible impression on the way that independent labels have operated ever since. As a direct result of its small but perfectly formed legacy, other music-loving entrepreneurs-with-attitude have set up

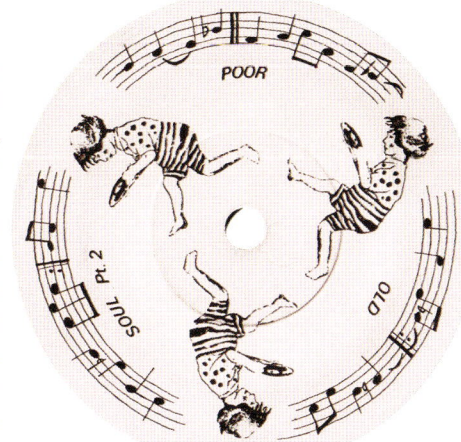

Top: Poor Old Soul by Orange Juice.

Middle: Simply Thrilled Honey by Orange Juice.

Bottom: It's Kinda Funny by Josef K.

Above, left: The Only Fun in Town by Josef K.

Above, middle: Pictures by Josef K.

Above, right: It's Kinda Funny by Josef K.

Below: Just Like Gold by Aztec Camera, with insert postcard.

Opposite, left: The Sound of Young Scotland.

Opposite, right: A collecion of responses to fan mail from the Orange Juice Fan Club, c. 1983. The fan club was maintained by Syuzen Buckley Ross, wife of Malcolm who played and wrote for the band.

record companies to challenge the majors at their own game – and plenty of them have succeeded. Creation Records took its lead from Postcard with Alan McGee, another Glaswegian gunslinger, at the helm. With Oasis, Teenage Fanclub, My Bloody Valentine, Primal Scream and others, McGee took on Alan Horne's swagger, confidence and bravado and scaled the charts, making serious money and soundtracking the 1990s in the process. Would Creation have existed without Postcard? Possibly, but it would have looked and sounded very different.

Postcard's ethos has permeated the attitude of younger Scottish labels such as Glasgow's Chemikal Underground, Edinburgh's Song by Toad, Fife's Fence Records and the Isle of Eigg's Lost Map. Horne himself tried his hand at another label called Swamplands but had no real success there. Then he re-emerged with a revived Postcard between 1992 and 1997, releasing some Orange Juice back catalogue, bankrolling new releases by Paul Quinn (previously of Bourgie Bourgie) and The Nectarine No. 9 (featuring Davy Henderson from Fire Engines) and issuing a Jock Scot anthology and music from their initial inspiration, Vic Godard of Subway Sect. It was certainly good to have the label back, but its second life never garnered the same respect or unleashed the same impact on pop culture.

Horne has now retired from the music industry and lives as a relative recluse in Dundee, where he cares for his friend Paul Quinn who has multiple sclerosis. But his legacy is immense. His attitude, vision and ambition within an increasingly safe and careerist music industry at the start of the 1980s profoundly altered the modus operandi. So-called 'indie' culture, whether music, film, art or fashion, is now a worldwide phenomenon. Thanks to Horne's tiny, self-financed label, it can reasonably be argued that the roots of that indie culture are in Glasgow's West End. Like the best short-and-sharp pop songs, Postcard ignited, burned bright and then quickly disappeared. And, like the best pop songs, it got stuck under the skin of every generation since.

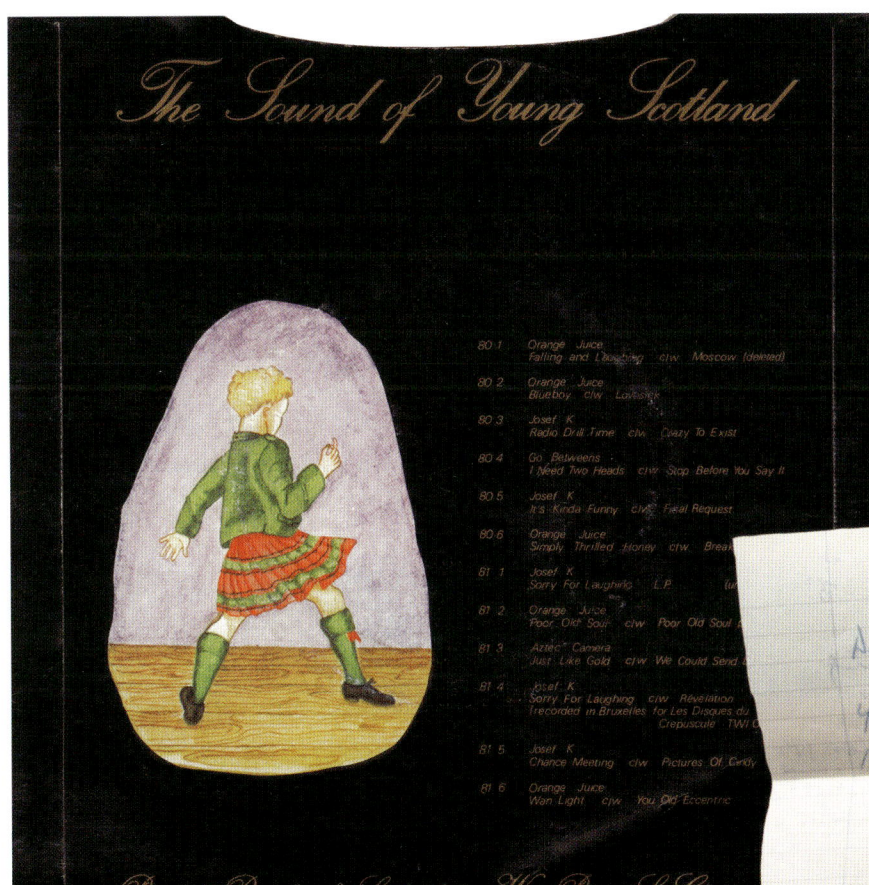

THE SECC
The Big Red Shed

Martin Cloonan

The Scottish Exhibition and Conference Centre (SECC) opened in 1985, the same year that Glasgow's much-loved Apollo closed. Its building coincided with attempts to rebrand Glasgow as a vibrant, post-industrial city in which the cultural industries were key components of economic regeneration. The SECC originally consisted of the main building with its various halls and a large parking area. A hotel, the Clyde Auditorium and the SSE Hydro were all later additions to the site. It is also the only Glasgow venue to have its own train station, Exhibition Centre.

In many ways the Apollo and the SECC's main building represent two different eras: one rough and ready but with masses of atmosphere, the other corporate and soulless, earning the nickname 'the Big Red Shed' (a name that was made somewhat redundant when the building was repainted grey in 1997). I know plenty of people who loved – genuinely loved – the Apollo, but it's hard to feel the same way about SECC's main building. Both the Apollo and the SECC have hosted some of the great names in popular music and have provided Glaswegians (and those who are Glaswegian for the night) with some cherished memories. But while the Apollo is regularly given the epithet 'legendary', it seems unlikely that any of the arenas in the SECC's main building will ever achieve that status.

However, perhaps that's not really the point. The building was designed to be practical, not soulful.

Authentic rock and roll experiences are not what the SECC and similar venues are about. They are multipurpose sites, built for a number

Right: The paint job that gave the SECC its nickname, pre-1997.

SECC
(and 'ARMADILLO' and SSE HYDRO)

Location   Exhibition Way, Glasgow, G3 8YW
Architect   SECC, The Parr Partnership (1985);
               'Armadillo', Sir Norman Foster (1997);
               SSE Hydro, Foster & Partners (2013)
Capacity   3000 – 12,500
Date opened   1985 – 2013
Music   Rock, Pop
website   www.secc.co.uk

of reasons. The SECC's full title is something of a giveaway on that front: 'exhibition and conference centre', not 'dance hall' or 'rock stadium'. The SECC main building was built as Scotland's national arena and it is important to recognise that, for better or worse, such arenas have transformed the UK concert industry. The SECC's Hall 4 can accommodate up to 12,500 people; venues of such capacity allow bands to perform to larger crowds. Once a band gets to a certain level of popularity, it makes much more economic sense to play to 10,000 people on one night at the SECC than, say, 4,000 people for two nights at the Barrowland Ballroom. For concert promoters and many bands, high-capacity venues are a good thing. For punters, they're something of a mixed blessing.

An arena-sized venue is also a marker of a city's prestige. It says, 'Yes, we're a real city and we can attract the biggest acts in the world.' The SECC was among the first of a series of such arenas built across the UK, generally with the help of large amounts of public money. These venues were designed to put cities on the map as destinations for all sorts of cultural and other events. They help cities to chase the tourist buck. Where Glasgow used to build ships on the Clyde, now it could provide world-class entertainment near to the Clyde. Of course, the fact that Edinburgh doesn't have an equivalent arena is a definite bonus for Glasgow.

At first the SECC was jointly owned by the Scottish Development Agency (which drew up initial plans for an arena in 1979), Glasgow District Council and Strathclyde Regional Council. Now it is operated by SEC Ltd, a private company in which Glasgow City Council owns 90.86% of the shares. Its location next to the Clyde, which the SECC's website describes as 'perfect' (although those stuck in its notorious car park queues following a show may beg to differ), is part of a broader trend to utilise riverside locations that has been replicated in cities across the globe. While the venue had financial difficulties in the early years – it didn't make a profit until 1993 – the SECC claims that

Right: Aerial view of Park Circus, in the foreground, with the view south to the River Clyde and SECC, 1994.

it has brought £342 million to Glasgow in its first 25 years. In 2004 alone its box offices sold 920,000 tickets, worth over £20 million.

While the aesthetics of gigs in arenas might leave something to be desired in terms of character, often the alternative would be no gig at all. Given the expense of going on the road with ever-increasing technical requirements and ever-more-expensive stage sets, certain acts almost have to play arenas. Put simply, no arena means no big acts coming to town – and I like big acts coming to my town. Take, for example, The Rolling Stones, who on their 2003 tour played the SECC with a stage that extended into the crowd and allowed the standing audience an up-close view. If the economies of scale provided by the SECC brought fans within inches of Keith Richards, then perhaps it can't be all bad.

The official opening night of the SECC on 7 September 1985 saw the venue play host to a gala concert by the Royal Scottish National Orchestra in Hall 1. The first public concert at the SECC was given by UB40 on 26 October 1985. The support act that night was Simply Red. The centre was officially 'opened' by the Queen the following month as part of the *Scottish Motor Show*. Since then many of the world's major acts have played the venue. Until the SSE Hydro opened,

Below: Queen's Dock in the 1950s, looking north – now the site of the SECC.

Right: Saltire Beat, perform to order outside the SECC.

it was *the* place in Scotland to see the sorts of acts that can sell out arenas but might struggle to sell out, for example, the 90,000 capacity Hampden Park. The SECC also played major roles in some key events in Glasgow's regeneration process. Hall 4 hosted the Grand International Show as part of the *Glasgow Garden Festival* in 1988, while in 1990 the city's status as European City of Culture saw it used for performances by the Bolshoi Ballet and Luciano Pavarotti. The same year, Miles Davis trod the SECC stage as part of the *Glasgow Jazz Festival*.

Like any venue, the SECC keeps its own records. The record-holders for the longest run by a single act are from the city itself: Wet Wet Wet played ten nights in 1995. The equivalent record for a solo act is held jointly by Kylie Minogue, who played five nights as part of her 'Showgirl' tour in 2005, and Rod Stewart, who also played five nights in 2005.

The experience of attending a show in the main building at the SECC is largely dependent on who is playing and how the venue is laid out – in particular how much seating is used. For those who like standing and being able to participate, even if only by hopping from one foot to another, the seated tickets in Hall 4 can feel somewhat distant, more like watching a film in an enormous church hall than being part of something special. To draw on my own experience of SECC gigs: I've been mesmerised (P J Harvey supporting Morrissey in 2004, Neil Young in 2001); impressed (Girls Aloud, 2008); frightened (the Sex Pistols in 2007); alienated (the Arctic Monkeys in 2011 – great band, bad audience) and simply awed (Bob Dylan, repeatedly). Some gigs there I've enjoyed, some not so much – which makes it a bit like any other music venue.

The sheer size and design of Hall 4 in particular mean that audiences can struggle to truly lose themselves in the music in the ways they might be able to at other venues. The hangar-like space of the venue makes audience members conscious of their surroundings. Rather than the music transporting them elsewhere, the cavernous scope of the hall constantly reminds listeners of exactly where they are. However, the main building has a certain amount of flexibility: smaller bands can play in Hall 3, which holds just under 6,000 people, and Hall 4 can be reconfigured to host a range of events. (The disadvantage here is that those wishing to include the SECC in a tour have often found it already booked for a wedding convention or a science conference.)

The best proof of the main building's limitations is provided by the fact that two new purpose-built arenas have been built directly beside it: the Clyde Auditorium which opened in 1997 and the SSE Hydro which opened in 2013. Smaller acts can now play the 3,000-capacity Clyde Auditorium which is generally referred to as 'the Armadillo' because of its unique design by Norman Foster, now well known as one of the world's leading architects. The Auditorium was built to complement the SECC's provision for live entertainment. It quickly became one of the most recognisable buildings on Clydeside and is one of the iconic images of modern Glasgow, alongside the third and latest venue on the SECC site, the SSE Hydro. The Hydro was also designed by Norman Foster to provide a venue for live indoor entertainment and sporting events – no conferences, no international exhibitions. The upper part of the

building is clad in translucent material, allowing daylight to come in and the front of the building to glow at night. The venue boasts 'superb sightlines' to the stage from each of the 12,000 seats and acoustics 'of the highest standard' and in this respect, the Hydro outdoes the arenas of the SECC's main building by miles.

All this is not meant to decry the original SECC venue. It has hosted some of the greats in music, from The Rolling Stones and The Who to Miles Davis and Pavarotti. One example from many: in 2003 The Rolling Stones played two nights (1 and 3 September) as part of their 'Licks' tour which accompanied their *40 Licks* greatest hits compilation. Tickets cost £65, which was seen as pretty steep for the time (though not a record for the SECC – Pavarotti charged £75 in 1990). The Stones had a main stage from which they could go to a smaller stage situated in the middle of the crowd, allowing the luckiest members of the crowd to get within touching distance. The Stones played some obscure songs: in addition to stalwarts such as 'Satisfaction', 'Brown Sugar' and 'Honky Tonk Women', fans also got to hear less familiar material such as 'Live With Me' and Otis Redding's 'That's How Strong My Love Is'. For those (like me) with a long-term love of the band, these two nights were truly special.

It may be all but impossible to love the venues in the SECC's main building, but it is obviously easy for fans to love the acts that have played there. The SECC has brought some of the very best acts in the world to Glasgow; without it, these acts might never have visited the city. Some thanks, at least, are due to the Big Red Shed.

Top: 'The Armadillo'

Above: SECC walkway which crosses the Expressway to the Exhibition Centre train station.

SUB CLUB

Malcolm Jack

The explosion of electronic dance music in the late 1980s shook few British cities harder than it shook Glasgow. Arguably the last major music and youth culture movement of the 20th century, it was unique in being conveyed not by recording artists but by DJs. It was powered by the repetitive, euphoric synthetic beats of house and techno. And the enormous surge in popularity of house and techno was inextricably intertwined with the emergence of a new drug called MDMA, or Ecstasy. Together the drug and its music provided formative experiences for a generation. Dance music established the cult of the DJ, prompted a notorious media and legislative backlash and effectively created clubbing as we understand it today.

With world-famous venues such as Sub Club as its standard-bearers, the clubland on the banks of the Clyde has become renowned not just on the UK but on the international stage. Every week Glasgow welcomes big-name touring DJs and floods of visiting revellers, and in turn sends its home-grown DJs out to perform everywhere from New York to Tokyo. Most patrons spill out onto Glasgow's pavements at the 3 am curfew and typically reconvene in somebody's home for impromptu after-parties that run past dawn.

What makes Glasgow, after only London and maybe Manchester, the key British city in the story of electronic dance music? Major players on the scene for the past 30 years offer a variety of thoughtful explanations: the unpretentious, upbeat attitude of Glasgow's clubbers; the relatively inexpensive cost of living and going out in the city; the presence of trendsetting hubs such as Rubadub, the electronic music record and technology shop. Or is it just that working-class

Left: Sub Club dancefloor

SUB CLUB

Location: 22 Jamaica Street, Glasgow G1 4QD
Date Opened: 1987
Capacity: 410
Music: House, techno, electro, disco, bass music and others
website: www.subclub.co.uk

Glaswegian mantra that says work hard and, come the weekend, blow-off steam harder?

Whatever the explanation, clubbing seems to be in Glasgow's DNA. To consider the history of Glaswegians gathering at the end of a working week to socialise, imbibe (legally or otherwise) and dance is to consider a history long preceding any kind of machine music. For example, what is arguably the city's most famous live music venue, the Barrowlands, started life as a ballroom and at the height of its 1930s and 1940s popularity was the hub of one of the most thriving swing dance scenes in Britain. In fact, read many of the other chapters in this book and you'll recognise a wider narrative of a city that is outgoing by nature, partial to a spot of excess, and perhaps seeking some escape from a day-to-day humdrum existence.

Created using synthesisers and drum machines, house music, acid house and techno originated in America – specifically in post-industrial cousins of Glasgow like Detroit and Chicago. House arose partly out of disco, channelling its euphoric feel and four-to-the-floor beats but in a more minimalist and repetitive style using all (or mainly) synthesised instruments. Techno was house's more progressive and involved descendant, defined in its earliest stages by futuristic titles and themes and by the sounds of the Roland TR-808 drum machine (also a staple of early hip hop). Acid house, with its characteristic squelchy bass-lines and psychedelic aesthetics, proved especially popular and influential in Europe, where it helped to break dance music into a global scene.

House was carried across the Atlantic by trend-setting DJs and music press tastemakers. At first it was heard in gay clubs (Glasgow's first gay club, Bennett's on Glassford Street, was perhaps the first place in the city to play electronic dance music). It arrived gradually: house from the early 1980s, techno later in the decade. It infiltrated a going-out scene in Glasgow that had already developed a pronounced rebellious streak. And that streak centred around one small subterranean venue in particular.

Accessible through an innocuous doorway on Jamaica Street, marked by little more than its iconic submarine logo, Sub Club – or 'The Subby' – launched in the early 1980s in a space that already had its own music history. The building was a speak-easy-style jazz club in the 1950s and 1960s. By the 1970s it had become a dinner-dance club called the Jamaica Inn, and in 1982 it morphed into a nightclub called Lucifer's. In 1983, the struggling Lucifer's invited an enterprising young promoter by the name of Graham Wilson and a group of his art student friends to launch a weekly alternative club night. They had hitherto run the Gang Hut at Maestro's on Scott Street (now the CCA bar). Sub Club was established, its name and logo both Wilson's inventions.

True to the post-punk-inspired DIY spirit of the times, Sub Club offered something defiantly different to other Glasgow nightclubs or 'discos' that rarely strayed far from chart pop. DJs such as Nick Peacock, Segun and James 'Harri' Harrigan played anything and everything non-mainstream – a scattershot of early hip hop and house, funk, jazz, soul, rare groove and punk. About 20 minutes every night would even be given over to one small group who regularly came requesting rockabilly. Wilson would each week decorate the club in different quirky ways, using everything from old copies of *Sounds* magazine to tinfoil. Daft stunts were common. One night, Wilson recalls, someone rode a motorbike down the stairs. The Subby was soon packed most nights; the single night turned into a week's residency, which eventually became several.

When Wilson, in partnership with publican Greg McLeod, took over the Lucifer's premises outright, Sub Club the venue was founded, officially opening its doors on 1 April 1987. But its reputation as a dance music mecca was still some way off. The place initially attracted a crowd centred around the Glasgow bands of the era: Orange Juice, The Bluebells, Lloyd Cole and The Commotions would often drink there. Wilson, who sold out to McLeod in 1989, later moved to London and enjoyed a successful music career himself with The Nightcrawlers. Sub Club's intuitively welcoming door policy would also take time to develop. It is ironic that, considering their vital parts in the club's story, both Harri and future Optimo DJ, Keith McIvor, were separately turned away by door staff when they first tried to visit.

The change that swept through clubland in the late 1980s was countrywide. The Hacienda in Manchester is well storied as the cradle of British acid house, but in a much smaller way you could have detected its arrival as far north as Aberdeen. It was there that the future Sub Club co-owner and manager, Mike Grieve, ran a nightclub called Fever from February 1989 until November 1991. He recalls the sudden preponderance of smiley T-shirts – effectively the logo of acid house – and a surge in the availability and popularity of Ecstasy.

The 'house bomb', as it's described by Stuart MacMillan (one half of electronic dance musicians/DJs Slam together with Orde Meikle) detonated in earnest during the legendary 'second summer of love', which broadly spanned 1988 and 1989. As they began playing near wall-to-wall acid house, clubs saw attendances skyrocket. Slam run an eclectic night called 'Black Market' at Fury Murrys on Maxwell Street from 1987, but in July 1988 made their debut proper with a swiftly well-attended, acid-house-heavy Saturday night residency at Tin Pan Alley on Mitchell Street. Newspapers were full of stories about a new youth craze. Slam's manager, Dave Clarke, recalls his dad reading an article in the paper and asking 'What are all these acid houses?' Dance music was breaking out into popular culture at large, carried by epochal Mancunian bands such as The Happy Mondays and The Stone Roses. Slam's fortunes, like those of many DJs around this time, were commensurately in the ascent.

In September 1988, as Sub Club began to lock into acid house's groove, they began a regular Friday night

Above, top: Jamiaca Street hoarding next to the club entrance.

Above: Front door signage.

Opposite, above: Sub Club interior.

Opposite, below: Harri Domenic Oscar promo graphic.

Below: Subculture poster.

Inset: Forthcoming gigs on Jamaica Street hoarding.

slot called 'Joy' (the original, less-than-subtle moniker 'Ecstasy' was dropped for obvious reasons), which would run until early 1992. In the summer of 1989, Slam embarked on a beer-brand sponsored tour of Scotland that peaked on 27 September with an infamous all-nighter at the 1,500-capacity Tramway. Some of the biggest names in acid house were present, from Hacienda DJ, Mike Pickering, to Detroit Techno pioneer, Kevin Saunderson, and live acts, Inner City and 808 State. A sensationalist advertising campaign had seen psychedelic posters enigmatically appear across cities around the UK and ensured that anticipation was at fever pitch. The event was massively over-attended – buses arrived from as far away as the Hacienda itself. As the crowd spilled out across Albert Drive at the end of the night, the police had to close the street and call in the riot squad.

The following day Slam flew to Ibiza to begin a DJ residency, returning to Glasgow some weeks later expecting the Tramway event's controversy to have killed the party for good. Far from it: acid house was bigger than ever, and Sub Club, like every venue that Slam played, was routinely full to capacity. In March 1990, the Tramway all-nighter was reprised at the SECC under more organised conditions, in collaboration with promoter Regular Music, drawing 3,500 revellers.

The following month Slam started DJing on Saturday nights at Sub Club as well as on Fridays. Sub Club teamed up with Harri for the fondly remembered 'Atlantis' club nights, which, following a slow start, exploded in popularity after they played the official after-party for The Stone Roses' Glasgow Green show that June. It ran until 1994, when Slam – now more focused on the forward-thinking possibilities of techno over party-friendly house – decided to concentrate their efforts at the newly opened Arches. There they

Right: Little Boots at Sub Club, 2009.

hosted weekly Slam Fridays between 1991 and 1998, then from 1998 to the present day a monthly techno night called 'Pressure'. They've also been back at Sub Club since 2004 with a monthly house night called 'Return To Mono'. With Domenic Capello joining him on the decks, Harri's Saturday night residency at Sub Club continued under the name 'Subculture' from 1994, and has remained a Glasgow institution ever since. It probably makes Harri an unofficial world-record holder: no one has yet claimed to have consistently DJed house music longer.

Where the Sub Club was 'shoe-box sized', with just one bar and years of history ground into its sticky carpet, The Arches, situated just around the corner, was something very different. Today it is one of Europe's leading multi-arts venues. In the late 1980s it was still a warren of dank, echoey, rat-infested railway arches beneath Central Station. It was partially redeveloped to host an exhibition, *Glasgow's Glasgow*, for Glasgow's year as European City of Culture in 1990 (itself a boon for clubbing, as 5am licenses became available year-long). Theatre director, Andy Arnold, then took on the space as a milieu for cutting-edge performing arts, opening in 1991 and cleverly identifying in Glasgow's burgeoning club scene a revenue stream to fund the rest of the enterprise. In April 1992, 'Friday Night With Slam' became the first resident club night. Almost every big name in the clubbing world has since played The Arches, helping to fund its diverse and innovative multi-arts programme.

By the early 1990s the public mood towards dance music culture had begun to sour. Police were cracking down heavily on large-scale illegal 'raves', held first in abandoned urban spaces such as old warehouses and factories then in the countryside anywhere from fields to quarries. A media backlash accompanied,

Below: On the decks at Sub Club.

and in 1994 the government passed the notorious Criminal Justice and Public Order Act that included an ill-defined clause prohibiting mass unsanctioned gatherings with music characterised by 'repetitive beats'. Ostensibly in a bid to tackle street violence, Glasgow District Licensing Board in June 1993 brought in the much-maligned curfew – a draconian ruling that drew closing times back to 2am and required anyone wishing to attend a nightclub to be inside by midnight, at a stroke stopping patrons from migrating between clubs over the course of a night. The curfew provoked street protests by outraged clubbers and its effects on Glasgow clubland were debilitating. Sub Club – sold by McLeod to the MacCrimmon family (father Kenny, sons Michael and Tony) in 1992 – suffered no less than anywhere else before restrictions were relaxed in 1995 (the curfew wasn't formally dropped until as late as 2009). Sub Club was finding increasing competition from other clubs as electronic dance music went firmly overground. Attendances at The Subby had dropped off sharply by the time Mike Grieve and Paul Crawford took over in 1994. Some Fridays the place wasn't even open.

In a bid to put down roots amid the heady uncertainty

Below: I Am – Standard Sub Club Tuesdays.

of the times, Slam had launched their own label, Soma Quality Recordings, in 1991. As well as releasing their own music with a lot of success, they also began to help break new talent in house and techno. This included a certain Daft Punk, today one of the world's biggest electronic dance artists, who released their first two singles on Soma and made their UK live debut at The Arches in January 1997. By July that same year, the Slam brand had grown so renowned that they were invited to organise and oversee a stage at the new and fast-growing *T in the Park* festival. The Slam Tent's first-year capacity of 4,000 has since doubled to 8,000, and they've booked acts from The Chemical Brothers to Orbital, DJ Shadow, 2 Many DJs and Leftfield.

Sub Club, meanwhile, was re-energised under new management, with refurbishments in 1996 and 1997 adding extra space and a second bar. Then in November 1997, Sub Club got the major shot in the arm it and Glasgow's club scene needed, courtesy of two DJs with a mission statement to 'break down the bullshit that exists in DJ culture'. The cult of the weekly club night 'Optimo (Espacio)' was such that it practically redefined the working week for Glasgow clubbers, as Sundays – it being on Sundays that it began and defiantly stayed – became the new Saturdays.

In the face of what they saw as an increasingly masculine, commercialised club culture, the Optimo DJs, Keith 'JD Twitch' McIvor and Jonnie 'JG Wilkes' Wilkes, sought to reconnect with clubbing's rebellious spirit of freedom and inclusiveness. They had met when McIvor co-ran the seminal Edinburgh techno night 'Pure, and their policy on the decks was unbridled eclecticism: you were just as likely to hear acid house and techno as you were post-punk, funk, psychedelia and experimental electronica. Another key contrast – and this more than anything probably opened them up to many new converts – was that they would invite up-and-coming

Above: Highlife, 2011.

Below: Interior.

Below: View from the decks.

bands to perform live, both from the Glasgow scene and further afield. Among them were Hot Chip, Franz Ferdinand, The Rapture, Peaches and LCD Soundsystem. It took about a year to build up a regular crowd, but once the 'collective light bulb went off', as McIvor puts it, Optimo began routinely selling-out, with queues snaking around the block whether people had work the next morning or not.

By 1999, Sub Club was going 'like a train', says Grieve, who was already beginning to plan his exit strategy with business peaking. Then in November that year came the fateful Sunday night when McIvor and Wilkes arrived at Sub Club as usual to see blue flashing lights illuminating Jamaica Street. The old post office building adjacent to the venue was on fire, but they were assured that all was under control and that they'd be in the club by midnight. Minutes later, as flames licked the night sky, all present could already tell that the wait was going to be longer – even if they could never have guessed just how long. In the end it was days, weeks, months, then years.

The Sub Club's closure due to extensive water damage incurred during that fire was a huge blow not just for the resident DJs but for the entire Glasgow scene (Soma had their offices above the venue and were likewise made homeless). Grieve admits that had he known then the nightmarish length of time it would take to get back in business, he'd have cut his losses and quit. As it was, with wrangles with insurers and niggling planning problems scuppering deadlines and dragging the rebuilding process out towards no sure end, Sub Club and its resident nights kept going in temporary locations – first in Planet Peach (now Cube) on Queen Street, then from 2001 in Mas on Royal Exchange Square.

Somewhat bravely, considering it was then still a wreck, Grieve, Crawford and backers eventually moved to buy Sub Club from the MacCrimmons, completing the deal in October 2002. A month later the venue finally reopened, almost three years to the day since the fire. Drawing upon their combined years of clubbing experience, the new, improved Sub Club was Glasgow's first custom-designed electronic dance music venue – probably the only one in Britain besides London's Fabric. It had a state-of-the-art sound system, a bass-frequencies-channelling Bodysonic dance floor and an official capacity of just 410. Sub Club celebrated its 25th anniversary in 2012 with its busiest year since 1991. Over its quarter-century it has welcomed an estimated two million guests, played over 25,000 hours of music and become the world's longest-running underground dance club.

Some key Glasgow club venues have shifted into musical history. Glasgow School of Art Students Association's The Vic reopened in 2014 after a major rebuild, but it will remain most fondly remembered by older patrons in its previous, scuzzier condition. New clubs have risen to prominence in recent years, such as La Cheetah, The Berkeley Suite and the SWG3 Studio Warehouse, which hosts the 'Electric Frog' dance music festivals. Optimo ended on 25 April 2010, when McIvor and Wilkes decided to quit on a high and concentrate on remixing, producing bands, releasing records on their Optimo Music label and DJing around the world. They still host occasional nights at Sub Club and elsewhere in Glasgow. In their footsteps have followed a younger generation who are re-inventing the scene anew. There are collectives such as LuckyMe and Numbers, and genres-spanning mobs of local labels, promoters, DJs and producers who are making waves around the electronic music world, led by rising stars such as Jackmaster, Éclair Fifi, Rustie and Hudson Mohawke.

British electronic dance music is still on much of a gravity-defying high. If one thing more than any other can explain Glasgow's centrality to the wider scene, it's surely the people: an inspiring, illogical mix of innovators, hedonists, misfits, motivators and miscreants who are enslaved to the beat with a passion and energy that often flaunts good sense. There's McIvor and Wilkes, who once didn't let a DJ set in Tokyo prevent them from making it back to Glasgow for Optimo the following night; there's Harri, 30 years and counting on the scene and still loathe to miss a single Saturday at The Subby; and not least, there's the city's indefatigable party people, who in their thousands every weekend define that Glasgow word 'gallus' by turning night into day and then back into night again. Now – where's the after-party?

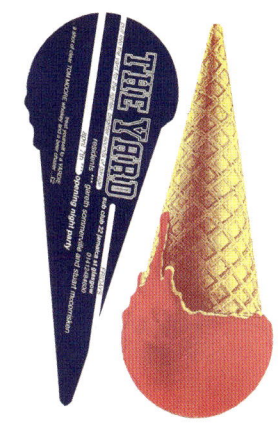

Above: Promo graphic for The Yard.

Below: The crowd during Eliphino's set, 2012.

VENUE · BAR · CAFE

King Tu
wah w
"BEST UK LIVE VENU

King Tuts
Glasgow, Scotland
Wah W

Left: KIng Tut's entrance.

Right: Promo badge to mark 15 years of the club.

KING TUT'S WAH WAH HUT

Vic Galloway

The lifeblood of any music community is its live venues, and one of the main reasons for Glasgow's ongoing blossoming as a cultural epicentre is the infrastructure of clubs and spaces available to local and touring acts. Since its inception and opening in 1990, one venue has been key to Glasgow's growing kudos as a global music hub: King Tut's Wah Wah Hut is regarded globally as one of the finest venues of its size anywhere – and for good reason.

Situated in central Glasgow at 272a St Vincent Street, King Tut's is surrounded, slightly incongruously, by offices, law firms, estate agents and residential properties. But it's well positioned in relation to train, bus and underground stations; is only a stone's throw from the nightly alcohol-induced mayhem of Sauchiehall Street; and is within reasonable walking distance of Glasgow's leafy, student West End. It might not be directly next door to other pubs or clubs, but it is easily accessible to almost anyone in the city centre. These details sound mundane but can make-or-break a venue that's trying to attract punters through the door.

In the 1970s and 1980s, the place was called Saints & Sinners: a low rent, low maintenance biker bar decked out in regulation chrome and red leather booths. One can imagine the beer and whisky flowing, the reek of leather and patchouli oil and the sound of classic blues rock on the shabby jukebox. The place must

KING TUT'S WAH WAH HUT

Location: 272a St Vincent Street, Glasgow, G2 5RL
Capacity: 300
Date opened: 1990
Music: Rock/Pop/Indie
website: www.kingtuts.co.uk/

have had character at the very least, but it remained somewhat unspectacular. In the early days of UK punk rock, one of Glasgow's few genuine safety-pinned combos, Johnny and the Self-Abusers (soon to rename themselves Simple Minds and achieve global success), wrote a song about the venue where they'd played their second gig. 'Saints & Sinners' appeared as their only single on Chiswick Records in August 1977: an adrenalised, speed-addled dash that's done and dusted in less than two minutes. Men and women of a certain vintage speak fondly of the place, but any nostalgia is usually forgotten when they realise how far it's come since then.

Cue DF Concerts, a fledgling but ambitious promotions company that started life in Dundee but soon realised that Glasgow was the place to be for anyone who wanted to have direct impact on Scotland's developing musicians and audience. In the late 1980s, the then DF boss, Stuart Clumpas, honed in on Saints & Sinners as a platform for promoting bands at small-sized club level, with nightly gigs staged at a reasonable hour and a reasonable price. Appropriating the unforgettable moniker, King Tut's Wah Wah Hut, from a New York City club on Avenue A that specialised in performance art in the early 1980s, DF gave a fresher, funkier image to the venue and everything it would soon stand for.

With a well-stocked bar, a pool table and cafe furniture shifted downstairs to leave a 300-capacity gig space above, Tut's immediately felt different with only limited redecoration. DF opened offices above and next door to the club, creating an in-house team spirit that pervaded promoters, sound engineers, bar managers and staff as the venue began to establish itself within the local consciousness.

From Tut's first official concert on 8 February 1990 – Geordie troubadour Martin Stephenson and his band The Daintees – it was clear that the new venture meant business. While Clumpas tended to liaise with bigger agents and touring acts, it was infamous Glasgow DJ, promoter and gob-on-a-stick, Tam Coyle, who would deal with most local artists. Coyle was the first of what would become a succession of hard-working, dedicated and knowledgeable promoters with their ear to the ground and their radar twitching for the next big thing. His first sell-out promotion was a hyped Manchester beat-combo-of-the-moment called The Charlatans; neighbourhood acts who could routinely pack the place included Glass Onion, featuring future members of Travis. Both groups went on to sell millions of records and play to crowds of thousands in the not-so-distant future. Another act to grace the King Tut stage in its first year was Blur, a band that would soon help to reshape UK guitar music and pop culture as a leading light of the Britpop movement. From the outset, the Tut's team was on the right track.

With wheels set in motion at the hands of Coyle and the ambitious forward-thinking Clumpas, the venue firmly rooted itself in a nationwide touring circuit and gained a unique reputation for looking after its visiting acts. Musicians were treated to a two-course meal, a small rider and a dressing-room – and, most important, to real friendliness and respect from the staff. This was the heyday of the UK 'toilet circuit': small venues of 100–300 capacity with erratic PA systems, sticky floors, watery beer and shabby interior decors that were poorly or thriftily maintained, easy to perform at and cheap for punters. Playing the circuit was (and still is) an essential right of passage for most touring acts.

All the while, King Tut's level of hospitality was rare to say the least. With countless bands crossing paths

Below: The King Blues crowd, in 2009.

Left: King Tut's iconic steps leading down to the club.

up and down the motorways of Great Britain, swapping stories with tour managers, agents and promoters, it was only a matter of time before Tut's was hoisted above the mire. Not only were artists treated well, but the Glasgow crowd often proved itself the liveliest and most appreciative of an entire tour.

Geoff Ellis, a go-getting, gruff-voiced Mancunian, replaced Coyle as promoter in 1992 and shortly after landed the club its most notorious evening. A Creation Records' line-up of local acts in May 1993 was headlined by 18 Wheeler; in the crowd was the label's mogul and impresario, Alan McGee. A bolshy Manchester quintet showed up unannounced and bullied their way onto the bill (or so the story goes), insisting that they play four songs. McGee's jaw dropped to the sound of 'Supersonic' and Oasis were signed straight after walking offstage. Thus began the most successful British band of the 1990s and 2000s. Was it some kind of divine synchronism? Would another venue have allowed the band to play? Was it just good fortune, or was the band especially talented? Whatever the case, the legend has stood King Tut's in good stead ever since.

News spread about Oasis, about the vibrant local music scene and the relative comforts afforded to touring bands, and a roll-call of soon-to-be-famous names was booked at Tut's on a weekly basis. Radiohead, Pulp, The Verve, Crowded House, Beck and Manic Street Preachers all trod the boards, each band set for massive success just around the corner. At their *T in the Park* headline set in 1999, James Dean Bradfield of the Manics dedicated a song to the venue: 'King Tut's was the first venue to treat us properly and give us hot food on tour,' he told the festival crowd.

Tut's was fast achieving iconic status. Of course there were other well-kent venues across the UK: TJ's in Newport, The Cockpit in Leeds, The Charlotte in Leicester, The Venue in Edinburgh, The Square in Harlow and various others. But Tut's was clean, tidy, well-organised and provided even the lowest-level bands with food and refreshments. It was a step above most other establishments of a similar size and garnered a reputation for just that. Soon it was a touring staple and a holy grail for local acts. Such repute was unheralded for a 300-capacity live club. Tut's became more than a grubby little gig: soon it was THE place to play.

And so the brand began to proliferate. DF Concerts launched *T in the Park* – Scotland's first major annual rock festival – in 1994 and named one of its featured tents in honour of Tut's. And, after 20 years of *T in the Park*, in 2013 the King Tut's Wah Wah Hut tent still replicates the role played by the venue itself: it provides a platform for developing acts on their way to playing the main stage. The vast success of the festival has

Below: Twin Atlantic play at King Tut's Wah Wah Hut a day after their biggest headline show to date sold-out at The ABC.

Above: Paloma Faith, 2009.

Below: First Tiger, 2009.

has only grown in stature since his arrival. He remembers being congratulated on his first sell-out show (Berlin electro-punks Atari Teenage Riot) and beams with pride when recounting the time he booked his childhood hero, Joe Strummer, with his new band, The Mescaleros, in June 1999.

Under McGeachan's watchful eye, a veritable hall of fame has passed through the venue's doors. Among many others, The Strokes, Muse, The Killers, Kasabian, Snow Patrol, Radiohead, Amy Winehouse, Jamie Cullum, Paramore, My Chemical Romance, Florence and the Machine, Paulo Nutini and Frightened Rabbit have all performed on the tiny Tut's stage. A special mention should go to Biffy Clyro, who were tirelessly championed by McGeachan, Tut's, DF Concerts and *T in the Park*. The band played the club about a dozen times on their way to mainstream success. But it's Glasgow indie-rockers Catcher who hold the record for the sheer number of Tut's bookings, with a staggering 41 appearances – so far.

In 2002, after the club underwent its first major refurbishment since transforming from Saints & Sinners, Stuart Clumpas retired from DF Concerts and moved to Australia on account of a diagnosis of Crohn's disease and a desire for change. Geoff Ellis scaled the dizzy heights and became CEO of DF Concerts, but Tut's has remained in the hands of McGeachan and various understudies – the equally committed Craig Johnston is now McGeachan's right-hand man. In the past decade the venue has diversified into promoting comedy, Saturday jazz matinees, a music networking social night called 'Your Sound' and two annual festivals of up-and-coming talent – *New Year's Revolution* in January and *Summer Nights* in July. It has started its own record label called King Tut's Recordings, which has released a number of largely rock-orientated regional acts including Twin Atlantic, The Xcerts, The Dykeenies and others.

McGeachan stresses that it's still the two-course menu, classy shower facilities, 7-foot fridge and graffiti-free dressing rooms (except on the allocated fridge door and toilet seat lid) that have made King Tut's stand apart from the vast majority of similar venues. But there must be more to it than that, judging by the accolades heaped upon the place year after year. The *Scottish License Trade News* named King Tut's the 'Licensed Music Pub of the Year' in 2001. *NME* magazine proclaimed it 'Britain's Best Small Venue' in 2011. Listeners of BBC Radio 1 voted it 'Best Live Venue' three years in a row as well as 'Best Launch Pad Venue' over

been good for the venue, naturally, but has also had a wider impact. More than 80,000 people now attend every year, and the King Tut's tent has introduced a mainstream audience to the joys of small concerts. If a show at King Tut's Wah Wah Hut becomes attractive to an infrequent gig-going audience, that same audience might also consider visiting one of Glasgow's other excellent small venues – the likes of Nice'N'Sleazy, Stereo, Broadcast, The Cathouse or The 13th Note. King Tut's might be the most visible, popular and populist of Glasgow's small venues, but it's also a catalyst, attuning its regulars to hearing cutting-edge grass-roots bands up close.

Dave McGeachan took over the reins as main booker in March 1999 and remains the man most closely associated with King Tut's. A fast-talking, wide-eyed Gourock-based music obsessive and local promoter, McGeachan had frequented the venue as a fan and enthusiast from the start and eventually befriended the booking team. The move was an obvious and natural one. Geoff Ellis was still involved in the Tut's team, but was also fast rising through the ranks of DF Concerts and taking a greater role in the ever-expanding *T in the Park*. With McGeachan's unfaltering work ethic and unending dedication to the venue, the place its lifespan. The 10th, 15th and 20th anniversary parties have been celebrated in style, with willing big names and surprise guests playing to packed audiences each time.

It should be pointed out that, unlike other small venues in Glasgow, King Tut's has the might of DF Concerts behind it to bankroll losses if and when they happen. DF are now Scotland's biggest promoters and can take risks in a way that others can't afford. The company also has sponsorship links with Tennent's dating back to the beginning of *T in the Park*. It's possible that a few similar-sized Glasgow venues do resent the fact that Tut's has both DF underwriting costs and a close relationship with Tennent's. There is a fiercely DIY/indie/punk ethos among some musicians and promoters in Glasgow, some of whom probably see King Tut's as too corporate. But they have their own venues and spaces and have created their own scene – one that is renowned across the world. Having DF Concerts and King Tut's operating in the way that they do is probably beneficial to Scotland's grassroots music scene and King Tut's serves as a bottom-feeder to the bigger stages in Glasgow and across Scotland. And anyway, corporate heft shouldn't undermine the venue's reputation.

Tut's has consistently led the way for other establishments to follow. Before it, most of Glasgow's entry-level venues either didn't exist or were poorly operated. Tut's has contributed to a nascent music scene that is now one of the healthiest in the world. What's more, it is still one of the best places in town to watch a new band strut their stuff.

Above: Paolo Nutini, 2006.

Left: Idlewild, 2008.

MONO
Going off the rails in a place where nothing's ever black and white

Neil Cooper

Onstage there's a young woman in a white jump suit having her head shaved by a young man in a leopardskin dress. David Bowie's 'Rebel Rebel' blares out the speakers while a young audience looks on. Even by the standards of the vegetarian cafe/bar/venue that is Mono, this Thursday teatime performance is an eccentric spectacle. The haircut performance marks the launch of the 2013 edition of the live art festival, *Buzzcut*, which has moved into Mono's speakeasy environs for the first time. If ever proof was needed, *Buzzcut*'s plethora of similarly off-the-wall events demonstrates that the venue's open-minded and inclusive policy goes miles beyond its left-field musical constituency.

Seated at a table over snacks, someone is opening up the gatefold sleeve of the vinyl edition of Bowie's new surprise album, *The Next Day*. The album has just been purchased from Monorail Music, the impeccably stocked record shop housed next to the bar and lovingly co-owned and run by Glasgow music legend Stephen McRobbie, aka Stephen Pastel, in partnership with Dep Downie, who also runs the Watts of Goodwill record label. McRobbie's band, The Pastels, has ploughed a wilfully individual furrow for some 30 years and has left its mark on at least two generations of Glasgow bands. Tucked away at the back of the room, the Good Press emporium sells limited-run

Above: Sunset at Mono, 2014.

MONO / MONORAIL MUSIC

Location: 12 Kings Court, Glasgow, G1 5RB
Capacity: 60
Date opened: 2002
Music: Multi Bands, DJs, Experimental, Indie, Lo-fi
website: www.monorailmusic.com

magazines, comics and arty books – all as appealingly tactile as the vinyl on sale in Monorail.

One of those records is the last-but-one copy of *Some Songs Side-by-Side*, a 2 x 12-inch box set compilation of eight Glasgow bands released in a collaboration between three micro-labels (RE:PEATER Records, Watts of Goodwill, and Stereo, run by Mono's sister venue of the same name). Whether any of the bands featured on the compilation are still with us by the time you are reading this remains to be seen, so fast-movingly fluid is the Glasgow scene. But for the record, Tut Vu Vu, Palms, Organs of Love, Gummy Stumps, Sacred Paws, The Rosy Crucifixion, Muscles of Joy, and Jacob Yates and the Pearly Gate Lock Pickers are still very much alive at the time of writing – although one or all of them could cross-fertilise and morph any minute into a new entity.

All of which goes some way to illustrating the fecund hub of activity that centres around Mono. The venue has roots tracing back through a welter of independently-minded initiatives in Glasgow – including the original 13th Note, the music department of John Smith's Bookshop on Byres Road, and the mid-1980s Splash One Sunday club nights. These tentacles reach right back to Postcard Records and the Third Eye Centre, Glasgow's multi-purpose arts lab that existed in Sauchiehall Street from 1972 to the early 1990s when it morphed into the more corporate-feeling Centre of Contemporary Arts (CCA).

As Glasgow's first multiple-arts space, the Third Eye fostered an environment where art forms crossed over in an open-minded spirit of collaboration and cooperation. Under its influence, a spate of independent, cooperatively run art spaces such as Transmission and Street Level developed throughout the 1980s, with Glasgow's music and art scene coexisting to the point of intimacy. Many visual artists formed bands or used music and sound as a key part of their practice. (It's no coincidence that the artwork that accompanies the *Some Songs Side-By-Side* box set are by the likes of Turner Prize winner, Richard Wright, Turner nominee, David Shrigley, and Tony Swain, all of whom have strong musical connections.) As the CCA has gradually stripped itself back to a rougher aesthetic, so Mono carries the Third Eye flame in a continuum of DIY artistic action.

Since the early 2000s, Mono, in conjunction with its sister bar, Stereo, has become one of the most significant

Inset, top: Mono interior atrium.

Inset, middle: Mono microbrewery.

Inset, bottom: DJ Jim at Mono, 2007.

venues in the city. Sitting on the edge of the Trongate in the network of converted railway arches that make up King's Court – vintage clothes shops, T-shirt printers and musical instrument sellers with a working railway track above – Mono hosts a regular stream of left-field artists without ever feeling like a workaday touring circuit. Special events are the norm. Take, for example, 2013's International Record Store Day, which saw hordes of music obsessives queueing from early morning, all intent on snapping up a limited edition purchase from Monorail Music. With such congestion, shoppers also had a chance to cast an eye over an installation entitled Seven Inch that consisted of seven-inch singles by imaginary bands dreamt up by 21 Glasgow-based artists. Each artist had created their own fictional 'single' in the form of a seven-inch double-sided label artwork. What their singles sounded like we'll never know.

Above: Perfect Pussy, 2014.

Below: Herman Dune, 2006.

Mono's live programme for the day culminated in a collaboration between Vic Godard and The Sexual Objects. Godard was the man whose band, Subway Sect, supported The Clash at the Edinburgh Playhouse during the Scottish leg of the May 1977 White Riot Tour. At the time Glasgow's concerned city fathers had banned all 'punk' gigs, so audience members at that Edinburgh show included Alan Horne, who would go on to found Postcard Records, and Horne's co-conspirator, Edwyn Collins, who with Alan Duncan would form Postcard's premier band, Orange Juice.

Also in attendance that night was Davy Henderson, who in 1980 formed the Fire Engines, arguably Scotland's most abrasively daring art-punk act. Henderson would later form the glossier Win, then the Nectarine No. 9, before briefly regrouping the Fire Engines to support The Magic Band, Sun Ra's Arkestra, and Franz Ferdinand. The latter owe much to the Fire Engines, as well as to the 'Sound of Young Scotland' that Alan Horne branded across his Postcard acts. Nowadays, Davy Henderson fires on all cylinders as frontman of The Sexual Objects; putting him on stage with Godard to play under the name Sectual Objects – as Mono did on International Record Day 2013 – was an inspired move. Their set of Velvet Underground covers mixed and matched several generations of influences and progeny in a way that typified Mono's ethos.

All of this is a far cry from how Glasgow used to be, when the only available small-scale venues were either spit-and-sawdust dives with unsympathetic landlords and the very real prospect of getting a kicking, or chrome-lined nightclubs more used to hosting weekend stag crowds than a radical new music community in search of somewhere safe to land. One such co-opted after-hours emporium was Daddy Warbucks, located just around the corner from Queen Street Station on West George Street. An indie club night called Splash One started taking over its glossy disco on Sunday nights in the mid-1980s. Essentially Splash One aspired to be Andy Warhol's Factory, putting on bands like The Pastels, The Shop Assistants, Primal Scream, The Soup Dragons, and The Jesus and Mary Chain between a relentless 1960s psych/post-punk soundtrack. As far as the club owners were concerned, it was just another hire – not the social movement signalling a nascent state of independence that in fact it was. A new model was needed.

Above: Monorail Music.

Below: Tuff Love, 2014.

Enter one Craig Tannock. A Glasgow music scene stalwart, Tannock had played in bands and run rehearsal studios including Tower Studios in Park Circus. Tannock had a knack of attracting good people around him, and Tower was run on a much friendlier basis than more commercially-minded operations. At Tower, the music and musicians came first – an ethos that Tannock took with him when he opened The Apollo, a small club space in a tenement building close to the site of the legendary Glasgow venue of the same name. Part rehearsal room, part venue, Tannock's Apollo allowed bands the luxury of practice rooms next door to a gig rather than in another part of the city.

The Apollo closed after the building above it flooded, but Tannock's egalitarian approach had already fostered a community spirit that helped sow the seeds for his next venture, the fancifully named 13th Note. Originally on Glassford Street, the 13th Note opened to an already thriving indie scene that – true to the term – was increasingly operating on its own terms. Labels like Chemikal Underground and Creeping Bent had inherited Postcard Records' mantle, while numerous micro-labels released a spate of limited-edition seven-inch singles. At the 13th Note, bands such as Urusei Yatsura, Bis and Mogwa were finding a natural home.

Some of 13th's booking was handled by Alex Huntly, who at various points was singer with The Blisters and The Karelia. As Alex Kapranos – lead singer of Franz Ferdinand – he would go on to take that band's brand of art-pop into the mainstream via a coup of pop entry-ism in excelsis.

For a time, the 13th Note was the centre of Glasgow's independent musical universe, with Tannock once again attracting a core of like-minded individuals to the cause. But eventually problems with the Glassford Street lease and structural faults in the building made it necessary for him to move out. The 13th Note shifted to King Street, close to Transmission and Street Level, and a second venue, the larger 13th Note club, opened on Clyde Street. As the venue moved and split in two, so too did some of the personnel and the vibe that went with the original 13th Note.

Sustaining two venues proved difficult, and operations were eventually wound up. The Clyde Street club was taken over by the UK-wide Barfly chain, while the King Street premises were adopted by new management who recognised a good thing and retain the 13th Note name to this day. Tannock opened West 13th on Kelvinhaugh Street in the West End, a small bar space that morphed into the first incarnation of Stereo before becoming The 78 in February 2007. Tannock has also managed to get back into the building that had housed his Apollo with a bar and club venue, the Flying Duck.

Stereo eventually moved to its current city-centre base in Renfield Lane. The two-floor space it occupies was designed by Charles Rennie Mackintosh, who also designed Glasgow School of Art. As a symbol of the criss-crossing between Glasgow's artistic endeavours it couldn't be more perfect. This has become even more so since Tannock opened The Old Hairdresser's in June 2011 directly opposite, and designed to complement, Stereo. The bijou space has become a hub for pop-up DIY gigs and live art events – yet again highlighting the promiscuous nature of the city's art and music scenes.

While all this was going on, Stephen McRobbie was working in the music department of the now-closed John Smith's bookshop next to Hillhead Underground on Byres Road. Although managed by Simon Black, Smith's, like Monorail Music later, was manned by a team of like-minded spirits brought together by a love of what they were selling and a loose-knit but instinctive affiliation with an independent ethos. The records stocked in the shop made up a treasure trove of free-thinking music past and present, local and international, and the shop attracted a core custom base of those in the know – as well as the odd star-struck Pastels pilgrim from Japan, where they and so many other Scottish bands have a devoted following.

When it closed at the end of the 20th century to become one more branch of Starbucks, John Smith's left a musical void, and McRobbie, alongside kindred spirit, John Williamson, decreed that they would find a new place to sell the sort of records that regular shops didn't stock. Like Tannock, Williamson was a Glasgow music scene stalwart who has variously been a journalist, a promoter, the manager of Belle and Sebastian, and an academic. In time he would become the quietly pragmatic Yang to Tannock's more mercurial Yin, as well as the obvious choice to provide the introductory text for *Some Songs Side By Side*.

With Tannock also on the hunt for a new venue in order to expand his existing operations beyond Stereo and The 78, the synergies between the two ventures proved irresistible. As soon as Tannock scouted the King's Court site – previously it had housed a Mexican restaurant – it was clear that a new era of grass-roots music activity was about to begin. Mono opened as a bar and cafe in October 2002, with Monorail Music launching in the same premises in December that same year.

While Stereo was initially the main focus for gigs, Mono eventually developed just as much of a focus for live music and is now on equal footing with its sister venue. In its first decade of existence, the musical landscape has shifted dramatically, so that a whole new generation of musicians, artists and – crucially – promoters have embraced a DIY ethos and a community-based ideology like never before. Nowhere is this captured better than in Mono.

All those involved in Mono and the assorted ventures that it houses are clearly kindred spirits. Their activities overlap and inspire each other, even as their businesses are kept separate, which helps to create a looser, less defined and more fluid relationship. Mono as a whole gets on well with its neighbours and hosts an annual exhibition by Project Ability, the Glasgow-based charity that enables adults and children with learning disabilities or mental health issues to create their own art. Other exhibitions have included a very telling show of posters and flyers from Splash One.

A dynasty of sorts has grown out of Mono. While young promoters such as Cry Parrot put on a series of small but imperfectly formed events there, it's telling that former personnel of West 13th, Stereo and

Mono now run Saramango, the vegetarian cafe at the CCA that has done much to recapture the atmosphere of the old Third Eye Centre. Altogether it adds up to something akin to a – whisper it – Socialist spirit that has been ingrained in the Glaswegian sensibility since the days of Red Clydeside.

For Mono's tenth anniversary in November 2012, the venue hosted a party featuring three acts. Muscles of Joy opened, followed by RM Hubbert, who would go on to win the 2013 'Scottish Album of the Year' award. While both have multiple links with Glasgow's art and music scenes, it was headliners Franz Ferdinand's first home-town appearance for four years that was most significant. They could have sold out the nearby Barrowlands several times over, so the fact that they were playing in a cafe/bar to a couple of hundred of their peers spoke volumes. In the songs, attitude and aesthetic that lived and breathed from Postcard Records onwards, here was a crucial umbilical link with Glasgow's musical past, present and future. The state of independence has been accomplished, and its living embodiment occupies a republic called Mono.

Top: Franz Ferdinand at Mono's 10th anniversary party, 2012.

Above: Edwyn Collins, 2009.

THE GLASGOW ROYAL CONCERT HALL

Tom Service

Left: The Glasgow Royal Concert Hall on completeion of contstruction.

Maybe it was just as well the boxing didn't happen. Cameron McNicol, director of the Glasgow International Concert Hall, spoke of his ambition in early 1990 that the multipurpose versatility of the building should accommodate badminton as well as Beethoven, snooker alongside Schubert, and boxing cheek-by-jowl with Brahms.

'There are certain people who think it will be outrageous to stage boxing in it. I'm not one of them,' McNicol said. Outrageous, maybe not; dangerous, quite possibly. Boxing and Glasgow's concert halls don't exactly have an auspicious history – witness a certain night in the autumn of 1962, an amateur pugilistic spectacle between Scotland and Romania, and a solo stray cigarette. But even if the boxing didn't end up as part of Glasgow Royal Concert Hall's agenda (the 'Royal' came as soon as the hall opened, an honour bestowed by Princess Anne), the hall's virtuosic multi-generic uses certainly did and have continued to do so. In the first year Glaswegians welcomed, among others, Runrig and the Berlin Philharmonic, The Blue Nile and the St Petersburg Philharmonic Orchestra.

Today, the Glasgow Royal Concert Hall (GRCH) is the home of the Royal Scottish National Orchestra (RSNO) and the *Celtic Connections* festival, of education and community projects, of pop and rock acts. Its place in the city's cultural life as the physical successor to St Andrew's Halls was assured as soon as the 2,500-seat auditorium opened in the autumn of 1990, one of the grand climaxes of Glasgow's year as European Capital of Culture. But whether the GRCH has always lived up to the expectations of the musical public and city planners' ambitions to become one of the key national and international venues for music, especially large-scale classical music, is another question.

But that's getting ahead of ourselves. There was already controversy around Glasgow about the hall during its planning and construction at the end of the 1980s – a controversy immortalised by the epithet 'Lally's Palais'. Pat Lally, leader of Glasgow District Council in the early 1990s and one of the larger-than-life figures in the city's local politics, had a dream. The new hall would be the most expensive, the most visible, and the most lasting legacy of Glasgow 1990. And it would be the people's hall – not least because £27 million of the people's money would pay for it. On 26 January 1990, Lally spoke of the new building as 'the Great Hall of the People of Glasgow' and said: 'We intend to ensure that it is for the privileged and the underprivileged, for the prosperous and the poor; to ensure that all of our citizens feel that this is their hall, and that they have the opportunity to enjoy performances in it.'

Lally was indirectly answering criticisms that the hall would mostly be putting on a programme of 'elitist' classical music, and that the district council had put up rents disproportionately fast to pay for the city's capital funding projects for 1990. (There was also an allegation that the council had sold off property at inflated prices specifically to generate the millions required by the concert hall's construction.) The hall's programme needed to be of sufficient international quality to impress audiences and critics, but it also needed to demonstrate that Lally's anti-elitist

GLASGOW ROYAL CONCERT HALL

Location: 2 Sauchiehall Street, Glasgow, G2 3NY
Architect: Sir Leslie Martin
Capacity: 4 halls; 2475, 600, 450 120
Date opened: 1990
Music: Multi, Choral, Classical, Folk, Celtic
website: www.glasgowconcerthalls.com

philosophy would translate into a genuinely popular venue. And, in 1990, all of its events needed to be cheap enough to make the hall feel like the centre of a festival city as much as merely – merely! – the heart of the city's musical life.

The location, at least, could hardly have been better chosen, at the corner of Buchanan Street and Sauchiehall Street. The new hall would be smack-bang between the city's great performing venues and cultural institutions: to the west the Theatre Royal, the Pavilion Theatre and the Royal Conservatoire of Scotland; to the south and east the City Halls and the Modern Art Gallery. But the GRCH would also be at the beating heart of the city's shopping district, and on a site that gives some of the best views south across Glasgow. Even though the behemothic Buchanan Galleries shopping centre now dominates the skyline to your left, the perspective granted from the stairs at the Buchanan Street entrance is still special. You feel as though you're on top of a great city that flows beneath you down the graceful slope of Buchanan Street.

Leslie Martin's striking but simple design – described by *The Herald*'s music critic, Michael Tumelty, as looming like a 'shinto shrine' over Buchanan Street's shops and malls – makes its greatest impact when you walk up from the underground station further down Buchanan Street. It's a welcoming mini-amphitheatre

Left: Lord Provost Pat Lally unveils the fourth mural at the Glasgow Royal Concert Hall. The painting is 'My Great Heart' (1996) by the celebrated Scottish artist Peter Howson.

Opposite: Transatlantic Sessions, Celtic Connections, 2015.

of sandstone, glass and steps; the other side of the building, facing the Buchanan Street Bus Station, is a less dramatic point of ingress, with columns of sandstone cladding and a wider flight of steps. With the completion of the Buchanan Galleries in 1999, that Buchanan Street elevation is now, according to your point of view, either swallowed up by the gigantism of the commercial excess that surrounds it, or at last a continuous immersive arc of architectural line and material that felt unfinished until the Galleries were built. (Pre-shopping mall, that eastern side of the hall presented a naked-looking wall of brick to the outside world).

However you feel about it, the exterior is an impressive sight. It's the interior that's more controversial, from the decoration to the foyer spaces to the ancillary auditoria, especially the Strathclyde Suite. And that's before you even get into the main hall. Maybe it's the carpets, maybe it's the swathes of marble, maybe it's the remarkable width of the foyers and the bars that surround the main auditorium, but the public spaces of the Glasgow Royal Concert Hall have always felt, to me, empty of function and purpose. The building's internal volumes don't lead you to the concert hall; they feel like bespoke lounges, bars and cafés, cast on a grand but anonymous scale. It's as if the hall is the supplementary part of the experience instead of the foyers.

Then there's the Strathclyde Suite, the smaller performance and reception space on the first floor. Successive generations of GRCH managers have fought vainly with its acoustic facelessness and atmospheric mediocrity. McNicol was optimistic about the Strathclyde Suite before the whole complex opened: 'It's the perfect shape for a small concert hall – shoebox shape – so I'm putting the acoustic engineers onto it now to see if they can come up with something.' They couldn't, or didn't. And although ensembles like the Scottish Ensemble, a host of string quartets, chamber groups from the RSNO, and dozens of others have tried over the years, the Strathclyde Suite looks and feels like what it is: a glorified conference room that doesn't work for acoustic music and which is best used as a

Below: The Scottish National Orchestra and the Royal Scottish Academy of Music at the Glasgow Concert Hall, in January 1963. The Hall, the former Gaiety Cinema at Anderston Cross, replaces the burnt out St. Andrew's Halls.

post-concert reception room or for hosting power-point presentations. Amplified music is another matter, but the suite has never become what McNicol originally thought it could be.

And so to the main hall, which seats 2,500 people in swathes of sumptuous blue-covered seats surrounded on three levels by the gentle, yellow-ish glow of the wood-veneer on the walls and stage. The first audiences to experience this space were not classical music crowds, but three gatherings who came to see a series of community concerts hosted by Bill McCue at the end of September 1990. As Andrew Young wrote in *The Herald*, the symbolism was clear: 'No effort is being spared to let the public become aware of the fact that the Glasgow International Concert Hall will be non-elitist.'

But that 'non-elitism' went hand-in-hand with another of the hall's ambitions: to develop a bigger audience for classical music (a project that Glasgow 1990 called Orchestras United). And the opening programme of orchestras and ensembles in the 1990–1991 season was indeed a high water-mark in Glasgow's musical life, resuscitating the remarkable international roster of orchestras and conductors who used to call Glasgow a home-from-home before the demise of St Andrew's Halls. The GRCH's official opening gala on 8 October 1990 featured the Royal Scottish Orchestra (as they were – briefly – called at the time) and their then principal conductor, Bryden Thomson. Later in the season Kurt Masur and the Leipzig Gewandhaus gave a televised cycle of Brahms symphonies and piano concertos with Alfred Brendel. There was the Bolshoi Orchestra, the Israel Philharmonic, the London Philharmonic and the Orchestra of the Age of Enlightenment. But the highlights were the two concerts that came just after the opening gala, in the Berlin Philharmonic's first visit to Glasgow since the 1950s. Under conductor, Kurt Sanderling, the Berlin Phil played programmes of Haydn and Shostakovich, of Mozart – the *Fourth Violin Concerto* with Frank Peter Zimmermann – and Bruckner's *Third Symphony*. For a teenage classical music fanatic and first-time Bruckner listener like me, these concerts were revelatory in their power and intensity. That Bruckner symphony is still scarred on my brain as opening up a world of experience and orchestral transcendence I could not have imagined possible; sitting above the violas in the GRCH's balcony that night was one of the defining moments in my musical life.

And that was just the first of the remarkable series of

international orchestras that the concert hall brought to Glasgow during those early 1990s seasons. No less memorable were Mariss Jansons and the St Petersburg Philharmonic in, for example, Shostakovich's *Seventh Symphony* and Mahler's *Second*; Riccardo Chailly and the Concertgebouw in Bruckner's *Fifth*; the sheer sumptuousness of the Vienna Philharmonic with Riccardo Muti in Bruckner's *Seventh* and Mozart's *34th*; the Russian-music thrill-ride of Valery Gergiev and his Mariinsky company in a concert performance of Tchaikovsky's opera *Mazeppa*. It felt in those early years of the GRCH that the world really was coming to Glasgow and at ticket prices that were affordable, to boot.

But the Berlin Philharmonic, to my huge personal disappointment, never came back. The problem with the sheer luxury and frankly life-enhancing power of performances like those was that they transcended the more mundane problems of the GRCH. The internal volume of the hall is unusually wide – wider than the more conventional shoe-box shapes of Symphony Hall in Birmingham and the Bridgewater Hall in Manchester, two British auditoriums that opened around the same time as Glasgow's, both of which have garnered more praise from musicians and audiences. The girth of the GRCH space diffuses the sonic and atmospheric impact of the acoustic. And while the sightlines from each of the seats in the hall gives unimpeded views of the stage, the experiences of sitting in the balcony

Top: This photograph shows pupils participating in the Children's Classic Concert, 1998. The concert was conducted by popular children's TV presenter Floella Benjamin.

Above: Evelyn Glennie is seen here in 2001 with her xylophone and drums during a concert and workshop for children.

as opposed to the stalls, in the upper echelons of the gallery compared to the first-floor level, or in the side-stall areas as opposed to the middle of the arena, are vastly different

The problem is that each area feels like a separate zone in the hall. And that amounts to a general lack of atmosphere when you're part of anything less than a sell-out crowd, which isn't the resident Royal Scottish National Orchestra's usual experience during their annual seasons, despite decades of initiatives. There's also an essential dryness to the GRCH's acoustic. The sound from the platform, especially at the lower end of the spectrum, is somehow anaesthetised before it reaches you (maybe it's the soft voluminousness of those comfortable seats). The experience of listening to orchestral music in the hall lacks a key ingredient of drama and involvement, and it's emphatically inadequate as a chamber music venue. In the early years, the management experimented with selling the space for celebrity recitals: violinist Pinchas Zukerman's already corporate performing style was rendered utterly anodyne in the gaping maw of the hall.

Sitting in the audience at the GRCH gives a sense of dislocation from the performers instead of the intimacy that the great auditoriums offer. And in the early years of Glasgow's new concert hall, it was as if the playing of the RSNO didn't communicate to the far reaches of the auditorium compared to the intensity of the international orchestras' performances. There were some scintillating exceptions – Messiaen's *Turangalîla Symphony* with Mark Wigglesworth and Joanna MacGregor, for example, in 1993 – but too often the playing of the hall's resident symphony orchestra couldn't get past the fundamental acoustic limitations of the auditorium.

There were institutional issues within the RSNO at that time as well. Bryden Thomson's contract was not renewed (he died in 1991, the year that the orchestra had obliged him to rescind his role), and his successor, Walter Weller, oversaw a period of complacent cosiness of repertoire and performance style. But the next generation of RSNO principal conductors has presided over an expansion of the orchestra's repertoire on the concert platform and its ambition within the audiences and communities of Glasgow. There are education projects, an ongoing tradition of children's concerts – some of the most accessible and successful in the country – and populist New Year's Day concerts.

The transformation of the orchestra's fortunes, and its relationship with the hall, is best symbolised by

Left: An aerial view of the almost-completed building.

current plans for the GRCH. In a £14-million development, the orchestra will move its administrative offices to the site, create a new rehearsal venue and space for education and community work, and open a new smaller hall that will – at last – render the Strathclyde Suite redundant for anything but conference-style events. It's a development that seems essential to the future of the orchestra and to embed the ensemble in the building at last. Hopefully it will also transform the musical possibilities of the building itself. With the support of politicians and city councillors, this development should mark the true fulfillment of the GRCH's possibilities as a home of orchestral music – with the proviso that the main hall still needs some acoustic improvement.

The GRCH's two decades of International Seasons came to an end in 2010 with a concert from the Basel Chamber Orchestra and pianist Angela Hewitt that Michael Tumelty reckoned worthy of only three of *The Herald*'s critical stars (Tumelty had preferred Joanna MacGregor's recent interpretations of Bach's keyboard concertos). That 20-year history of international orchestral intervention changed the terms of Glasgow's musical life. The seasons restored Glasgow to pride of place in the roster of UK cities regularly visited on the international touring circuit. They gave Scottish audiences the chance to experience some of the world's finest orchestras outside of the concentrated summer dose of internationalism that the Edinburgh International Festival provides.

Since 2009 and the formation of what's now known as Glasgow Life and the appointment of Svend Brown as its Director of Music, the GRCH has taken a new, project-based approach to the music-making it promotes. There's no formally branded 'international season', but instead a richer diversity of themes, events, musical experiences and repertoire. Brown told Michael Tumelty in 2010: 'I didn't want to destroy the achievements of the International Classical Season by any means. I can't afford to bring the big orchestras. But I can afford to bring the great soloists and, on occasion, to bring the large ensembles, which is why we have the Academy of Ancient Music doing the *Brandenburgs* and the London Sinfonietta doing Reich's *Music for 18 Musicians*. What I wanted to offer, above all, was range; so I took the decision to bow out of presenting the Bolshois and the Dresdens.' In practice, Brown's leadership has meant the presentation of a greater diversity

Opposite: From the back of the stage, during a rehearsal.

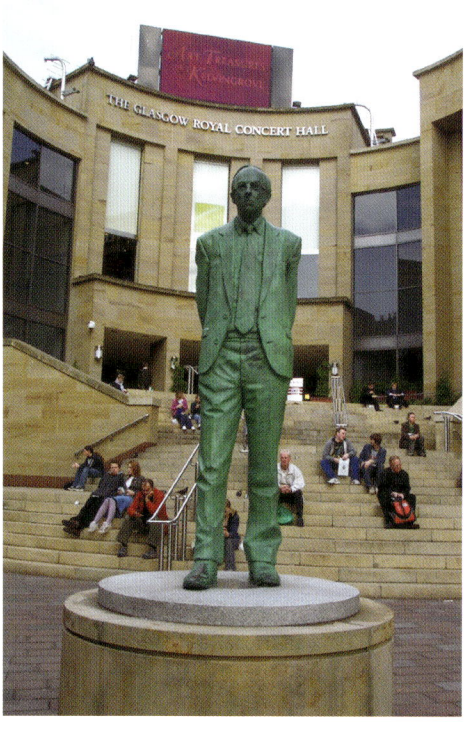

Above: Buchanan Street, with building work for Buchana Galleries in the foreground.

Top, right: The statue of Donald Dewar (1937–2000) in front of the Buchanan Street entrance.

Right: The Glasgow coat of arms adorns the wall of the concert hall.

of music-making across all of Glasgow's Concert Halls (Glasgow Life covers a sweep of the city's venues for music), above all in a new focus on contemporary music and early music events.

But among the GRCH's most successful partnerships, and one of its most successful incarnations as a venue, is what has happened there every year from 1994 during the darkest month of the Glaswegian winter. *Celtic Connections*, under its first artistic director Colin Hynd, began as a hibernal takeover of all of the GRCH's spaces – it even succeeded in making the Strathclyde Suite work as a venue for amplified and acoustic sets. Over a 20-year history from Wolfstone's first concert on 9 January 1994 to an epic celebratory concert that kicked off the 2013 festival, *Celtic Connections* has created new meanings, new audiences and new opportunities for an astonishing range of music and musicians. That 'Celtic' label now includes rap, rock, jazz, world and classical artists, as well as the core sessions of more traditional folk musicking. The 20th anniversary concert demonstrated some of that spectrum of music-making: Capercaillie (whose line-up includes the festival's artistic director since 2007, Donald Shaw) played alongside Eddi Reader, Chris Stout, Flook, Phil Cunningham and a string section helmed by BBC Scottish Symphony Orchestra violinist Greg Lawson.

Some have questioned the continual expansion of the definition of 'Celtic-ness' in the acts that Shaw has promoted: how did Tom Jones fit the bill, for example, when he played the festival in 2011? 'There was much talk about "what has Tom got to do with Celtic music apart from being Welsh?" The relevance was that he'd just recorded an album of great old-time Blues songs.

Once you start getting into old-time American blues, R&B, soul, you are going to find folk music right at the heart of it, if you look deep enough.' That's Shaw's essential ethos about the festival now: that it's more about the 'connections' than the 'Celtic'. The American connection, for example, has been among the strongest of the festival's musical bonds in the Transatlantic Sessions it convenes every year, steered by Aly Bain and Jerry Douglas. *Celtic Connections* now encompasses, you feel, the whole of Glasgow in venues from galleries to the Barrowlands, nightclubs to the Piping Centre, theatres, churches, and pubs to the Old Fruitmarket. Altogether the festival reaches an audience of over 100,000 every year. But the GRCH is still the centre from which the festival radiates its irresistible energy.

At times when you're part of the crowd seeing one of the headline acts of *Celtic Connections*, escaping the grey of Glasgow's January for the warmth and intimacy of, say, Eddi Reader singing Burns; when you're hearing Steve Reich's *Drumming* performed by Colin Currie and his ensemble; or when you're experiencing the RSNO at their best, then the GRCH really does feel like the 'Great Hall of the People' that Pat Lally dreamed of back in 1990. Yes, its acoustics are limited, and yes, there will always be issues around how to fill its yawning public spaces. But if the GRCH works it's because its audiences want it to, and because successive directors of the hall and artistic directors of its festivals have answered – or created – the city's demand for the highest quality and biggest range of music-making. It's the place where Glasgow consecrates its love of live music. And in that sense, whatever its flaws and its controversies, the Glasgow Royal Concert Hall is a worthy successor to St Andrew's Halls.

Above: Beethoven on Sauchiehall Street.

Inset, left: Bjorn Again bring a touch of Abba to Glasgow.

Below: 'Treacherous Orchestra' at Celtic Connections, 2015.

Acknowledgements

Glasgow UNESCO City of Music, Svend Brown, Kate Molleson, the contributors and Waverley Books would like to thank the following:

Dave Clarke, Ian Davison, Morrison Dunbar, Dep Downie, Lady Veronica Gibson, Mike Grieve, James 'Harri' Harrigan, Stuart Harris-Logan, Fiona Imlach, Stuart MacMillan, Ken McCluskey, David McGuiness, Eddie McGuire, Keith 'JD Twitch' McIvor, Stephen McRobbie, Donald Menzies, Alan Miller, Alasdair Roberts, Raymond Williamson, Graham Wilson, Catherine Lockerbie, Michael Gallagher, Winnie Tyrrell, Neil Fraser, Robert Pool, Bruce Kennedy, Ailene Hunter, John Wood, and the many photographers, amateur and professional, who responded to our *Flickr* enquiries.

Bibliography

Beranek, Leo: *L. Music, Acoustics and Architecture;* John Wiley & Sons Inc, New York, 1962.

Birkin, Kenneth: *Hans von Bulow: A Life for Music;* Cambridge University Press, New York, 2011.

Collinson, Francis: *The Traditional and National Music of Scotland;* Routledge & Kegan Paul London, 1966.

Farmer, Henry George: *A History of Music in Scotland;* Da Capo Press Inc, 1970 (Hinrichsen Edition Limited 1947).

Finnegan, Ruth: *The Hidden Musicians: Music-making in an English Town;* Wesleyan Publishing House, 2013.

Fisher, Joe: *The Glasgow Encyclopedia;* Mainstream Publishing, Edinburgh & London, 1994.

Harvey, Hamilton: *Franz Ferdinand and the Pop Renaissance;* Reynolds & Hearn, 2005.

Hay, Marianne H.: *Glasgow Theatres and Music Halls: A Guide;* Glasgow Room Publications No. 15, The Mitchell Library, Glasgow, 1950.

Hogg, Brian: *All That Ever Mattered: The History of Scottish Rock and Pop;* Guinness Publishing, 1993.

Imlach, Hamish; McVicar, Ewan: *Cod Liver Oil and the Orange Juice, Reminiscences of a Fat Folk Singer;* Mainstream Publishing, 1992.

Inglis, Jim: *The organ in Scotland before 1700;* Schagen, 1991.

Livingstone, Rev. Neil (Editor: *The Scottish Metrical Psalter of A.D. 1635, Reprinted in Full from the Original Wor;* Glasgow, 1864.

Maitland Club, Glasgow: *Miscellany of the Maitland Club, Vol. 1, issued in 2 parts;* Printed at Edinburgh 1833, 1840.

Marwick, J. D. (Editor): *Extracts from the Records of the Burgh of Glasgow Vol. 1, 1573–1642;* Corporation of Glasgow (Records of the Burgh of Glasgow originally published by the Scottish Burgh Records Society, Edinburgh, 1914).

McQuaid, John: *Music and the Administration after 1560;* from The Innes Review, Vol. 3. Edinburgh University Press, 1952.

McQuaid, John: *Musicians of the Scottish Reformation c.1560–1650;* PhD Thesis, University of Edinburgh, 1949.

McVicar, Ewan: *One Singer One Song: Old and New Stories and Songs of Glasgow Folk;* Glasgow City Libraries and Archives, 1990.

McVicar, Ewan: *Katherine Campbell. Traditional Scottish Songs and Music;* Leckie & Leckie, 2001.

McVicar, Ewan: *Doh Ray Me, When Ah Wis Wee: Scots Children's Songs and Rhymes;* Birlinn Ltd, 2007.

McVicar, Ewan: *A B C My Grannie Caught A Flea: Scots Children's Songs and Rhymes;* Birlinn Ltd, 2014.

Mollison, David. Melody—The Soul of Music: *An Essay Towards The Improvement Of The Musical Art;* The Courier Office, Glasgow, 1798.

Moohan, Elaine: *The Sacred Music Institution in Glasgow, 1796–1805 in Notis musycall: Essays on Music and Scottish Culture in Honour of Kenneth Elliott;* (Editors: Gordon Munro, Stuart Campbell, Greta-Mary Hair, Margaret A. Mackay, Elaine Moohan, Graham Hair). Musica Scotica, Glasgow, 2005.

Munro, Ailie: *The Folk Music Revival in Scotland;* Kahn and Averill, London, 1984.

Munro, Gordon: *Scottish Church Music and Musicians, 1500–1700;* PhD Thesis, University of Glasgow, 1999.

Munro, Gordon: *The Scottish Reformation and its Consequences' in Our awin Scottis Use: Music in the Scottish Church up to 1603;* (Editor: Sally Harper). Universities of Glasgow and Aberdeen, 2000.

Munro, Gordon: *"Sang Schwylls" and "Music Schools": Music Education in Scotland, 1560–1650' in Music Education in the Middle Ages and the Renaissance;* (Editors: Russell E. Murray Jr., Susan Forscher Weiss and Cynthia J. Cyrus). Indiana University Press, 2010.

Old Glasgow Club Transactions, Vol. 2 1908–13; Aird & Coghill Printers, Glasgow, 1909.

Old Glasgow Club Transactions, Vol. 3 1913–18. Aird & Coghill Printers, Glasgow, 1919.

Purser, John: *Is the Red Light On?;* BBC Scotland, Glasgow, 1987.

Purser, John: *Scotland's Music;* Mainstream Publishing (with support from the Scottish Arts Council, Edinburgh), 1992.

The British Minstrel, William Hamilton, Glasgow, 1843.

The Euing Collection, Glasgow University:

Brown, William: *A collection of psalm tunes, in four parts;* Glasgow, 1700.

Bruce, Thomas: *The Common Tunes: Scotland's Church Musick Made Plain;* 1726

Duncan, Gideon: *True Presbyterian, or a brief account of the new singing, its author, and progress in general;* Glasgow, 1755.

Ferguson, W. M.: *Catalogue of Euing's Musical Collection;* Glasgow, 1878. Accessed in The Euing Collection, Glasgow University.

Holden, John: *'An essay towards a rational system of music';* Glasgow, 1770.

Programmes from the 1821 Glasgow Music Festival

Tobin, Eddie; Kielty, Martin: *Are Ye Dancin'?;* Waverley Books, 2010.

*****Various at *The Glasgow Herald*. Seligmann, J.:** *'Musical Progress of Glasgow during the Last Fifty Years';* 1893

Walker, Alan: *Hans von Bulow: A Life and Times;* Oxford University Press, New York, 2009.

Wilkie, Jim: *Blue Suede Brogans: Secret Life of Scottish Rock Music;* Mainstream Publishing, Edinburgh, 1990.

Williamson, John; Cloonan, Martin; Frith, Simon: *Mapping the Music Industry in Scotland: A Report;* Commissioned by Scottish Enterprise, 2003.

Wilson, Conrad: *Playing for Scotland: The History of the Royal Scottish National Orchestra;* HarperCollins, 1993.

Wilson, Conrad: *Scottish Opera: The First Ten Years;* HarperCollins, 1972.

Wodrow, Robert: *Collections upon the Lives of the Reformers and Most Eminent Ministers of the Church of Scotland Vols. 1 and 2;* Maitland Club, Glasgow, 1834 and 1845.

www.glasgowapollo.com

Picture Credits

Cover, Page 3, Page 4: Gramophone, Traffic Cone and Scottie Dog, concept and arrangement by Waverley Books © elements: Vilmos Varga, Viktorija Reuta, Photohunter/Shutterstock

Front Endpaper: Plan Of Glasgow, 1888, © National Library of Scotland

Page 7: Glasgow Orpheus Choir concert in the Winter Gardens at the People's Palace circa. 1910 © CSG CIC Glasgow Museums and Libraries Collections

Page 8: Colour lithograph poster by Charles Rennie Mackintosh (1868–1928) for The Scottish Musical Review, 1896 © CSG CIC Glasgow Museums and Libraries Collections

Page 9: Crowd at Queen's Park Bandstand, summer 1955 © CSG CIC Glasgow Museums and Libraries Collections

Page 10: Govanhill Recreation Ground, early 20th century © CSG CIC Glasgow Museums and Libraries Collections

Page 11: Phonographs advertisement, 1909 © CSG CIC Glasgow Museums and Libraries Collections

Page 11: Hungarian composer and pianist Béla Bartók arriving in Glasgow for his St Andrew's Halls concert November 1933 © Glasgow Evening News

Page 12: Gig on the Green © Greater Glasgow and Clyde Valley Tourist Board

Page 13: Sir Alexander Gibson photographed with the SNO, Kelvin Hall, 1975 © CSG CIC Glasgow Museums and Libraries Collections

Page 14: View of The Piping Centre with the Theatre Royal to the right (pictured 2012, pre-extension) © Mark Mechan

Page 14: View of The Pavilion Theatre, with Cineworld (site of The Apollo) with The Glasgow Royal Concert Hall in the distance © Mark Mechan

Page 16: Glasgow Cathedral, viewed from W. Cathedral Square © RCAHMS (A Brown and Company Collection). Licensor www.rcahms.gov.uk

Page 17: Glasgow, Antique Map detail, late 16th century © National Library of Scotland. Licensor www.scran.ac.uk

Page 18: Glasgow Cathedral Precinct Map © John Durkin, designed by Michael Healey

Page 18: Vicars Choral Stone, commemorating Bishop Andrew Muirhead © CSG CIC Glasgow Museums and Libraries Collections

Page 19: Page of 'Gradual' © CSG CIC Glasgow Museums and Libraries Collections

Page 20: Noted Breviary, Liturgical Fragment © CSG CIC Glasgow Museums and Libraries Collections

Page 21: Engraving, Glasgow Cathedral – Part of the Crypt © University of Strathclyde. Licensor www.scran.ac.uk

Page 22: Engraving of Glasgow Cathedral seen from the Necropolis © University of Strathclyde. Licensor www.scran.ac.uk

Page 22: Watercolour 'On the outskirts of Glasgow with the Cathedral beyond' artist unknown, circa. 1840 © CSG CIC Glasgow Museums and Libraries Collections

Page 23: The Cathedral, flood-lit for Christmas, © Newsquest (Herald & Times). Licensor www.scran.ac.uk

Page 25: City Halls, exterior © Mark Mechan

Page 26: Candleriggs, looking towards City Halls © Newsquest (Herald & Times). Licensor www.scran.ac.uk

Page 26: BBC SSO at City Halls – photograph taken before their New Year 2015 tour in China © BBC, photo John Wood

Page 27: Andrew Manze conducting the BBC SSO © BBC, photo John Wood

Page 28: BBC SSO playing the Bernard Herrmann score for 'Psycho', live © BBC, photo John Wood

Page 29: Glasgow City Hall poster, 1892 © CSG CIC Glasgow Museums and Libraries Collections

Page 29: Matthias Pintscher conducting over 100 amateur musicians and strings of the BBC SSO © BBC, photo John Wood

Page 30: City Halls, Fruitmarket © RCAHMS (Reproduced courtesy of J R Hume). Licensor www.rcahms.gov.uk

Page 31: City Halls, Fruitmarket, interior prior to refurbishment © Crown ©: RCAHMS. Licensor www.rcahms.gov.uk

Page 31: City Halls, Fruitmarket, refurbished, resounding to Celtic Connections © Glasgow Life

Page 32: Interior, City Halls, 1987 © Bruce Kennedy

Page 33: City Halls from Candleriggs © Newsquest (Herald & Times). Licensor www.scran.ac.uk

Page 33: City Halls Blue Plaque © Mark Mechan

Page 34: Poster-covered wall of The Scottish College of Dramatic Art in Glasgow, 1955 © Getty Images

Page 36: Athenaeum, Glasgow, built 1796 as Assembly Rooms © Glasgow City Libraries, Information and Learning. Licensor www.scran.ac.uk

Page 37: Liberal Club, Glasgow, altered in 1928 for RSAMD © Crown ©: Royal Commission on the Ancient and Historical Monuments of Scotland. Licensor www.scran.ac.uk

Page 38: 'Opening Soiree of the Glasgow Athenaeum, Charles Dickens in the Chair, City Hall, 1847' by William Simpson © Glasgow Museums. Licensor www.scran.ac.uk

Page 39: The Athenaeum, Nelson Mandela Place © William Young. Licensor www.scran.ac.uk

Page 40: Royal Scottish Academy of Music and Drama, Glasgow © Royal Fine Art Commission for Scotland. Licensor www.scran.ac.uk

Page 40: Construction work in progress, Royal Scottish Academy of Music and Drama, Glasgow © Royal Fine Art Commission for Scotland. Licensor www.scran.ac.uk

Page 40: The Queen Arcade from Renfrew Street, 1956 © Newsquest (Herald & Times). Licensor www.scran.ac.uk

Page 41: Alexander Gibson Opera School, Royal Scottish Academy of Music and Drama, Cowcaddens Road, Glasgow © Architecture on Disc. Licensor www.scran.ac.uk

Page 41: The Royal Conservatoire of Glasgow signage (Gaelic) © Mark Mechan

Page 42: Scotia Variety Theatre programme, 1892 © CSG CIC Glasgow Museums and Libraries Collections

Page 43: The Scotia Bar, street view © Mark Mechan

Page 44: Postcard photograph of Marie Loftus © CSG CIC Glasgow Museums and Libraries Collections

Page 44: The Scotia Bar interior © Francesco Basso

Page 45: The Scotia Bar, 'smoke break' © Przemek Oracz

Page 46: The Scotia Bar,' notice', exterior wall © Mark Mechan

Page 47: Theis Juul Langlands and Michael Graubæk © Gareth Talbot

Page 48: Scotia Folk, Fontana LP cover courtesy of Jim McLean © Alison Chapman McLean

Page 49: Gerry Rafferty © Brunton Hunter

Page 50: Theatre Royal, 254–90 Hope Street, auditorium roof © University of Strathclyde. Licensor www.scran.ac.uk

Page 51: Theatre Royal programme, 1935 © CSG CIC Glasgow Museums and Libraries Collections

Page 52: Playbill for a production of *Der Freischütz* at the Theatre Royal, York Street, in 1830 © Glasgow University Library. Licensor www.scran.ac.uk

Page 52: View of The Theatre Royal, Queen Street, after it burned down 1829 © Glasgow City Libraries. Licensor www.scran.ac.uk

Page 52: Theatre Royal, Queen Street, 1805 © Glasgow University Library. Licensor www.scran.ac.uk

Page 53: Theatre-bill for a benefit performance at The Theatre Royal, Queen Street, 1826 © Glasgow University Library. Licensor www.scran.ac.uk

Page 53: Engraving pre-1852: view of The Theatre Royal, Dunlop Street © Glasgow City Libraries. Licensor www.scran.ac.uk

Page 53: The Theatre Royal, Dunlop Street, redeveloped upper storey © Glasgow City Libraries, Information and Learning. Licensor www.scran.ac.uk

Page 54: The Theatre Royal, Hope Street, view towards proscenium arch © RCAHMS (Scottish Colorfoto Collection). Licensor www.rcahms.gov.uk

Page 55: The Theatre Royal, Hope Street, view from SSW © Crown ©: RCAHMS. Licensor www.rcahms.gov.uk

Page 55: Theatre Royal Hope Street, main entrance © Crown ©: RCAHMS. Licensor www.rcahms.gov.uk

Page 56: Title page of 'The Courier' in-house magazine, 1935 © Glasgow University Library. Licensor www.scran.ac.uk

Page 56: Programme cover for 'Scottish Opera Magazine', Winter 1967 © Glasgow University Library. Licensor www.scran.ac.uk

Page 56: Theatre Royal, Hope Street, plasterwork detail © Mark Mechan

Page 57: Theatre Royal, Hope Street, Ticket Office Window © University of Strathclyde. Licensor www.scran.ac.uk

Page 57: Theatre Royal, Hope Street, Foyer © University of Strathclyde. Licensor www.scran.ac.uk

Page 57: Theatre Royal Playbill for the pantomime 'Cinderella', 1930 © Glasgow University Library. Licensor www.scran.ac.uk

Page 58: John Mauceri at Theatre Royal 1986 © The Scotsman Publications Ltd. Licensor www.scran.ac.uk

Page 58: Pat Hoys, Billy Connolly and Alexander Gibson outside Theatre Royal 1978 © The Scotsman Publications Ltd. Licensor www.scran.ac.uk

Page 58: Theatre Royal ticket © Robert Pool, The Robert Pool Glasgow Collection

Page 59: Theatre Royal, Hope Street, interior view to the right of the Proscenium © University of Strathclyde. Licensor www.scran.ac.uk

Page 59: Theatre Royal, extended 2014, exterior © Mark Mechan

Page 59: Theatre Royal, The Sackler Staircase © Mark Mechan

Page 60: Stage of the Empire Theatre, 1963, as the curtain falls for the final time © Newsquest (Herald & Times). Licensor www.scran.ac.uk

Page 61: Variety Show programme, 1963 © CSG CIC Glasgow Museums and Libraries Collections

Page 62: Stanley Baxter in the 5 past 8 Show in the Empire Theatre © The Scotsman Publications Ltd. Licensor www.scran.ac.uk

Page 62: Laurel and Hardy, April 1950 © The Scotsman Publications Ltd. Licensor www.scran.ac.uk

Page 62: Empire Theatre, June 1930 © CSG CIC Glasgow Museums and Libraries Collections

Page 63: Empire Theatre reopening, The Auditorium, 1931 © CSG CIC Glasgow Museums and Libraries Collections

Page 63: Programme cover for 'Variety at the Empire', 1950 © Glasgow University Library. Licensor www.scran.ac.uk

Page 63: Andy Stewart, singer in his dressing room at Empire Theatre, 1957 © The Scotsman Publications Ltd. Licensor www.scran.ac.uk

Page 63: Red Army ensemble of singers and dancers and musicians at Empire Theatre, 1959 © The Scotsman Publications Ltd. Licensor www.scran.ac.uk

Page 64: Empire Theatre, (Empire Palace) poster © CSG CIC Glasgow Museums and Libraries Collections

Page 65: Glasgow Empire Christmas Show 1956, Programme Cover © Glasgow University Library. Licensor www.scran.ac.uk

Page 65: Harry Lauder with fellow entertainers, circa 1945 © Glasgow University Library. Licensor www.scran.ac.uk

Page 66: The Great Hall, St Andrews Hall, from the platform, looking north toward the rear balcony © T & R Annan & Sons Ltd

Page 67: Campbell Douglas & Sellars' drawing of the Granville Street facade of St Andrew's Halls, from the north-west, 1880 Courtesy of Bruce Kennedy

Page 68: St Andrew's Halls, exterior from Granville Street © T & R Annan & Sons Ltd

Page 69: St Andrew's Halls, section drawing © Bruce Kennedy

Page 70: Opening night concert at St Andrew's Halls, 1877 © CSG CIC Glasgow Museums and Libraries Collections

Page 71: Photograph of the statues for the west frontage of St Andrews Hall, being carved in Mossman's studio © T & R Annan & Sons Ltd

Page 71: St Andrew's Halls, detail from The Builder Magazine, 1880 © CSG CIC Glasgow Museums and Libraries Collections, courtesy of Bruce Kennedy

Page 72: View of Lounge (or Gallery) on the Ballroom floor of St Andrew's Halls © CSG CIC Glasgow Museums and Libraries Collections

Page 73: The Great Hall, St Andrew's Halls looking south towards the platform © T & R Annan & Sons Ltd

Page 74: John Barbirolli, on the podium with the Scottish Orchestra, St Andrew's Halls, 1933 © Royal Academy Of Music

Page 75: St Andrew's Halls, detail from The Builder Magazine, 1880 © CSG CIC Glasgow Museums and Libraries Collections, courtesy of Bruce Kennedy

Page 75: Promenade Concert Programme courtesy of Bruce Kennedy

Page 76: West frontage of St Andrew's Halls following the 1962 fire © CSG CIC Glasgow Museums and Libraries Collections

Page 76: Fire at St Andrew's Halls – Glasgow – Firemen tackle the blaze, 1962 © The Scotsman Publications Ltd. Licensor www.scran.ac.uk

Page 76: Boxing in St Andrew's Halls in Glasgow © The Scotsman Publications Ltd. Licensor www.scran.ac.uk

Page 77: Salvaged instruments following the fire at St Andrew's Halls, 1962 © The Scotsman Publications Ltd. Licensor www.scran.ac.uk

Page 78: Statuary, St Andrew's Halls © Bruce Kennedy

Page 79: Statuary, St Andrew's Halls © Bruce Kennedy

Page 79: St Andrew's Halls, composers' names carved into stonework © Mark Mechan

Page 80: Townhead Primary School, Rottenrow © Crown ©: RCAHMS. Licensor www.rcahms.gov.uk

Page 82: Rottenrow Primary School © CSG CIC Glasgow Museums and Libraries Collections

Page 83: Outdoor activities at Kennyhill Special School, 1916 © CSG CIC Glasgow Museums and Libraries Collections

Page 83: 19th-century photograph of Balmano Brae © Glasgow University Library. Licensor www.scran.ac.uk

Page 84: 'Skipping' © Raymond Townsend, by permission of Karina Townsend

Page 84: 'Finger games' © Raymond Townsend, by permission of Karina Townsend

Page 85: 'Bools' © Raymond Townsend, by permission of Karina Townsend

Page 85: 'One-two-three a-leerie' © Raymond Townsend, by permission of Karina Townsend

Page 86: The Pavilion, Harry Lauder playbill, 1913. By permission of University of Glasgow Library, Special Collections

Page 87: Pavilion Theatre by night 1981 © The Scotsman Publications Ltd. Licensor www.scran.ac.uk

Page 88: Pavilion Theatre, Lex McLean programme © CSG CIC Glasgow Museums and Libraries Collections

Page 88: The Pavilion, Renfrew Street signage © Mark Mechan

Page 89: Pavilion Theatre poster, 1904 © CSG CIC Glasgow Museums and Libraries Collections

Page 89: The Pavilion, Renfrew Street stonework detail © Mark Mechan

Page 90: The Wooltoun Jazz Band on stage at The Pavilion Theatre © Dave Young. Licensor www.scran.ac.uk

Page 90: Victor Borge at The Pavilion, 1975 © The Scotsman Publications Ltd. Licensor www.scran.ac.uk

Page 91: Programme cover for the Pavilion Theatre © Glasgow University Library. Licensor www.scran.ac.uk

Page 91: Pavilion Theatre, 1979 © The Scotsman Publications Ltd. Licensor www.scran.ac.uk

Page 92: Poster for George Mozart at the Pavilion Theatre, 1913 © Glasgow University Library. Licensor www.scran.ac.uk

Page 92: Outside The Pavilion, Johnny Beattie and Maidie Murray, Launching 'The Chic Murray Story', 1989 © The Scotsman Publications Ltd. Licensor www.scran.ac.uk

Page 93: The Pavilion, Renfrew Street, foyer mosaic floor detail © Mark Mechan

Page 94: Barrowlands dance hall in 1960 © Newsquest (Herald & Times). Licensor www.scran.ac.uk

Page 95: Barrowland in lights (detail) © Robert Sweeney

Page 96: Simple Minds at Barrowlands, February 2012 © Ian Brown

Page 96: Enter Shikari at Barrowlands, 2011 © Stuart Westwood Photography

Page 97: Barrowland Ballroom, Gallowgate, photographed in 1935 (roofline of man pushing a barrow) © CSG CIC Glasgow Museums and Libraries Collections

Page 98: Firemen at Barrowland Ballroom, 1958 © The Scotsman Publications Ltd. Licensor www.scran.ac.uk

Page 98: A view of the fire-gutted Barrowland Ballroom, 1958 © The Scotsman Publications Ltd. Licensor www.scran.ac.uk

Page 99: Glasgow Barrowlands © Murray McMillan

Page 99: Brownbear Rehearsals, Glasgow Barrowlands showing dancefloor, 2014 © Murray McMillan

Page 99: Barrowlands Ballroom dancefloor 1935 © CSG CIC Glasgow Museums and Libraries Collections

Page 100: Barrowland in lights © Robert Sweeney

Page 100: Barraloadasoul 'Alldayer' event, 31st May 2014 © Gregor Miller

Page 100: Barrowland today © Mark Mechan

Page 101: Inside the dressing room at Barrowlands © Christopher Anderson

Page 101: Belle and Sebastian © Takeshi Suga

Page 102: Amy Macdonald at Barrowlands, January 2010 © Paul Monaghan

Page 102: Iggy Pop ticket © Robert Pool, The Robert Pool Glasgow Collection

Page 102: Saw Doctors ticket © Mark Mechan

Page 102: Carrie MacNeil, The Vatersay Boys © www.scottish-images.co.uk, courtesy of Ron Cowan

Page 103: Twin Atlantic – Barrowlands, 2011 © Mark Forrer

Page 103: Barrowlands plaque © Mark Mechan

Page 105: BBC Broadcasting House, Queen Margaret Drive, stairwell and vaulted ceiling © Crown ©: RCAHMS. Licensor www.rcahms.gov.uk

Page 106: North Park House, BBC Broadcasting House, Scotland HQ, 1980, from Queen Margaret Drive © CSG CIC Glasgow Museums and Libraries Collections

Page 107: BBC Broadcasting House, Queen Margaret Drive, ground floor © Crown ©: RCAHMS. Licensor www.rcahms.gov.uk

Page 107: BBC Broadcasting House, Queen Margaret Drive, entrance hall © Crown ©: RCAHMS. Licensor www.rcahms.gov.uk

Page 107: BBC Broadcasting House, Queen Margaret Drive, Mackintosh Courtyard © Crown ©: RCAHMS. Licensor www.rcahms.gov.uk

Page 108: Junior Kirkintilloch Choir sing for BBC Radio's 'Children's Hour in 1946 © Getty Images

Page 109: Jimmy Shand and his band – May 1956 – playing 'The Kilt Is My Delight' for the BBC © The Scotsman Publications Ltd. Licensor www.scran.ac.uk

Page 110: Lonnie Donegan appearing in the film 'Six Five Special' in 1957 © Getty Images

Page 111: Lulu, singer, performing at Celtic Park, 1990, recorded by the BBC © Alan Wylie

Page 111: Mr Peter Mooney, conductor of the Glasgow Phoenix Choir © The Scotsman Publications Ltd. Licensor www.scran.ac.uk

Page 111: BBC Headquaters Pacific Quay © Mark Mechan

Page 112: The National Piping Centre, from the top of Hope Street © Mark Mechan

Page 114: Seamus MacNeill © The College Of Piping

Page 114: The College Of Piping, Otago Street © Mark Mechan

Page 114: The College Of Piping, brass plate © Mark Mechan

Page 115: The Piping Centre, Roddy MacLeod, lunchtime recital © The Piping Centre

Page 116: Pipers at The World Pipe Band Championships at Glasgow Green © Glasgow City Marketing Bureau

Page 116: The Piping Centre, Museum © The Piping Centre

Page 117: Drummers at The World Pipe Band Championships at Glasgow Green © Glasgow City Marketing Bureau

Page 117: The National Piping Centre, entrance © Mark Mechan

Page 118: Mick Jagger performing with the Rolling Stones at the Apollo, 1976 © Getty Images

Page 119: Rolling Stones Concert Ticket © Bruce Reeve

Page 120: The Apollo, previously Green's Playhouse © CSG CIC Glasgow Museums and Libraries Collections

Page 120: Jack Bruce performing at the Apollo in Glasgow © Alan Wylie

Page 121: Billboard advertising Billy Connolly at the Apollo, 1975 © Newsquest (Herald & Times). Licensor www.scran.ac.uk

Page 121: Billy Connolly Concert Programme, Apollo, 1975 © Robert Pool, The Robert Pool Glasgow Collection

Page 122: Golden Earring live in concert 1974 at The Apollo © Robert Pool, The Robert Pool Glasgow Collection

Page 123: Apollo concert ticket collage © Robert Pool, The Robert Pool Glasgow Collection

Page 124: Apollo theatre fire continues to smoulder, 1988 © The Scotsman Publications Ltd. Licensor www.scran.ac.uk

Page 125: Apollo theatre demolition, 1989 © The Scotsman Publications Ltd. Licensor www.scran.ac.uk

Page 125: Apollo demolition site © David Holgate

Page 125: Apollo concert tickets © Robert Pool, The Robert Pool Glasgow Collection

Page 126: Inset, photo of Alex Fleming © Grand Ole Opry

Page 127: Glasgow's Grand Ole Opry © Gerry McLaughlin

Page 128: Grand Ole Opry exterior, 1983 © Grand Ole Opry

Page 128: Sheriff's Star © J. Helgason/Shutterstock

Page 129: Boot and Star, Grand Ole Opry © Glasgow Film Festival

Page 129: Grand Ole Opry, sign, dancers in foreground © Glasgow Film Festival

Page 129: Barley Scotch of Hayseed Dixie at The Grand Ole Opry, 2010 © Andy Murray

Page 130: Grand Ole Opry, fiddle player from The Moonshiners © Glasgow Film Festival

Page 130: Concert Ticket, Franz Ferdinand © celticblade, under Creative Commons Licence

Page 130: Grand Ole Opry interior © Glasgow Film Festival

Page 131: Glasgow cowboys, 1989 © The Scotsman Publications Ltd. Licensor www.scran.ac.uk

Page 131: Grand Ole Opry, line dancers © Glasgow Film Festival

Page 131: Grand Ole Opry, Exterior © Brian Smith – gable-end photography

Page 131: Cowboy Boots © Steve Collender/ Shutterstock

Page 132: Detail from Postcard Records Album cover © Robert Pool, The Robert Pool Glasgow Collection

Page 133: West Princes Street © Mark Mechan

Page 134: Poor Old Soul', vinyl record © Robert Pool, The Robert Pool Glasgow Collection

Page 135: 'Cat' logo courtesy of Robert Pool

Page 136: Josef K photo set, 1981 © W. Keith Milne

Page 136: Josef K album cover and inner sleeve 'The Only Fun In Town' © W. Keith Milne

Page 137: Single record sleeve, and lower record labels © Lenny Lane

Page 137: Record label (top) © Robert Pool, The Robert Pool Glasgow Collection

Page 138: Josef K record label (left) © W. Keith Milne

Page 138: Josef K record labels (centre and right) © Lenny Lane

Page 138: Aztec Camera 'Just Like Gold' with insert postcard © Lenny Lane

Page 139: 'Sound Of Young Scotland' single © Robert Pool, The Robert Pool Glasgow Collection

Page 139: Fan Mail and Orange Juice Postcard © Dolina Thomson

Page 140: Simple Minds ticket © Robert Pool, The Robert Pool Glasgow Collection

Page 141: SECC – Big Red Shed © SECC, courtesy of Kirsten McAlonan

Page 142: Aerial view of Park Circus, in the foreground, with the view south to the River Clyde, 1994 © CSG CIC Glasgow Museums and Libraries Collections

Page 143: Queen's Dock in the 1950s, looking north – now the site of the SECC © CSG CIC Glasgow Museums and Libraries Collections

Page 144: 'Saltire Beat' outside the SECC © Mark Mechan

Page 144: James Brown; Bon Jovi tickets © Robert Pool, The Robert Pool Glasgow Collection

Page 145: The Armadillo © Mark Mechan

Page 145: Bob Dylan; Fun Lovin' Criminals tickets © Robert Pool, The Robert Pool Glasgow Collection

Page 145: SECC Walkway © Mark Mechan

Page 146: Sub Club Dance Floor © R.H. Thompson under Creative Commons Licence

Page 148: Sub Club interior © Sub Club

Page 148: Sub Club 'harri dominic oscar' graphic © Sub Club

Page 149: Jamaica Street hoarding © Mark Mechan

Page 149: Sub Club front door signage © Mark Mechan

Page 150: Little Boots at the Sub Club, 2009, © Stephen Hughes

Page 150: Sub Club Poster graphic © Sub Club

Page 150: Forthcoming gigs on hoarding © Mark Mechan

Page 151: DJ at Sub Club © Calum Barr

Page 152: Standard Sub Club Tuesdays © Robyn Ramsay

Page 153: Highlife at the Sub Club © Duncan Harvey

Page 153: Sub Club interior © Calum Barr

Page 154: View from the decks © Sub Club

Page 155: The crowd during Eliphino's set in Sub Club, 2012 © R.H. Thompson under Creative Commons Licence

Page 155: Sub Club 'cone image' © Sub Club

Page 156: King Tut's entrance © Mark Mechan

Page 157: King Tut's badge © Robert Pool, The Robert Pool Glasgow Collection

Page 158: The King Blues crowd at King Tut's Wah Wah Hut. © Christina Riley

Page 159: King Tut's Wah Wah Hut steps © Cornelius Körner

Page 159: 'Twin Atlantic' live at Tut's © Jessica Newell

Page 160: First Tiger © Ingrid Mur

Page 160: Paloma Faith at King Tut's © Lydia Milne

Page 161: Paulo Nutini at King Tut's 2006 © Fiona McKinlay

Page 161: Idlewild at King Tut's, 2008 © Takeshi Suga

Page 163: Sunset at Mono, Glasgow, 2014 © Matthew McAndrew

Page 164: Mono interior, atrium © James Cadden

Page 164: Mono microbrewery © James Cadden

Page 164: DJ Jim at Mono, 2007 © Stacey Shackford

Page 165: Perfect Pussy at Mono © Matthew McAndrew

Page 165: Herman Dune, live at Mono © Susie Young

Page 166: Tuff Love at Mono, Glasgow, 2014 © Matthew McAndrew

Page 166: Monorail Music © James Cadden

Page 167: Franz Ferdinand © Ingrid Mur

Page 167: Edwyn Collins, Mono 2009 © James Cadden

Page 168: The Glasgow Royal Concert Hall, Buchanan Street © Royal Fine Art Commission for Scotland. Licensor www.scran.ac.uk

Page 170: Transatlantic Sessions, Celtic Connections © Alan McAteer, courtesy of Glasgow Life

Page 171: Lord Provost Pat Lally with a Peter Howson painting © Newsquest (Herald & Times). Licensor www.scran.ac.uk

Page 172: SNO and the Royal Scottish Academy of Music at The Glasgow Concert Hall, in January 1963 © Newsquest (Herald & Times). Licensor www.scran.ac.uk

Page 173: Children's Classical Concert at The Glasgow Royal Concert Hall, 1998 © Gerry McCann

Page 173: Evelyn Glennie at Glasgow's Royal Concert Hall © Gerry McCann

Page 174: From the back of the stage, during a rehearsal at The Glasgow Royal Concert Hall © Newsquest (Herald & Times). Licensor www.scran.ac.uk

Page 175: The Glasgow Royal Concert Hall, under construction © Newsquest (Herald & Times). Licensor www.scran.ac.uk

Page 176: Statue of Donald Dewar (1937–2000), The Glasgow Royal Concert Hall in the background © CSG CIC Glasgow Museums and Libraries Collections

Page 176: Buchanan Street, building work for Buchanan Galleries in foreground © Royal Fine Art Commission for Scotland. Licensor www.scran.ac.uk

Page 176: Glasgow Coat Of Arms above The Glasgow Royal Concert Hall signage © Mark Mechan

Page 177: Beethoven poster © Mark Mechan

Page 177: Treacherous Orchestra © Colin Goldie, courtesy of Glasgow Life

Page 177: Bjorn Again ticket © Mark Mechan

Page 178: Glasgow Royal Concert Hall, interior wall © Ron Grosset

Page 182: Metronome © Evan Fariston/Shutterstock

Building / Location Factboxes throughout the book: various elements © Sociologas, Hein Nouwens, Karin Hildebrand Lau, Avesun, squarelogo, Dmitry Naumov, Thomas Bethge, Andrey_Kuzmin, Daniel Schweinert, Olga Kovalenko, Tatiana Popova, guidocava, Dn Br, Viktor Gladkov, Lou Oates/Shutterstock

Endpaper: Glasgow Map © Glasgow City Marketing Bureau

Index

Symbols

2 Many DJs 153
5SC 77, 78, 104
13th Note, The 160, 164, 166
18 Wheeler 159
78, The 166, 167
101 Scottish Songs 45
808 State 150

A

ABC 101
Abstainers' Union 24, 26, 28, 76
Academy (O2, Carling), the 101
Academy of Ancient Music 175
AC/DC 121, 122, 124
Active Society for the Propagation of New Music 12, 75, 76
Adams, Richard 10
Admiral Fallow 101
Aird, James 9
Albina, Madame 75
Alexander Gibson Opera School 39, 41, 58
Alex Harvey Big Soul Band 13
Alhambra, The 88, 89, 92, 93
Allan Glen's School 45
Allan, James 74
Amalgamated Musicians' Union. SEE Musicians' Union
Anderson, Freddy 44
Anderson, Sandra 129
Andrew Hook Centre for American Studies 128
Animals, The 32
Apollo Memories 121
Apollo, The 13, 14, 119, 119–124, 124, 140, 166
Arches, The 14, 124, 150, 151, 153
Arctic Monkeys 101, 144
Armadillo, the. SEE Clyde Auditorium
Armstrong, Louis 61, 63, 64
Army School of Piping 113
Arnold, Andy 151

Assembly Rooms, the 10, 36
Atari Teenage Riot 160
Athenaeum 36, 39. SEE Royal Conservatoire of Scotland, The
Aztec Camera 13, 135, 136, 137

B

Bach, Johann Sebastian 38, 175
Backhaus, Wilhelm 75
Bain, Aly 47, 89, 177
Baker, Josephine 64
Barber, Samuel 56
Barbirolli, John 74, 78
Barras. SEE Barrowland Ballroom
Barrowland Ballroom 13, 84, 95, 95–103, 96, 97, 98, 100, 101, 103, 124, 142, 148, 167, 177
Barrowlands. SEE Barrowland Ballroom
Bartók, Béla 10, 12, 75
Basel Chamber Orchestra 175
Bassey, Shirley 106
Battlefield Band 45, 49
Baxter, Stanley 62, 108
Bay City Rollers 122
Bayliss, Mrs (one-time owner of Scotia Bar) 89
BBC Alba 111
BBC Home Service 106
BBC Scotland 104–111. SEE ALSO British Broadcasting Corporation (BBC)
BBC Scottish Singers 104
BBC Scottish (Symphony) Orchestra 12, 14, 24, 26, 27, 28, 29, 30, 77, 78, 104, 106, 107, 109, 176
Beastie Boys, The 100
Beatles, The 45
Beattie, Johnnie 92
Beck 159
Beecham, Sir Thomas 67
Belle and Sebastian 130, 137, 167
Bell's Pottery 107
Benjamin, Floella 173

Bennett's 149
Beranek, Leo 67
Berkeley Suite, The 155
Berlin Philharmonic 169, 173
Bernstein, Leonard 58
Bertini, Gary 56
Besch, Anthony 54, 56
Best, WT 71
Biffy Clyro 101, 160
Big Country 100
Bill Haley & His Comets 98
Billy Blue and the Bluebirds 96
Bis 166
Bishop's Castle 9
Bjorn Again 177
Black, John 22
Black Sabbath 119
Black, Simon 166
Black Watch Regiment 114
Blake, Norman 130
Blisters, The 166
Blondie 122
Blue Angels, The 49
Bluebells, The 136, 149
Blue Nile, The 169
Blur 101, 158
Blythman, Morris 45, 46
BMX Bandits 13, 137
Bogle, Eric 47
Bolshoi Ballet 144
Bolshoi Orchestra 173, 175
Borge, Victor 90
Boston Symphony Orchestra 74
Boswell Sisters 64
Botanical Gardens 11
Boult, Adrian 77
Bourgie Bourgie 139
Bowie, David 101, 124, 134, 162
Boyd, Joe 48
Boy Hairdressers 137
Bradfield, James Dean 159
Braham, John 24
Brahms, Johannes 72

Braithwaite, Warwick 52
Brendel, Alfred 173
Bridgewater Hall 173
British Broadcasting Company 77
British Broadcasting Corporation (BBC) 78
British Minstrel 10
British National Opera Company 52, 78
Broadcast 160
Broderick, Big Mick 44, 48, 49
Brodsky String Quartet 41
Broomhill Bums 46
Brown, James 120
Brown, Svend 175
Bruce, Dave 90
Bruce, Frank 90
Bruce, Keith 11, 15, 35
Brydon, Roderick 30, 52
Buchan, Janie 45, 46
Buchan, John 22
Buchan, Norman 12
Buchan, Norrie 45, 46
Buffalo Bill's Wild West Show 128
Builder, The 71
Bullock, Ernest 38
Bülow, Hans von 69, 70, 76, 79
Burnett, Duncan 8, 22
Burns Night 76
Burns, Robert 10, 177
Buzzcocks, The 132
Buzzcut 162
Bygraves, Max 122
Byrd, William 22

C

Caledonian Theatre, The 10
Calloway, Cab 63
Calvinism 23
Camera Obscura 137
Campbell, Alex 13, 48, 49
Campbell, Bobby 45
Capello, Domenic 151
Capercaillie 176

Captain America 137
Carl Rosa touring opera company 52
Carrick, John 30
Carrodu, John 71
Carruthers, Herbert 77, 78
Cash, Johnny 120
Catalani, Angelica 10, 52
Catcher 160
Cathouse, The 160
CCA bar 149
Celibidache, Sergiu 75
Celtic Connections 14, 30, 32, 109, 114, 169, 176, 177
Celtic FC 13, 83
Celtic Park 111
Central Station 64, 68, 90, 151
Chailly, Riccardo 173
Chaliapin, Feodor 75
Chapel Royal at Stirling 23
Charing Cross 52
Charlatans, The 158
Charles, HRH Prince of Wales 39, 115
Charlotte, The 159
Cheape, Hugh 113
Chemical Brothers 153
Chemikal Underground 14, 139
Chevalier, M. Gaston 92
Chicken Factory 49
Chic Murray Story: The Best Way to Walk, The 92
Chisholm, Erik 12, 52, 75
Choral Union. SEE Glasgow Choral and Orchestral Union
Christian (Chris McClure) 122
Chuck Wagon 126
Church of Scotland 23
Cineworld 14, 124
Citizens Theatre 39, 79
City Chambers. SEE Glasgow City Chambers
City Hall (Halls). SEE Glasgow City Halls
City of Glasgow Bank 72
City Theatre 10, 52
Clapton, Eric 122
Clarke, Dave 149
Clark, John S 29
Clash, The 100, 121, 122, 165
Classics Unwrapped 109
Cleveland Orchestra 76
Clive's Incredible Folk Club 13, 48

Cloonan, Martin 15, 140
Close Lobsters 13, 137
Clumpas, Stuart 158, 160
Clutha 13, 49
Clyde Auditorium ('the Armadillo') 140, 144
Cochran, Eddie 63
Cockpit, The 159
Cole, Lloyd 130
Cole, Nat 'King' 61, 62
Coles, Cecil 106
College of Piping 12, 113–117
Collegiate Church of St Mary and St Ann 18, 22
Collins, Edwyn 134, 137, 165
Commercial College 35
Commonwealth Games 55
Connolly, Billy 13, 44, 45, 47, 49, 58, 85, 89, 122
Cooper, Alice 122
Cooper, Neil 15, 162
Copland, Aaron 39
Corea, Chick 14
Corner House, The 46
Corries, The 47
Coyle, Tam 158, 159
Craig, Charles 56
Crawford, Paul 152, 154
Creation 139
Crosby, Bing 64, 65
Crowded House 159
Cry Parrot 167
Cullum, Jamie 160
Cunningham, John 69
Cunningham, Phil 47, 109, 176
Cunningham, Tommy 14
Cure, The 100
Currie, Colin 177

D

Daddy Warbucks 165
Daft Punk 153
Daintees, The 158
Dalcroze Eurhythmics 38
Daly, Steven 135
Davies, Peter Maxwell 30
Davis, Miles 122, 144, 145
Davison, Ian 45, 82
Deacon Blue 137

Deep Purple 122
Del Amitri 137
Del Mar, Norman 78
Dennistoun Palais 96
Denver, Bert 65
Denver, Nigel 45
Devlin, Vivien 62
Diana, Princess of Wales 39
Dickens, Charles 38
Dickson, Barbara 47, 122
Dillon, James 33
Directory for Public Worship 23
Donaldson, David 55
Donegan, Lonnie 13, 45
Douglas, Jerry 177
Dowds, Bobby 62
Downie, Dep 162
Drummond, Pete 119
Dubliners 13
Duncan, Alan 165
Duncan, Gordon 117
Dunlop Street 53
Dutta, Prakriti 107
Dykeenies, The 160
Dylan, Bob 13, 101, 144

E

Easton, Sheena 89
Ebert, Peter 56
Éclair Fifi 155
Edinburgh International Festival 51, 55, 58, 109
Elizabeth II, Queen 38
Ellington, Duke 64
Ellis, Geoff 159, 160
Emerson, Lake & Palmer 119
Empire Palace 61, 64
Empire Theatre, The 61–65, 62, 64, 88, 93
Empress Playhouse 93
English National Opera (ENO) 52
Euing, William 10
European City of Culture 14, 151, 169
Evening News 63

F

Fabric 154
Factory 132
Fairweather, John 119

Fame, Georgie 122
Fence Records 139
Fever 149
Finian's Rainbow 93
Firebird 33
Fire Engines 139, 165
Firkusny, Rudolf 107
First Draw and Western Re-enactment 126
Fisher, Archie 45, 46, 109
Fisher, Ray 45, 46
Fitzgerald, Ella 76, 106, 120
Five Past Eight Show, The 62, 93
Fleming, Alex 126, 129
Flook 176
Florence and the Machine 160
Flying Duck, The 166
Forde, Florrie 88
Foster, Norman 142, 144
Frame, Roddy 135
Francie and Josie 93
Franz Ferdinand 14, 130, 131, 137, 154, 165, 166, 167
Frightened Rabbit 101, 160
From Here to Eternity 65
Fruitmarket. SEE Old Fruitmarket
Fulton, Rikki 93
Furtwängler, Wilhelm 75
Fury Murrys 149
Fyffe, Will 11, 65, 88, 90

G

Gaiety Theatre 29, 61, 64
Gallacher, George 13
Gallagher, Noel 130
Gallery of Modern Art 170
Galloway, Vic 13, 15, 108, 132, 157
Gandhi 91
Gang Hut (Maestro's) 149
Gang of Four, The 132
gangs 83
Gardner, Ava 65
Garland, Judy 61, 64, 65
Gaughan, Dick 13
Gaybirds, The 96, 97
Gaye, Marvin 120
General Post Office 36, 68
Gentlemen's Subscription Concerts 10
George VI, King 38

Gergiev, Valery 173
Gibson, Sir Alexander 12, 13, 29, 52, 53, 55, 56, 58, 69, 78, 79
Gigli, Beniamino 75
Gig on the Green 12
Gilbert, WS 70
Girls Aloud 144
Glasgow Cathedral 17–23
Glasgow Choral and Orchestral Union 69, 70, 71, 72, 74, 77
Glasgow Citizen 79
Glasgow City Chambers 68
Glasgow City Corporation 74, 76, 79
Glasgow City Halls 11, 12, 14, 24–33, 69, 70, 76, 107, 170
Glasgow Concert Hall 29
Glasgow Fair 89
Glasgow Festival 11, 69
Glasgow Folk Centre 47
Glasgow Folk Club 13, 47
Glasgow Garden Festival 144
Glasgow Grand Opera Society 52
Glasgow Green 12, 13, 48, 89, 97
Glasgow Gunslingers 126
Glasgow International Concert Hall. See Glasgow Royal Concert Hall
Glasgow International Jazz Festival 14, 89, 144
Glasgow Larks 10
Glasgow Mechanics Union 11
Glasgow Music Festival 76
Glasgow Orchestral Society 76
Glasgow Orpheus Choir 6, 11, 49, 76, 77
Glasgow Phoenix Choir 111
Glasgow Public Halls Company 74
Glasgow Resident Orchestra 70
Glasgow Royal Concert Hall 14, 24, 29, 32, 169–177
Glasgow School of Art 14, 36, 155, 166
Glasgow's Miles Better 14
Glasgow Socialist Women's Choir 49
Glasgow University. See University of Glasgow
Glass Onion 158
Glen, Alexander 114
Glennie, Evelyn 173
Glen, Thomas 114
Global Gathering 109
Go-Betweens, The 135, 136

Godard, Vic 139, 165
Golden Earring 122
Gordon, Harry 65, 89, 90
Gordon, Joe 45
Govanhill Recreation Ground 10
Graham, Davy 13
Grand International Show 144
Grand Ole Opry 126–131
Graubæk, Michael 47
Gray, Alasdair 14
Great Scotch Concerts 28
Green's Playhouse 119, 124
Grieve, Mike 149, 152, 154
Gummy Stumps 164

H

Hacienda, The 149, 150
Haig, Paul 135
Hair 93
Half Past Eight Show, The 88, 93
Hallé, Charles 27, 72
Hall, Robin 45, 108
Halstead, Philip 36
Hampden Park 144
Hanley, Cliff 93
Happy Mondays, The 149
Hardy, Oliver 62
Harewood, Lord 58
Harper, Edward 36
Harrigan, James 'Harri' 149, 150, 151, 155
Harrison & Harrison 23
Harvey, Alex 13, 44, 122
Harvey, Jonathan 33
Harvey, P J 144
Harvey, Tam 13, 44
Havergal, Giles 39
Havergal, Henry 38, 39
Hawkins, Coleman 64
Haydn 173
Heifitz, Jascha 75
Hemmings, Peter 53, 55, 56
Henderson, Davy 139, 165
Henderson, Hamish 13
Hendrix, Jimi 119
Henschel, George 74
Heron, Mike 48
Hewitt, Angela 175
High Flying Birds 130
Hindemith, Paul 75

Hipsway 137
His Majesty's Theatre, Aberdeen 51
Hofmann, Josef 75
Hogmanay concerts 76
Holst, Gustav 38
Holt, Harold 75
Hope, Bob 64
Horne, Alan 132, 134, 139, 165
Horne, Lena 64
Horowitz, Vladimir 75
Hot Chip 154
House, Jack 62
Hoys, Pat 58
Hubbert, RM 167
Huberman, Bronislaw 75
Hudson Mohawke 155
Hue and Cry 13
Human League 132
Humblebums 13, 44, 47
Huntly, Alex 166
Hutton, Betty 64
Hydro, The (SSE) 119, 140, 142, 143, 144, 145
Hynd, Colin 176

I

Ibbs and Tillett 75
Ice Cube 101
Imlach, Hamish 13, 45, 46, 48, 49
Incredible String Band, The 13, 48
Inner City 150
International Celebrity Subscription Concerts 75
International Record Store Day 165
Iona Community 45, 46
Iona Records 48
Israel Philharmonic 173
I Was There: The Story Of The Glasgow Apollo 124

J

Jack, Malcolm 15, 147
Jackmaster 155
Jacob Yates and the Pearly Gate Lock Pickers 164
James VI, King 6, 22
Jansch, Bert 13, 47
Jansons, Mariss 173
Järvi, Neeme 30

Jesus and Mary Chain, The 13, 137, 165
Joachim, Joseph 73
Joe Gordon Folk Four 46
Johnny and the Self-Abusers 13, 158. See also Simple Minds
Johnston, Arthur 48
Johnston, Craig 160
Jones, Grace 101
Jones, Tom 176
Josef K 135, 137
Joy Division 135
JSD Band 45
Jullien, Louis Antoine 24
Just for Seamus 117

K

Kapranos, Alex 137, 166
Karelia, The 166
Kasabian 160
Kaye, Danny 61, 64, 65, 76
Keel, Howard 64, 93
Kelly, Michael 14
Kelvingrove Park 12
Kelvin Hall 13
Kemble, Charlie 65
Kemp, Andrew 22
Kennedy, Bruce 69
Kennyhill Special School 83
Kent, Enoch 45
Kentigern 45
Kentigern, Saint. See St Mungo
Keppie, John 107
Kerr, Alison 15, 61
Kerrang! 100
Kibble Palace 11
Kielty, Martin 121
Killers, The 160
Kings, Queens and People's Palaces 62
King Stephen Overture 71
King's Theatre, The 51, 52, 56
King Tut's Wah Wah Hut 14, 124, 157–161
Kinloch, Maggie 40
Kinloch, William 22
Kiss 124
Knox, John 21
Koussevitsky, Serge 77
Kyle, Danny 47

L

Lacey, Kenneth 28
La Cheetah 155
Lally, Pat 169, 177
Lambert, Hendricks and Ross 93
Lambeth, Henry 69, 70, 71
Lamond, Frederic 11
Lamour, Dorothy 64
Lanark 14
Landowska, Wanda 75
Langlands, Theis Juul 47
Lanza, Mario 64, 76
Last, Bob 132
Last Show At The Apollo, The 122
Lauder, Harry 64, 65, 88, 89, 90, 106
Laurel, Stan 42, 62, 89
Laurie, Cy 49
Laurie's Acoustic Music Bar 49
Lawson, Greg 176
LCD Soundsystem 154
Leftfield 153
Lennon, John 13
Lewis, TC 71
Liberace 65
Liberal Club, The 36, 37
Lind, Jenny 10, 52
Liszt, Franz 69
Lloyd Cole and The Commotions 149
Lloyd, Marie 88
Locarno 96
Loftus, Marie 44
Logan, Ella 93
Logan Family, the 42
Logan, Jimmy 92, 93, 108
London Philharmonic 173
London Sinfonietta 175
Lorne, Tommy 91
Lost Map 139
Louis de France 23
Love and Money 137
Lucifer's 149
LuckyMe 155
Lulu 13, 89, 93, 106, 111
Lumsden, David 39
Lynn, Vera 97

M

Macbeth, Allan 36
MacColl, Ewan 45
MacCrimmon, Donald Bàn 116
MacCrimmon, Kenny 152, 154
MacCrimmon, Michael 152, 154
MacCrimmon, Tony 152, 154
MacCulloch, Gordeanna 45, 49
MacDonald, Alistair 46
Macdonald, Hugh 11, 15
MacFarren, George 76
MacGregor, Jimmie 45, 108
MacGregor, Joanna 174, 175
MacGyurmen, John 116
Mackenzie, Alexander 76
Mackintosh, Charles Rennie 8, 36, 107, 166
Mackintosh, Iain 49
Maclean, Dougie 46, 49
Maclean, Jim 46, 49
MacLeod, Roddy 117
MacMillan, Stuart 149
MacNaughtan, Adam 45, 49
MacNeill, Seumas 114, 116, 117
Macrae, Josh 45, 46
Maestro's 149
Magic Band, The 165
Manhattan School of Music 39
Manic Street Preachers 159
Manns, August 72
Manze, Andrew 27
Mariinsky 173
Marland Bar 13, 47
Martell, Lena 89
Martin, Leslie 170
Martinu, Bohuslav 107
Martyn, John 13, 47, 89
Mas 154
Massacre of Glencoe 46
Masur, Kurt 173
Matcham, Frank 64
Mauceri, John 58
McCalmans 47
McCartney, Paul 122
McClure, Chris 122
McClymont, David 134
McCormick, John 75
McCue, Bill 56, 173
McCulloch, Gordeanna 12
McGeachan, Dave 160
McGeachy, Iain 13, 47
McGee, Alan 139, 159
McGinn, Matt 13, 45, 46, 48
McGoldrick, Michael 32
McGregor, Billy 96, 97
McIver, James 95
McIver, Margaret 95, 97
McIvor, Keith 149, 153, 154, 155
McKellar, Kenneth 106
McKelvie, Harry 11, 90
McLaughlin, John 89
McLean, Alison Chapman 49
McLellan Galleries 28, 77
McLeod, Greg 149, 152
McNaughtan, Adam 12, 13
McNicol, Cameron 169, 172, 173
McPeake, Frank 44
McPeake, Frank 'Middle Francie' 44, 45
McPeake, James 44
McRobbie, Stephen 162, 166, 167
McVicar, Ewan 12, 15, 42, 81, 86
Mecca 122
Medtner, Nicolai 75
Meikle, Orde 149
Melody Maker 13
Menuhin, Yehudi 49, 75, 79
Mercury, Freddie 121
Mercury Prize 14
Mescaleros, The 160
Metallica 101
Metropole, the 88, 93
Millar, Edward 22
Miller, Bill 65
Milne, Alasdair 108
Milroy, Jack 93
Minogue, Kylie 144
Mitchell, Donald 78
Mitchell Library 67, 79
Mogwai 14, 130, 166
Molleson, Kate 14
Mono 162–167
Moody-Manners Opera Company 52
Moohan, Elaine 15, 17
Mooney, Peter 111
Moore and Burgess Minstrels 76
Morgan, Tommy 89, 91
Morrissey 144
Moss Empires 61, 63
Move, The 119
Mozart 173
Mozart, George 92
Muirhead, Bishop Andrew 18
Mungo, Saint 17
Munro, Gordon 15, 21
Murray, Chic 92
Murray, George 24
Murray, Maidie 92
Muscles of Joy 164, 167
Muse 160
Music Acoustics and Architecture 67
Musica Nova 12
Musicians' Union 11
Musician, The 109
Music Makars, The 109
Muti, Riccardo 173
My Bloody Valentine 139
My Chemical Romance 160

N

National Museums of Scotland 113
National Piping Centre 12, 113–117, 177
Necropolis, The 22
Nectarine No. 9 139, 165
New Metropole 93
New Year's Revolution 160
Nice'N'Sleazy 160
Nightcrawlers, The 149
Noakes, Rab 47
North Park House 104, 107
Numbers 155
Nutini, Paulo 160

O

Oasis 101, 130, 139, 159
Ocean Colour Scene 101
O'Connor, Des 62
Old Fruitmarket 14, 30, 32, 177
Old Grey Whistle Test 122
Old Hairdresser's, The 166
Ono, Yoko 13
Optimo 153, 154, 155
Orange Juice 46, 134, 135, 136, 137, 139, 149, 165
Orbital 153
Orchestra of the Age of Enlightenment 173
Organs of Love 164
Orpheus Choir. See Glasgow Orpheus Choir

P

Pachmann, Vladimir de 73
Pacific Quay 107
Paderewski, Ignacy Jan 73
Palms 164
Panopticon 89
pantomimes 11, 52, 54, 89, 90, 91, 92, 93
Paramore 160
Parsonage Choir, The 129
Parsons, Gram 129
Parton, Dolly 128
Pastel, Stephen (Stephen McRobbie) 162
Pastels, The 137, 162, 165, 167
Patti, Adelina 75
Pavarotti, Luciano 144, 145
Pavilion Theatre, The 14, 86–93, 124, 170
Peabody Institute 40
Peaches 154
Peacock, Nick 149
Pearston, Thomas 114
Peel, John 13, 14
penny geggies 89
People's Palace 6, 97
Pere Ubu 135
Philharmonic Hall, Liverpool 69
Phoenix Choir. See Glasgow Phoenix Choir
Piano Society, the 75
Piatti, Signor 27
Pickering, Mike 150
Pink Floyd 119
Pintscher, Matthias 29
Piping Centre 14
Piping Live 114
Piping Times 12, 114
Piping Today 114
Placebo 19
Plague of Fiddlers 49
Planet Peach 154
Plaza 96
Poets, The 13, 44
Postcard Records 13, 132–139
Pountney, David 56
Powrie, Ian 108
Prager, Sammy 64
Presley, Elvis 128
Primal Scream 137, 139, 165
Provand's Lordship 18
Pulp 101, 159

Purcell School 40
Purser, John 12, 104, 113

Q

Quarrymen. See also Beatles, The
Queen Arcade, The 40
Queen's Park bandstand 9
Queen Street Station 165
Quinn, Paul 139

R

Rachmaninov, Sergei 75
Radcliffe, Jack 65
Radiohead 101, 159, 160
Radio nan Gaidheal 111
Raff, Joachim 70
Rangers FC 83
Rankl, Karl 78
Rapture, The 154
Ravel, Maurice 75
Rayment, Malcolm 29
Reader, Eddi 176, 177
Red Army, The 63
Red Clydeside 46
Redding, Otis 145
Red Hackle Whisky 114
Reed, Lou 120
Reformed Kirk 21
Reich, Steve 175, 177
Reinhardt, Django 64
Reivers, The 46
REM 101
Reynolds, Simon 134
Richard, Cliff 122
Richards, Keith 143
Richman, Jonathan 135
Richter, Hans 36
Ries, Herr 27
Riverdance 44
Riverside Club 49
Roberton, Sir Hugh S 76
Roberts, Dame Jean 79
Robeson, Paul 12
Rogers, Kenny 128
Rolling Stones, The 120, 143, 145
Rosenthal, Moriz 75
Ross, Annie 93
Ross, Diana 120

Ross, Malcolm 135
Ross, Ricky 108
Rosy Crucifixion, The 164
Rothesay, Duke of. See Charles, HRH Prince of Wales
Rottenrow Primary School 81–85, 82
Rough Trade 132, 136
Rowdy A 128
Royal Academy of Music, London 39
Royal College of Music, London 38
Royal Colosseum Theatre 52
Royal Conservatoire of Scotland, The 11, 35–41, 58, 114, 170
Royal Princess's Theatre 11, 90
Royal Scottish Academy of Music and Drama (RSAMD). See Royal Conservatoire of Scotland, The
Royal Scottish National Orchestra (RSNO) 12, 15, 36, 72, 143, 169, 172, 174, 177
Royal Scottish Orchestra 173
Rubadub 147
Rubinstein, Artur 75
Runnicles, Donald 14, 33, 41
Runrig 169
Rush 122
Russell, Margaret 95
Rustie 155

S

Sacred Music Institution 23
Sacred Paws 164
Sadler's Wells Opera 52
Saint Magnus Festival 109
Saints & Sinners 157, 158, 160
Sanderling, Kurt 173
sang school (song school) 17, 18, 19, 21, 22
Sarasate, Pablo 72
Saraste, Jukka-Pekka 30
Saturday Evening Concert 24
Saturday Popular Concerts 72
Saunderson, Kevin 150
Sayer, Leo 122
Scars 132
Schick, Stephen 33
Schnabel, Artur 75
School of Music 35, 36
Schools Ballad Club 12
Schreurs, M 27

Schumann, Elisabeth 75
Scotia Bar 12, 13, 42–49, 89, 93
Scotia Folk 42, 44, 49
Scotia Music Hall 44
Scotia Variety and Music Hall 42, 44
Scot, Jock 139
Scotland Street Museum 81
Scott, Bon 121, 122. See also AC/DC
Scottish Ballet 56
Scottish Chamber Orchestra 12, 56
Scottish Enlightenment 9
Scottish Ensemble 172
Scottish Exhibition and Conference Centre (SECC) 14, 29, 101, 124, 128, 140–145, 150
Scottish First Draw Association 126
Scottish Home Service 104, 109. See BBC Scotland
Scottish Motor Show 143
Scottish Musical Review, The 8
Scottish National Academy of Music 36
Scottish National Jazz Orchestra 41
Scottish National Orchestra (SNO) 13, 14, 29, 74, 78, 79
Scottish Opera 11, 41, 51, 53, 54, 55, 56, 58
Scottish Opera Magazine 56
Scottish Orchestra 74, 75, 76, 77, 78
Scottish Philharmonia 56
Scottish Pipe Band Association 12
Scottish Psalter 22
Scottish Radio Orchestra 104
Scottish Television 45, 46, 51, 53, 55, 56
SECC. See Scottish Exhibition and Conference Centre
Sectual Objects 165
Segun 149
Sellars, James 69
Sensational Alex Harvey Band 44, 122
Service, Tom 11, 15, 24, 169
Sex Pistols 144
Sexual Objects, The 165
Shadow, DJ 153
Shand, Jimmy 108
Sharkey, Jeffrey 39
Shaw, Donald 176, 177
Shawe-Taylor, Desmond 56
Shepherd, Robbie 108
Sherwin, Manning 97
Shikari 96

Shop Assistants, The 137, 165
Shrigley, David 164
Simonon, Paul 122
Simple Minds 13, 96, 98, 100, 137, 158
Simply Red 143
Simpson, William 38
Sinatra, Frank 61, 65, 76
Sinclair, Calum 45
Slam 149, 150, 153
Sloan's Bar (Sloan's Oddfellows Music Hall) 89
Smiths, The 100
Snow Patrol 160
Social Reform Society 11
Soma Quality Recordings 153, 154
Song by Toad 139
Sons and Daughters 130
Soul, David 122
Soup Dragons, The 13, 137, 165
Spagnoletti, Paolo 10
Splash One 164, 165, 167
SSE Hydro. See Hydro
St Andrew's Episcopal Church 9, 23
St Andrew's Halls 10, 11, 24, 27, 28, 29, 33, 52, 67–79, 173, 177
St Andrew's in the Square 49
Star Folk Club 48
Status Quo 120, 122
Stephenson, Martin 158
Stereo 160, 164, 166, 167
Stevenson, Sir Daniel 36
Stewart, Andrew 111
Stewart, Andy 63, 93, 108
Stewart, John 19
Stewart, Matthew, laird of Castlemilk 19
Stewart, Rod 144
Stiff Little Fingers 101
Stillie, Thomas Logan 69, 72
Stock Exchange 68
Stockhausen, Karlheinz 78
Stone Roses, The 149, 150
Stout, Chris 176
St Petersburg Philharmonic Orchestra 169, 173
Stramash 49
Strathclyde Concertos 30
Strathclyde Suite 172, 175, 176
Strauss, Johann 56
Strauss, Richard 76

Street Level 164, 166
street songs 81–85
Strokes, The 160
Strummer, Joe 122, 160
Struthers, William 21
STV. See Scottish Television
Style Council 122
Sub Club, The 147–155
Subway Sect 134, 139, 165
Sullivan, Arthur 70
Summer Nights Festival 160
Sun Ra's Arkestra 165
Susskind, Walter 78
Swain, Tony 164
Swamplands 139
Swarowsky, Hans 78
SWG3 Studio Warehouse 155
Symphony Hall, Birmingham 173
Szell, George 75, 76

T

Talich, Vaclav 77
Talking Heads 135
Tangerine Dream 124
Tannahill Weavers 47
Tannock, Craig 166, 167
Tausch, Julius 72
Tectonics 33
Teenage Fanclub 13, 130, 137, 139
Television 135
Temperance Halls 89
Theatre Royal, Hope Street 54, 55
Theatre Royal, Queen Street 52
Theatre Royal, The 10, 11, 14, 51–58, 170
Thin Lizzy 122
Thomas Beecham touring opera company 52
Thomson, Alexander 'Greek' 69
Thomson, Bryden 173, 174
Tilley, Vesta 64
Timberlake, Justin 101
Tin Pan Alley 149
TJ's, Newport 159
Top Ten Club 13
Tower Studios 166
Townhead Primary School 81
Tracey, Edmund 78
Tramway, The 150

Transmission 164, 166
Travelling Folk 109
Travis 158
T Rex 122
Trojans, The 56
Tron Kirk 22
Tumelty, Michael 170, 175
Tut Vu Vu 164
Twin Atlantic 160
Twist 98

U

U2 100
UB40 143
Underground, Glasgow 93
UNESCO City of Music 14, 40
University of Glasgow 12, 36
Urusei Yatsura 166

V

Vänskä, Osmo 30
variety theatres 76, 86, 93
Vaselines, The 137
Vaughan, Sarah 14
Velvet Underground, The 134, 135, 165
Venue, The 159
Verbrugghen, Henri 36
Verve, The 159
Vic, The 155
Victoria Bar 49
Vienna Philharmonic 173
Vieuxtemps, Monsieur 27
Vincent, Gene 63
Virtue, Graeme 13, 15, 95, 119
Volkov, Ilan 33

W

Wagnerian Denhof Opera Company 52
Walker, Alan 70
Wallace, John 39
Wallace, Robert 117
Waller, Fats 64
Walton, William 76
Warhol, Andy 165
Watson, Bruce 100
Wayfarers 45
Wee Back Room (Scotia Bar) 49
Wee Man Bar 49

Weingartner, Felix 77
Weller, Paul 122
Weller, Walter 174
Wells Cathedral School 40
West 13th (The 78) 166, 167
Wet Wet Wet 13, 14, 137, 144
Wham! 122
Whistlebinkies 12, 49
Whistlin' Kirk 23
White Heather Club 46, 108
Whitman, Slim 93
Whittaker, William Gillies 38
Who, The 119, 145
Wigglesworth, Mark 174
Wilde, Kim 122
Wilkes, Jonnie 'JG Wilkes' 153, 154, 155
Williamson, John 130, 167
Williamson, Robin 48
Willis, Dave 65, 89, 91
Wilson, Conrad 10, 15, 51
Wilson, Graham 149
Wilson, Robert 93, 108
Win 165
Winehouse, Amy 160
Wings 122
Wolfstone 176
Wood, John 26, 27, 28, 29
Wood, Thomas 23
Worcester, Battle of 116
World Pipe Band Championships 12
Wright, Mrs 10
Wright, Richard 164

X

Xcerts, The 160

Y

Young, Andrew 173
Young, Neil 144
Ysäye, Eugene 73

Z

Zimmermann, Frank Peter 173
Zoo 132
Zukerman, Pinchas 174